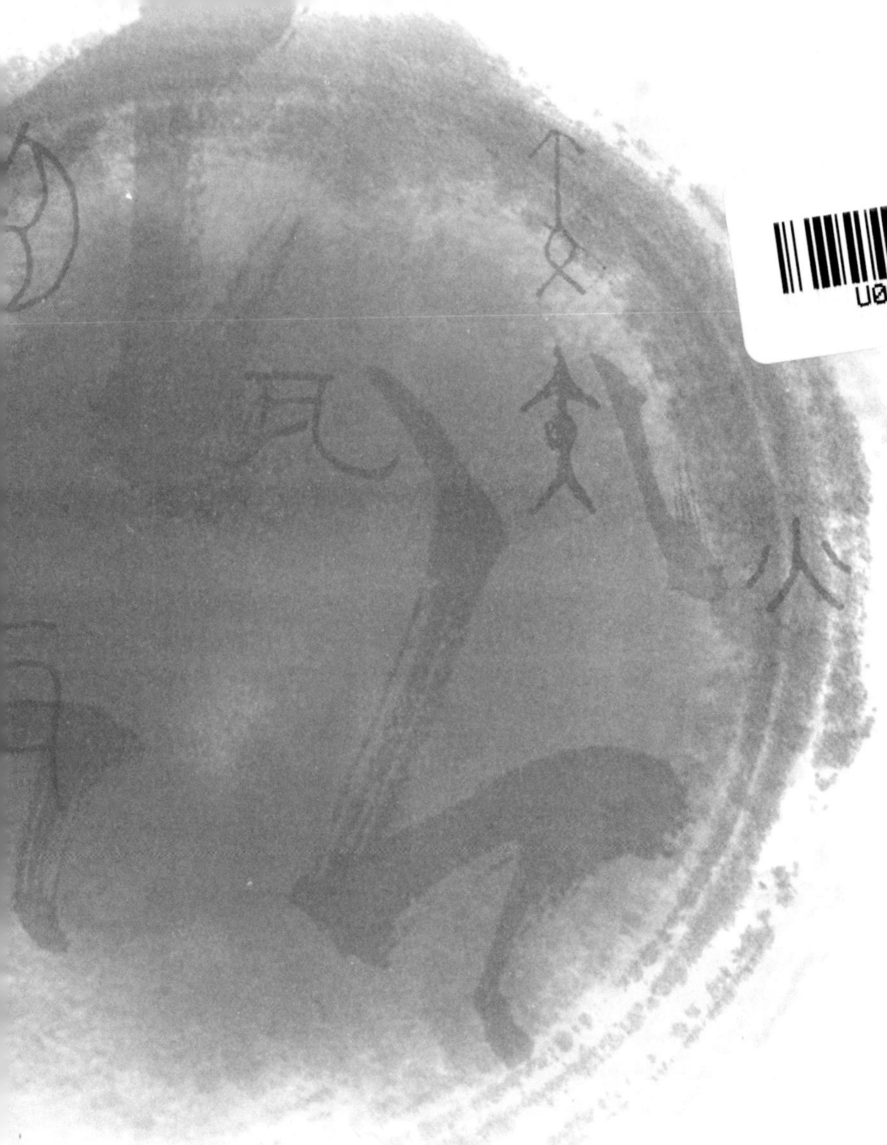

北大版海外汉语教材

汉字部首教程（第二版）

[美]沈禾玲（**Helen H. Shen**）
王　平（**Ping Wang**）　编著
[美]蔡真慧（**Chen-hui Tsai**）

Learning 100 Chinese Radicals (Textbook)

(Second Edition)

北京大学出版社
PEKING UNIVERSITY PRESS

图书在版编目(CIP)数据

汉字部首教程 / (美) 沈禾玲，王平，(美) 蔡真慧编著. —2版. —北京：北京大学出版社，2020.1
北大版海外汉语教材
ISBN 978-7-301-30764-9

Ⅰ.① 汉… Ⅱ.① 沈… ② 王… ③ 蔡… Ⅲ.① 汉字—部首—对外汉语教学—教材 Ⅳ.① H195.4

中国版本图书馆CIP数据核字（2019）第262491号

书　　名　汉字部首教程（第二版）
　　　　　HANZI BUSHOU JIAOCHENG (DI-ER BAN)
著作责任者　[美] 沈禾玲　王　平　[美] 蔡真慧　编著
责任编辑　孙艳玲　路冬月
标准书号　ISBN 978-7-301-30764-9
出版发行　北京大学出版社
地　　址　北京市海淀区成府路 205 号　100871
网　　址　http://www.pup.cn　新浪微博：@ 北京大学出版社
电子信箱　zpup@pup.cn
电　　话　邮购部 010-62752015　发行部 010-62750672　编辑部 010-62753374
印 刷 者　三河市北燕印装有限公司
经 销 者　新华书店
　　　　　889 毫米 ×1194 毫米　16 开本　34.5 印张　883 千字
　　　　　2009 年 7 月第 1 版
　　　　　2020 年 1 月第 2 版　2020 年 1 月第 1 次印刷
定　　价　138.00 元（含课本、练习册及部首卡片）

前　言

《汉字部首教程》是专门为外国学生编写的汉字部首学习教材。汉语不同于英语或其他以罗马字母为书写符号的语言，它的书写形式是用笔画组成的方块符号，称为"汉字"。汉字的特点是形体与其所代表的意义有很强的联系。从结构上讲，汉字可以分为独体字与合体字两种。独体字的字形具有整体性，从结构上不能分拆。合体字的字形具有可分拆性，从结构上可以分出独体字或其他部件。

独体字中许多就是汉字的部首。什么是部首？如果从书写的形式上对合体字进行分类，我们就会发现很多合体字含有相同的基本字，比如合体字岩、屿、峡、峰都含有相同的基本字"山"，而且这些合体字的意思都与"山"有关系，我们就称"山"为部首。有了部首，我们就可以在字典中把含有相同部首的汉字放在一起，便于查找。这种以部首为序来查找字典中的汉字的方法，我们称为部首检字法。

在这本教材中，我们介绍了100个高频率部首。所谓高频率部首，是按照部首在汉字中出现的频率来计算的，一个特定的部首出现在汉字中的次数越多，它的频率就越高，对我们学习包含这个部首的汉字的帮助也越大。部首在汉字中的主要作用是表示汉字的字义，但是有时候，它们也表示汉字的字音，比如部首"刂"在"刚"中是表义的，但是在"到"中却表示该字的读音。因此，学习高频率部首，可以帮助我们记住很多合体字的形、义、音。

本教材介绍的100个高频率部首是根据《现代汉语词典》（商务印书馆，2005）所收的9999个汉字统计出来的。根据这100个部首在常用字中表义、表形和表音的情况以及那些常用字在汉语作为第二语言的初级课本中的出现频率，我们删去了10个部首：一丨丿丶亠冖髟罒耒虍（虎），另外补上了10个部首：匚户工止寸夊矢斤舌身。下面是本教材要介绍的100个部首（根据频率排列）：

水、艸、口、木、手、人、金、心、土、月、糸、虫、言、女、竹、火、王、

日、石、鱼、山、足、鸟、疒、辵、衣、犬、目、刀、邑、宀、禾、马、贝、车、阜、示、食、酉、八、页、巾、门、广、大、米、田、十、彳、革、攴、戈、尸、穴、力、舟、囗、雨、厂、又、牛、皿、夂、羽、羊、弓、歹、小、欠、子、隹、耳、白、骨、立、见、厶、毛、卜、齿、方、黑、殳、儿、彡、气、勹、爪、瓦、走、匚、户、工、止、寸、夊、矢、斤、舌、身

本教材共有十一课。第一课介绍部首知识，让同学们对汉字的部首有一个大体的了解。第二到十一课，每课详细介绍十个部首。每一课的内容大致如下：

1. 部首的古字形。对每一个部首，我们列出甲骨文、金文或者小篆的书写形式，使同学们对汉字部首的象形与表义的特点有一个具体形象的了解。
2. 部首的起源及形成。通过对部首的起源和形成的介绍，我们可以让同学们懂得汉字的发展跟人们对自然界和社会事物的认识以及文化的形成和发展有密切的关系。揭示部首的文化内涵，有助于同学们对部首进行有意义的记忆。
3. 语言文化拓展。因为多数部首来源于独体字，为了加深同学们对该基本字的印象，我们尽可能为每个基本字提供一个含有该字的成语故事、寓言故事、民间故事、传说或其他生动有趣的故事以及相关语言文化知识等，使同学们能在语境中深化对该基本字的了解和记忆。

本教材的特点在于，我们不光介绍部首知识，同时设计相应的练习对学到的部首知识进行巩固并学习如何运用该知识去习得汉字的方法，因此本教材配有练习册和练习网站。针对每一课内容，练习侧重于两个方面：

1. 部首练习。每一个部首都有相应的练习。练习的设计采取从单项到综合，从简单到复杂，既对每个新学的部首进行单项练习，也对前面学过的部首进行复习。
2. 部首复习和测验。在学完每课后，学习者可以对部首进行综合练习并做有关测验。综合练习部分将对本课学到的十个部首进行系统复习。复习完以后，学习者可以做测验题来检查自己是否已经掌握。教师应该在确信学习者已经掌握了这一课的部首知识的基础上介绍下一课部首知识。

另外，本教材配套的部首练习网站 https://asian-slavic.uiowa.edu/asll/chinese-language-program/radical-practice 提供互动式练习并配有图片、音乐及部首笔画书写顺序动画，使学习者在轻松愉快的氛围中达到进一步巩固课堂中学到的部首知识的目的。

本教材的编写和练习设计遵循认知规律，让学习者对部首进行有意义的学习，从而提高学习效率。教材最后附有100个部首检索。检索采用音（拼音）、形（笔画）、义（英文）三种方法，并标出每个部首在教材中的页码，便于查找。

我们建议将本教材作为汉语课的补充教材使用，每一到两个星期介绍十个部首。部首教学要跟汉字教学紧密结合起来，这样，学习者可以把学到的部首知识应用到汉字学习中去。在汉字教学中尽量让学生通过辨认生字中的已知部首并讨论它对学习合体字的义或音的作用来巩固部首知识。久而久之，学生就能自觉地运用部首知识去习得新字了。当然，教师也可根据课程的要求灵活使用本教材。

本教材第一版由北京大学出版社在2009年出版，受到了广大汉语学习者的厚爱，在此我们表示感谢。根据读者的反馈，第二版对部分内容进行了修订以更方便读者使用。

沈禾玲　王　平　蔡真慧

2019春于美国艾奥瓦城

Preface

Learning 100 Chinese Radicals is a textbook specifically designed for foreign learners of Chinese. Unlike English or other languages, which use Roman letters to phonetically represent words, the written form of Chinese uses strokes to form square block symbols that we refer to as "characters." While western alphabets use written symbols to represent sounds only, in Chinese the written symbols signify meanings in addition to pronunciation. In other words most characters have obvious connections with the meanings they represent. This is a unique feature of the Chinese writing system.

In terms of structure, characters can be classified into two categories—integral characters and compound characters. Integral characters are visually compact representations, often derived from ancient pictographs. They cannot be broken down into two or more meaningful parts, but must be read as a whole. Compound characters consist of at least two or more integral characters or other components.

Radicals were originally integral characters. What does "radical" mean? If we analyze compound characters, we find that many characters with conceptually related meanings contain the same integral character. For example, the compound characters 岩 (*cliff*), 屿 (*islet*), 峡 (*gorge*), and 峰 (*summit*) all contain the same integral character 山 (*mountain*). Since 山 gives us information about the meaning category of these compound characters, we call 山 as a radical for these compound characters, thus, radicals are root characters. Once we have established a finite set of key radicals, we can then classify all compound characters according to their radicals, and thereby create a reference system to be used in dictionaries. The process of using an index of radicals to classify and look up characters in a dictionary is known as "the radical index method."

In this textbook, we will introduce 100 high-frequency radicals. The high-frequency radicals are those that appear most often in compound characters. Learning the high-frequency radicals facilitates the study of the compound characters. While radicals usually signify the meanings of compound characters, sometimes they also indicate pronunciation. For instance, the radical 刀（刂 ⺈）(pronounced as "dāo") indicates the meaning of the compound character 刚 which means tough, but it also cues the sound for the character 到 (dào). Therefore, learning high-frequency radicals can help students learn the pronunciations, meanings, and graphic representations of many compound characters effectively and eff iciently.

Each radical's frequency of appearance in this textbook was computed through an analysis of the 9999 character entries listed in the *Modern Chinese Dictionary* (《现代汉语词典》), published by the Commercial Press in 2005. We have made an adjustment based on an analysis of their frequency in cuing the meaning, shape, and sound in compound characters—in other words—their usefulness in terms of decoding and memorizing compound characters. We have also modified the list based on an analysis of the compound characters used in beginning level Chinese textbooks for nonnative Chinese learners. Specif ically, we have eliminated 10 radicals [一丨丿丶亠冖髟罒耒虍（虎）] from the list and added another 10 (匚户工止寸夊矢斤舌身). Below are the 100 radicals (in order of frequency from high to low) that we will introduce in the textbook:

水、艸、口、木、手、人、金、心、土、月、糸、虫、言、女、竹、火、王、日、石、鱼、山、足、鸟、疒、辵、衣、犬、目、刀、邑、宀、禾、马、贝、车、阜、示、食、酉、八、页、巾、门、广、大、米、田、十、彳、革、攴、戈、尸、穴、力、舟、囗、雨、厂、又、牛、皿、夂、羽、羊、弓、歹、小、欠、子、隹、耳、白、骨、立、见、厶、毛、卜、齿、方、黑、殳、儿、彡、气、勹、爪、瓦、走、匚、户、工、止、寸、夊、矢、斤、舌、身

The book consists of 11 lessons. Lesson 1 gives an overview of the development and use of the radical system, to give students a general understanding of the radical method before

they begin to work on the 100 radicals individually. Lessons 2~11 present detailed information on the 100 radicals. Each lesson introduces 10 radicals. The content of each lesson is outlined below:

1. The ancient form of the radical: For each radical, we illustrate the radical as it appeared in its oldest form—in oracle bone inscription, bronze vessel inscription, or small seal style. This will help learners understand the form-to-meaning connection in each radical.
2. The origin and development of the radical: In this section, we present an etymological account of the radical. Through this learners can observe the connection between Chinese script and Chinese culture. Because they were created by the ancient people, so characters suggest how people in Ancient China understood the natural world. Further, each character's form and meaning evolved along with changes in Chinese society and thought. Therefore, characters are like evolving time capsules. They offer a window into ancient and historic Chinese culture and ideology. Presenting radicals in this meaningful way will help learners remember radicals.
3. Linguistic and cultural development: As we mentioned earlier, radicals were originally integral root-characters, and most radicals can still stand alone as integral characters in modern Chinese. In this book we provide an idiom, parable, folk-tale, interesting story or relevant knowledge of language and culture that uses the radical as an integral character. We thereby embed the radical in an entertaining context to facilitate memorization.

In addition to the textbook, there is also a workbook which contains a set of exercises for each radical. In these exercises students can practice recognizing radicals within compound characters and apply their new radical knowledge to the task of learning new compound characters. The workbook features two types of exercises:

1. Individual radical exercises: For each radical, we provide a set of corresponding exercises—both drills and tasks—to reinforce new knowledge. These exercises help students develop the skill of breaking down new characters into component radicals for

easier memorization. In addition, these exercises recycle previously introduced radicals to reinforce learning. The exercises are sequenced according to the pedagogical principle of ascending difficulty.

2. Radical reviews and quizzes: At the end of each lesson we provide a review section to recap the 10 radicals covered in that lesson, and a quiz to assess learners' proficiency with the 10 radicals. By analyzing the results of these quizzes, instructors can identify the strength and weakness of students' learning. It is advised that the instructor make sure that students have attained mastery of old radicals before introducing new ones.

In addition, the textbook provides companying website: https://asian-slavic.uiowa.edu/asll/chinese-language-program/radical-practice, on which the exercises provide animated stroke order for each radical and check learners' application of radical knowledge in character learning. The exercises are accompanied with pictures and music, all of which allows learners to practice radicals in an interactive and pleasant environment to reinforce radical knowledge learned from the previous lessons.

This textbook is designed in accordance with cognitive theories on the learning of Chinese characters, which demonstrate that radical learning is most effective when lessons are interesting and meaningful. At the end of this book, we provide three indexes of the 100 radicals introduced in the book, one organized by pronunciation (using *pinyin* phonetic transcriptions), one by stroke count, and one by English translation. In each index the page number of each radical is recorded so that they can be easily located in this book.

We suggest that this textbook be used as a supplemental material to a regular Chinese textbook. It is best to introduce 10 radicals in every one or two-week period so that students have enough time to digest them. We further suggest that radical instruction be integrated with character learning; thus, students can apply the learned radical knowledge to learning new characters. When introducing new characters of a given lesson, we should try our best to have students identify the known radicals in the new characters and discuss their roles in learning the meaning or sound of the new characters. This kind of practice, for a long run, will not only reinforce the radical knowledge students have learned but also help students gain

automaticity of using radical knowledge in learning new characters.

The first edition of this textbook was published by the Peking University Press in 2009. After its publication, we received highly favorable feedback from our users. We hope the second edition will be appreciated by more learners internationally wide.

Helen H. Shen, Ping Wang, and Chen-Hui Tsai

Iowa City, U.S.A., Spring 2019

目 录

Contents

第一课　汉字部首知识
Lesson 1　Basic Knowledge of Chinese Radicals

部首概念的产生
The Origin of the Radical

汉字部首起源于基本字，那么是谁最先提出部首这个概念的呢？中国东汉时期学者许慎（约58—约147）把9353个汉字按字体形状分类，把含有相同结构成分且意义有关联的合体字归为一类，这样，9353个字被分成540类，其中每类汉字中结构相同的部分也称为基本字，放在这一类字的首位，并称它为部首。利用这540部，许慎编著了中国第一部篆书字典《说文解字》。后来南朝的学者顾野王（519—581）根据许慎的方法，编写了中国第一部楷书字典《玉篇》，共有部首542部。到了明代，梅膺祚编了一本字典《字汇》(1615)，把部首精简到214部。后来，清代的张玉书、陈廷敬等编的《康熙字典》(1716）也用214部。汉语大词典出版社出版的《标准汉语字典》(2000) 收了201部。2005年商务印书馆出版的《现代汉语词典》也为201部。我们现在学习部首一般都学201部。我们在这本书中，将介绍其中的100个。

Originally, radicals were root characters. How did these root characters become radicals, and who invented the term "radical?" In the Eastern Han Dynasty, a scholar named Xu Shen (58?—147?) classified 9,353 compound characters into 540 categories based on the common root characters they contained. He grouped together characters containing the same root character and wrote their common root character as their heading. Xu Shen referred to

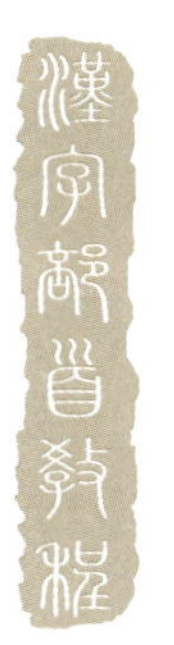

this common root character as a "radical." Xu Shen identified 540 radicals. His groundbreaking method—classifying characters based on their shared component, allowed him to compile the first Chinese character dictionary. It was written in small seal script and titled *Shuowen Jiezi* (*Character and Word Annotations*). Later, in the Southern Dynasty, another scholar, named Gu Yewang (519—581), compiled another character dictionary using Xu Shen's method. This dictionary was named *Yu Pian* (*Jade Articles*) and was written in regular script listing 542 radicals. Mei Yingzuo, a scholar in the Ming Dynasty, compiled a dictionary named *Zihui* (*Collection of Characters*) published in 1615 and reduced the number of radicals to 214. The *Kangxi Character Dictionary*, published in 1716, retained the 214 radicals. Modern Chinese linguists further analyzed the 214 radicals and made a further deduction from 214 to 201. This 201 radical system is what is used today in prominent Chinese dictionaries, such as the *Biaozhun Hanyu Zidian* (*Standard Chinese Character Dictionary*), published by the Modern Chinese Dictionary Publishing House in 2000. Another commonly used dictionary, the *Xiandai Hanyu Cidian* (*Modern Chinese Dictionary*) published by the Commercial Press in 2005, also uses the 201 radical system. In this textbook, we introduce 100 of the 201 radicals.

部首形体的演变
The Evolution of Written Structure of Radicals

现在我们使用的部首很多都起源于古代，但是，古代的写法和现代有着很大的差别，因为在不同历史阶段汉字书写形式发生了变化，因此，部首的书写形式也发生了变化。汉字部首的形体演变大致可以分为五个阶段：甲骨文、金文、小篆、隶书、楷书。从甲骨文到小篆，我们称为古文字阶段，虽然部首的形体有变化，但是依然保存着象形特点。隶书以后，我们称为今文字阶段，部首的笔画已不再是曲线形，而是直线形，因此现代汉字已不再是象形文字，而是用笔画组合而成的抽象符号。下面是部首“目”从甲骨文到楷书的形体变化过程：

Although many radicals used in modern Chinese originated in ancient China, the written forms of the modern radicals differ dramatically from their ancient forms. This is because throughout different stages of Chinese history the entire Chinese writing system has undergone great stylistic changes. From its conception to today the Chinese writing system, along with the radicals contained within, has passed through five different writing styles: Oracle bone inscription, bronze vessel inscription, small seal script, official style, and regular style. The first three styles, oracle bone inscription, bronze vessel inscription, and small seal script are classified together as ancient scripts because, although they are very different in appearance, they still retain more pictographic forms. We refer to the character styles after the official style as modern scripts as the strokes in these two styles are no longer curved. The straightened strokes of the modern scripts diminish the pictographic characteristics of the characters. Therefore, the modern Chinese script is not a pictographic writing system, rather, it is a system of abstract symbols composed of strokes. Consider, for example, the historical evolution of the radical 目:

甲骨文　　Oracle Bone Inscription：

金文　　Bronze Vessel Inscription：

小篆　　Small Seal Script：

隶书　　Official Style：

楷书　　Regular Style：目

虽然“目”起源于象形文字，像人的一只眼睛，但是历史上书体的演变使它逐渐失去象形的特点直到成为结构化和抽象化的符号，所以现在我们看到这个汉字很难根据字形猜测它所代表的意义。

While the original character looked like a picture of an eye, the pictograph became more and more stylized and abstract, until a reader could no longer guess its meaning.

部首的结构特点

The Physical Feature of Radicals

因为汉字是一种表意文字，大部分部首最初的形体都是仿照实物画出来的，人们用这些形状来表示部首所代表的意义。我们称它们为象形字，也就是部首的写法像它所表示的物体的形体。上面提到的“目”是按眼睛的形状写出来的，下面的“犬”也是。如果你看了下面的两张图片，你就会知道“犬”就是“狗”，“犬”字是按“狗”的形状画的。

Chinese writing originated from pictographs. If we track down the origins of each radical, we will find that they began as pictures of physical things—people, animals, and objects. This is the reason that many Chinese characters have strong meaning-script correspondence. Consider, for example, the oracle bone inscription for the radical 目 mentioned above. We can guess that its meaning is “eye” just by looking at it. The two pictures below are another example. They are the origins of the radical 犬. After viewing the following two pictures, you can probably guess the meaning of the radical 犬, which is *dog*.

（内蒙古阴山岩画·犬）
The rock painting of the Yin Mountain in Inner Mongolia

（金文·犬）
Bronze vessel inscription

下面是部首“犬”从甲骨文到楷书的字形变化：

The evolution of the radical 犬 is illustrated below:

甲骨文：　　金文：　　小篆：

隶书：**犬** 楷书：犬

“犬”字，甲骨文描画成一只头朝上，尾巴朝下，腿朝左或朝右的狗。因为狗的尾巴常常是上卷的，金文就更突出了这一可以区别于其他动物的特点，尾巴更明显地向右上翘起，所以是个象形字。“犬”到小篆以后，就逐渐失去了狗的形象。

如果我们能够知道一个部首的古文字形体以及它在历史上的变化，那么我们就能很容易地记住这个部首的字形和它代表的意义。如部首“山”的古文字形 像山峰，“水”的古文字形 像流水，“日”的古文字形 像太阳，“人”的古文字形 像侧立的人。

In the oracle bone inscriptions, we can tell that the top portion of the symbol is the head of the dog and the bottom portion is the tail. The two lines on the left are the legs. Just as real dogs' tails tend to curl, their representation in oracle bone inscription features a curved tail. The curl is even more exaggerated in the bronze vessel inscriptions. In the small seal and regular script styles however, the pictographic nature of the characters is obscured and we can no longer guess that 犬 means *dog*.

If, however, we equip ourselves with the knowledge of evolution of radical forms from their conception to today, it will be much easier for us to memorize the shape and meaning of their contemporary forms. Here are a few more examples: the radical 山 (*mountain*) is derived from the pictograph which depicts three mountain peaks; the radical 水 (*water*) in its ancient pictographic form resembles flowing water; the radical 日 means *sun* and its pictographic form looks like a round sun; and the radical 人 means *person* and its pictographic form looks like a profile of a person.

部首的变体

Alternative Versions of Radicals

部首成为合体字的部件时，由于在整个汉字中所处的位置不同，常常会有不同的写法。我们把在组合汉字过程中没有发生形体变化的部首叫作"正体部首"，发生变化的部首叫作"变体部首"。正体部首和变体部首只是在形体上有差别，读音和意义完全相同。例如"犬"是正体部首，构成的汉字如"哭"；"犭"是"犬"的变体部首，构成的汉字如"狗"。"心"是正体部首，构成的汉字如"思"；"忄"和"⺗"是"心"的变体部首，构成的汉字如"情"和"慕"。本书选用的100个汉字部首，首先介绍的是正体，然后将变体用括弧［ ］标出，如"水［氵氺］"。

20世纪50年代，中国政府开始推行简化字。随着汉字的简化，有些部首也相应被简化了，比如合体字"餅"的简体形式是"饼"。我们可以看到左边的部首"飠"在简体字中写成了"饣"。正体部首的简体形式、繁体形式，我们也在括弧中标出，如"食［飠饣］""鱼［魚］"。

When radicals are used to form a compound character, they can be placed in different positions relative to other components in the compound—such as above, below, or to the left or right side of the other components in the compound. In order to fit into the square block shape of contemporary compound characters the radical is often given an alternative, truncated version. We call these condensed forms "alternative versions" of the radical, while characters that retain their original shape are called "regular versions." The regular and alternative versions of a radical differ in shape but not in the meaning and sound it represents. For example, the alternative version for 犬 is 犭. In the character 哭 the radical 犬 appears in its regular version, but in the character 狗 it appears in its alternative version, standing on the left side of the compound character. The regular version of the radical 心 (*heart*) is used in its regular version in compound characters such as 思. But 心 also has two alternative versions—忄

and 小, which are used in compound characters like 情 and 慕. In this textbook, we will introduce both the regular and alternative versions of each radical. The alternative versions are indicated with brackets such as 水［氵氺］. Of course, some radicals do not have alternative versions.

In the 1950s, the government of the People's Republic of China, in an attempt to expand literacy, promoted the use of a more simplified form of Chinese characters. Just as many integral characters were simplified, many radicals were also transformed into simpler forms. To cite an example, the simplified version of the compound character 餠 is 饼. The radical 飠 in the left part of character is written as 饣 in the simplified system. In this textbook, we indicate the simplified and traditional versions of regular radicals in brackets, such as 食［飠 饣］、鱼［魚］.

部首在汉字中的位置
The Position of Radicals in Compound Characters

部首在合体字中可以处在各种位置，下面是常见的部首在合体字中的位置：

1. 部首在左边。例如：氵→江。
2. 部首在右边。例如：攵→政。
3. 部首在中间。例如：口→哀。
4. 部首在上边。例如：宀→室。
5. 部首在下边。例如：土→堑。
6. 部首在外边。例如：门→闯。

在学合体字时，先找出已经学过的部首，不仅可以帮助我们很快记住合体字的字形，而且还可以帮助我们记住字义。如果一个部首在合体字中表示字音，那么，我们还可以利用这个部首来记住合体字的发音。

As stated above, radicals can appear in several different positions within a compound character. Below we have listed the common positions for radicals in compound characters:

1. The left side of a compound character: 氵→江。
2. The right side of a compound character: 攵→政。

3. The middle of a compound character: 口→哀。

4. The top of a compound character: 宀→室。

5. The bottom of a compound character: 土→堑。

6. Half-encircling another radical or integral character: 门→闯。

When we learn a new compound character, identifying familiar radicals contained within will help us memorize both the form and the meaning of the new character. Sometimes radicals also serve as phonetic cues for a compound character—indicating that the compound character has a pronunciation same or similar to the radical. In these cases, identifying the radical will also help to learn the pronunciation of the compound character.

前面我们提到汉字部首起源于基本字，部首是合体字里标示该字字义类别的成分，而部件是由笔画组成的构字单位，一般由两个或两个以上的笔画构成。如“件”的部首是“亻”，组成部件是“亻”“牛”；又如“清”的部首是“氵”，组成部件是“氵”“青”，“青”的组成部件是“龶”“月”。可见，部件是对汉字形体结构所作的分析，不同于部首的概念。

In the previous sections, we mentioned that radicals were originated from root characters. In a compound character, the radical often signifies the meaning category of the compound character. The component is a unit combined by two or more than two strokes. For example, the radical of 件 is 亻, and the components of 件 are 亻 and 牛; the radical of 清 is 氵, and the components of 清 are 氵 and 青, the components of which are 龶 and 月. So component is the analysis of the character's form, which is different with the radical.

部首的意义分类
Classifying Radicals by Their Meanings

《现代汉语词典》列出201部，其中大部分为表义部首，如“木”，少数为不表义的部件，如“一”。如果我们要记住所有的表义部首，最好的方法是对部首按照它们所代表的意义进行分类。根据对表义部首起源的分

析，大部分的部首可以被分类，下面列举的仅仅是几个分类的例子：

In the "Preface" section, we mentioned that the *Xiandai Hanyu Cidian* (*Modern Chinese Dictionary*) uses the 201 radicals system. Most of them are semantic radicals, such as 木, and a few of them are just components of characters, such as 一. The best way to memorize the semantic radicals is to organize these radicals into groups according to common meanings. The table below presents one way to organize major radicals:

类别 Category	部首 Radicals				
人体 Human body	人 (rén) person	大 (dà) big	子 (zǐ) boy	女 (nǚ) female	身 (shēn) body
动物 Animals	犬 (quǎn) dog	牛 (niú) cattle	马 (mǎ) horse	羊 (yáng) goat	鱼 (yú) fish
植物 Plants	禾 (hé) grain	艸 (cǎo) grass	木 (mù) tree	米 (mǐ) rice	竹 (zhú) bamboo
器物 Objects	贝 (bèi) seashell	皿 (mǐn) container	酉 (yǒu) alcohol	刀 (dāo) knife	弓 (gōng) bow
天文 Astronomy	日 (rì) sun	月 (yuè) moon			
地理 Geography	山 (shān) mountain	土 (tǔ) soil; earth	邑 (yì) city	阜 (fù) hill	

在学习时，我们最好自己对部首进行意义分类，每学一个新部首，把它列入一个意义类，等学完全部部首时，这些部首就会登记在每个同学自己的认知系统中，变成自己的知识体系。

As the number of radicals we have learned increases, we shall be able to reclassify radicals into new meaningful categories based on our own individual cognitive characteristics and styles. This, in turn, will facilitate compound character memorization.

部首的本义和引申义

The Original and Extended Meanings of a Radical

每个部首起源时都代表一定的意义，我们称为本义。随着语言的发展，一个部首逐渐有了好几个意义，后来产生的这些意义都与本义有关联，我们称为引申义。例如“火”是汉字的常用部首，“火”的本义是火焰。用“火”部组成的合体字与“火”存在着意义上的密切联系，比如“煌”是光辉、“燥”是被火烘了以后那种“干”的感觉。“火”作为一个独体字，可以跟许多其他字组合表示与“火”不同但是有关联或相似的一些事物，如：

上火：发炎　　　动火：发怒

了解了部首的本义与引申义的关系以后，我们知道学习部首的本义，不仅能帮助我们学习部首的引申义，还可以让我们很快记住那些含有相同部首的合体字的字义以及那些用部首作为基本字所组成的词或词组的意思。

Originally, each radical was an integral character created to represent some meaning. We refer to the original meaning of a radical as its "basic meaning." As Chinese language and writing developed, each radical's meaning expanded to represent several different concepts. This means that a single radical may have several different meanings, though they are all related to the same basic meaning. We refer to the meanings that the radical accrued over time as "extended meanings."

The original and extended meanings of the integral character 火 (*fire*) illustrate this phenomenon. 火 is a high-frequency radical. Its basic meaning is *fire.* A compound character with 火 as its radical, its meaning often has a close connection with 火, such as the compound character 煌, means *glory*, while the character 燥 means *dry* (after being baked in a fire). So 火 takes on the extended meanings of glory and dryness.

The same diffusion of meaning occurs when the basic character 火 combined with other characters to form a word or phrase. That is, the meaning of a word or phrase is sometimes conceptually distant from fire but still related to fire as illustrated below:

上火 (to inflam)　　　　动火 (to get angry)

To effectively use radicals in the task of memorizing new characters, we need to know both the radical's basic meaning as well as its extended meanings. To grasp a radical's extended meanings it is very helpful to consider examples of compound characters that use that radical, or phrases in which the radical is used as integral character, just as we have done above with 火.

部首与社会文化的关系

Radicals and Their Relation to the Chinese Culture and Society

语言是随着社会和文化的发展而发展的，自然，中国古人的人生观、宇宙观、宗教信仰、文学艺术、风土人情等都会在汉字的创造中有所反映。部首作为最古老的汉字，反映着当时的中国社会和文化。比如，部首“父”最初的形状像一只手抓住一个形状尖利的石头，反映出当时的男人是在外面用石头打击动物，获取食物，或是用石头打击敌人，保护部落的安全。从这个部首的形状，我们还可以推知，当时也许处在石器时代。因此，学习部首不仅可以帮助我们学汉字，而且还可以帮助我们学习中国的文化和历史。

While the Chinese language developed along with Chinese society and culture, the characters, like graphic time-capsules, still reflect the lifestyle, ideology, and beliefs of the ancient Chinese' creators. They also offer insight into areas of Chinese culture such as fine arts, literature, customs and conventions. This is especially true for radicals, which were derived from the oldest integral characters. For example, the ancient pictographic form of the

radical 父, looks like a man holding a stone axe. We can imagine that males were often working outdoors and using tools like axes to catch animals, harvest food, or attack enemies in order to protect their tribe. We could also infer that China was in the Stone Age at the time of the character's inception. Because characters capture the unique way ancient Chinese conceptualized their world, learning radicals not only helps us learn Chinese characters, but also introduces us to Chinese culture and history.

学了这一课，大家可能对部首知识以及为什么要学习部首有一个大致的了解了。希望在学完所有课文以后，大家能掌握100个高频率部首并自觉运用部首知识去学习新的汉字。

另外，我们要说明的是，本教材采用双语编写，但是英文部分有时候不是中文部分逐字逐句的直接翻译，而是对中文文本做了一些简化处理，因为中文部分是为那些已经有一定汉语基础知识的汉语高级学习者而编写的，而英文部分是为零起点的汉语初级学习者编写的，所以就内容来说，相对容易一些，虽然中英文表达的意思是基本一致的。

我们期望你在探索部首知识的过程中收获快乐！

By now, we hope that you have had a general understanding of why students of Chinese need to learn radicals. We certainly hope that after completing all of the lessons in this book, you will have a deep understanding of the 100 high-frequency radicals and that you will use your radical knowledge to acquire more Chinese characters.

This book provides both Chinese and English texts. You may notice that on some occasions, the English text is not strictly sentence by sentence translation from the Chinese text, rather it simplifies the content expressed in the Chinese text. The reason for this is that the Chinese text is designed for advanced learners who have accumulated considerable amount of linguistics knowledge, but the English text is designed for beginner learners who have zero or little Chinese linguistics knowledge.

We hope you enjoy your exploration of Chinese radicals!

练习 Exercises

一、讨论 Discussion

1. 为什么我们说最初的部首大多是象形字？请举例回答这个问题。Why do we refer to the earliest radicals as pictographs?
2. 部首最早是谁总结出来的？现代汉字部首有多少个？Who summarized the concept of the radical? How many radicals are there in modern Chinese?
3. 学部首为什么能帮助学习汉字？Why does studying radicals help us learn Chinese characters?

二、表一列出100个部首，它们的次序是根据部首在合体字中出现的频率排列的，也就是说第一个部首“水”在合体字中出现的次数最多。请根据表一，回答问题。Table 1 lists 100 high-frequency radicals. Their order is based on their frequency rates—how frequently these radicals appeared in the compound characters. That is, the radical 水 has the highest frequency among all radicals. Please answer the questions below based on Table 1.

1. 部首“目”和“人”的频率哪个高？哪个对学习合体字更有帮助？Which radical “目” or “人” appears more frequently? Which of the two will help us learn more compound characters?
2. 从表一中至少找出三个在第一课中提到的部首，说说这三个部首的意思。Please find at least three radicals mentioned in this lesson from Table 1 and explain their meaning.

表一　按频率排列的100部首

Table 1　100 radicals according to their frequency

编号	拼音	部首	编号	拼音	部首	编号	拼音	部首	编号	拼音	部首
1	shuǐ	水（氵 氺）	26	yī	衣（衤）	51	pū	攴（攵）	76	jiàn	见（見）
2	cǎo	艸（艹）	27	quǎn	犬（犭）	52	gē	戈	77	sī	厶
3	kǒu	口	28	mù	目	53	shī	尸	78	máo	毛
4	mù	木（朩）	29	dāo	刀（刂 ⺈）	54	xué	穴	79	bǔ	卜（⺊）
5	shǒu	手（龵 扌）	30	yì	邑（阝在右）	55	lì	力	80	chǐ	齿（齒）
6	rén	人（亻）	31	mián	宀	56	zhōu	舟	81	fāng	方
7	jīn	金（钅）	32	hé	禾	57	wéi	囗	82	hēi	黑
8	xīn	心（忄 ⺗）	33	mǎ	马（馬）	58	yǔ	雨（⻗）	83	shū	殳
9	tǔ	土	34	bèi	贝（貝）	59	hǎn chǎng	厂	84	rén ér	儿
10	yuè	月（月）	35	chē	车（車 ⻋）	60	yòu	又	85	shān	彡
11	mì	糸（糹 纟）	36	fù	阜（阝在左）	61	niú	牛（⺧）	86	qì	气
12	huǐ chóng	虫	37	shì	示（礻）	62	mǐn	皿	87	bāo	勹
13	yán	言（讠）	38	shí	食（飠 饣）	63	bīng	仌（冫）	88	zhǎo	爪（爫）
14	nǚ	女	39	yǒu	酉	64	yǔ	羽	89	wǎ	瓦
15	zhú	竹（⺮）	40	bā	八（丷）	65	yáng	羊（⺷ ⺶）	90	zǒu	走
16	huǒ	火（灬）	41	xié yè	页（頁）	66	gōng	弓	91	fāng	匚
17	wáng	王（玉）	42	jīn	巾	67	è dǎi	歹（歺）	92	hù	户
18	rì	日（曰）	43	mén	门（門）	68	xiǎo	小（⺌）	93	gōng	工
19	shí	石	44	yǎn guǎng	广	69	qiàn	欠	94	zhǐ	止
20	yú	鱼（魚）	45	dà	大	70	zǐ	子	95	cùn	寸
21	shān	山	46	mǐ	米	71	zhuī	隹	96	zhǐ	夂
22	zú	足（⻊）	47	tián	田	72	ěr	耳	97	shǐ	矢
23	niǎo	鸟（鳥）	48	shí	十	73	bái	白	98	jīn	斤
24	nè	疒	49	chì	彳	74	gǔ	骨	99	shé	舌
25	chuò	辵（辶）	50	gé	革	75	lì	立	100	shēn	身

第二课　水、艸、口、木、手、人、金、心、土、月

1. 水 [氵 氺]（shuǐ）部 Water

古字形

“水”是象形字，其古文字始终保持着它的象形性：弯曲的波纹，像水流的形状。作为部首，“水”通常位于汉字的左侧，写作“氵”，俗称“三点水”，例如“汉”；有时位于汉字的下面，写作“水”，例如“泉”。水部的字多与水有关，例如“汉语”的“汉”字，本是中国古代一条著名的河流的名称，刘邦做皇帝后立国号为“汉”。汉朝是中国历史上一个统治时间很长的统一王朝，影响深远，现在所说的“汉族”“汉语”之“汉”都是由此而来。

Ancient form

水 is a pictograph. The ancient form of 水 looks like a flowing river. When 水 is used as a radical standing on the left of a compound character, it is written as 氵 which is called sān diǎn shuǐ (three drops of water), for example, 汉. It can also be placed at the bottom of a compound character, such as 泉. The character 汉 (hàn) has the 氵 radical, because 汉 is the name of an ancient river —the Han

River. The Han Dynasty is one of the dynasties which maintained long-term hegemony and brought significant influence in shaping the Chinese history. Han people are known as 汉族 (Hànzú; *Han Nation*) and their language is referred as 汉语 (Hànyǔ; *Chinese*).

故事 Story

水中捞月 (Shuǐ zhōng lāo yuè)
水 water 中 in 捞 catch 月 the moon

Once upon a time, there was a group of monkeys. One night they were sitting in a big tree admiring the moon. One monkey asked: “How can we capture the moon?” Another monkey answered: “Perhaps we need to climb to the top of a mountain.” All of the monkeys agreed and so they climbed up a mountain. However, when they reached the top they were disappointed to find that the moon was still high in the sky, well beyond their reach. Later, after they descended the mountain, one monkey saw the reflection of the moon on the surface of a nearby lake: “Look, the moon is in the water! We can get it!” All the monkeys were excited; again they tried to catch the moon, and again were unable to reach it. Finally, they all jumped into the water, and the moon was broken by the ripples. 水中捞月 is an allegory for people who make impractical or vain efforts. This is similar to the English expression: crying for moon.

2. 艸 [艹] (cǎo) 部 Grass

古字形

“艸”是象形字，古文字像一棵棵生长茂盛的青草。“艸”在现代汉语中只用作部首，不单独成字。作为部首，“艸”通常位于汉字的上面，写作“艹”，俗称“草字头”。艸部的字多数是名词，一般用于指称除树木以外的植物，例如“花”“芽”。

Ancient form

艸 is a pictograph. Its ancient form looks like two stalks of grass with sprouting leaves. 艸 means *grass*. In modern Chinese, 艸 is no longer an independent character. It is used only as the radical in compound characters. When it appears at the top of a compound, it is written as 艹 which is called cǎo zì tóu (grass head). Characters containing the 艹 radical often have meanings related to grass or plants, such as 花 (huā; *flower*) and 芽 (yá; *sprout*).

故事 Story

草船借箭 (Cǎo chuán jiè jiàn)
草 straw 船 boat 借 borrow 箭 arrows

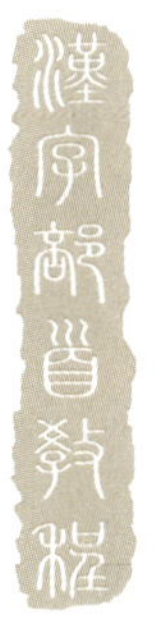

草船借箭 is a story from the Chinese novel *Three Kingdoms*. Cao Cao commanded his army to conquer the rival state of Wu. At that time, General Zhou Yu, and State Chancellor Lu Su worked for Sun Quan, and Military Councilor Zhuge Liang, worked for Liu Bei. They needed to work together to defeat Cao Cao's army. Zhou Yu envied Zhuge liang's outstanding abilities and wisdom. So he decided to set Zhuge Liang up to fail. He ordered Zhuge to prepare 100 thousand arrows within ten days for his army. But Zhuge promised to produce the arrows in just three days. If Zhuge could not get the arrows ready, then Zhou Yu could blame him for ruining their chances of winning the battle. In order to ensure Zhuge would fail, he also informed the military carpenters not to provide enough materials for making arrows. To witness Zhuge's failure, Zhou Yu sent Lu Su to help Zhuge. Zhuge was happy to accept Lu Su's help. Together they prepared twenty big boats, and outfitted each with two rows of scarecrows.

Early in the morning of the third day, Zhuge invited Lu to join him in collecting 100 thousand arrows. Lu was very puzzled but accompanied Zhuge to the riverside. It was very foggy that morning. Zhuge asked his soldiers to sail the twenty boats toward the north bank of the river where Cao's army was encamped. When the boats were close to Cao's military fort, Zhuge ordered his soldiers to shout loudly and beat their drums as if they were going to attack Cao's army. Due to the fog, Cao Cao could not tell these scarecrows were not real soldiers. Deceived, he ordered his archers to shoot at the enemy boats. After a while, the fog began to fade, so Zhuge ordered his men to sail the boats back to the south bank. When the boats returned they found more than 100 thousand arrows in the scarecrows. When Lu Su reported the whole story to Zhou Yu, Zhou Yu recognized that Zhuge was a brilliant strategist and accepted that he could never compete with him.

3. 口（kǒu）部 Mouth

古字形

“口”是象形字，古文字像人的口形，本义指人的嘴巴。由此引申为指称人的数量单位，例如“三口之家”。“口”也用来泛指进出的通道，例如“出口”“入口”等。作为部首，“口”通常位于汉字的左侧，有时位于汉字的下面、中间。口部的字多与口的动作有关，例如“吃”“喝”“叫”“告”“问”等。

Ancient form

口 is a pictograph. The ancient form of 口 depicts a person’s mouth. Therefore, 口 is also used as measure word for person, such as 三口之家 (sān kǒu zhī jiā; *a family with three people*). The other meaning of 口 is *gateway* such as in the words 出口 (chūkǒu; *exit*) and 入口 (rùkǒu; *entrance*). As a radical, it usually appears on the left side of a compound and sometimes at the bottom or in the middle of a compound. Characters with 口 often have meanings related to the actions of the mouth. This is exemplified in the characters 吃 (chī; *to eat*), 喝 (hē; *to drink*), 叫 (jiào; *to call*), 告 (gào; *to tell*), and 问 (wèn; *to ask*).

故事 Story

口蜜腹剑 (Kǒu mì fù jiàn)

口 mouth 蜜 honey 腹 stomach 剑 dagger

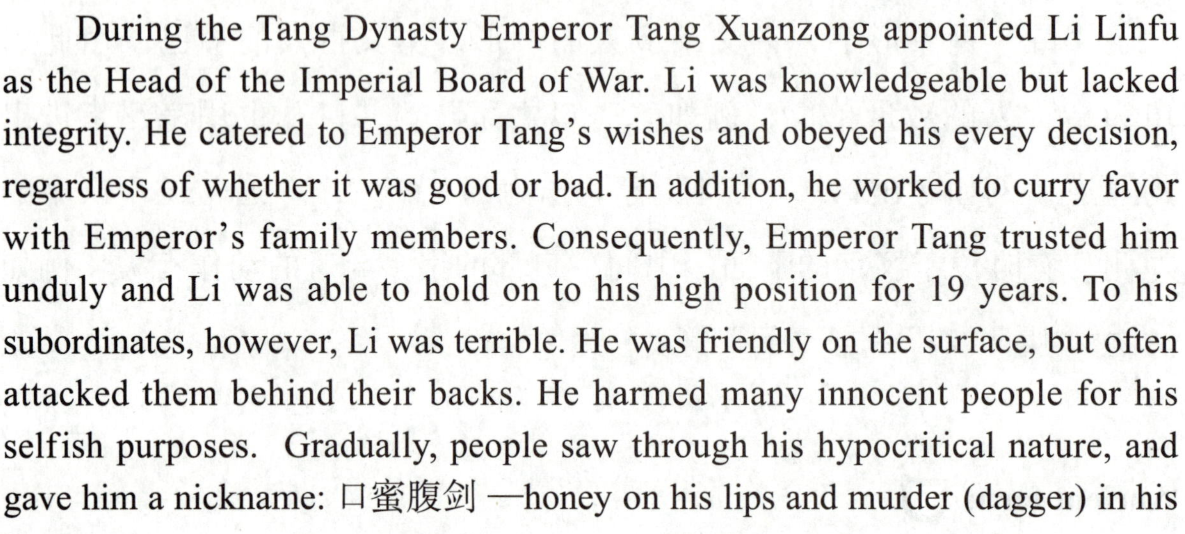

During the Tang Dynasty Emperor Tang Xuanzong appointed Li Linfu as the Head of the Imperial Board of War. Li was knowledgeable but lacked integrity. He catered to Emperor Tang's wishes and obeyed his every decision, regardless of whether it was good or bad. In addition, he worked to curry favor with Emperor's family members. Consequently, Emperor Tang trusted him unduly and Li was able to hold on to his high position for 19 years. To his subordinates, however, Li was terrible. He was friendly on the surface, but often attacked them behind their backs. He harmed many innocent people for his selfish purposes. Gradually, people saw through his hypocritical nature, and gave him a nickname: 口蜜腹剑 —honey on his lips and murder (dagger) in his heart.

4. 木 [朩] (mù) 部 Tree

古字形

“木”是象形字，古文字像树木之形：上为树枝，中为树干，下为树根。“木”的本义指树木。作为部首，“木”通常位于汉字的左侧，有时也位于汉字的其他部位。木部的字有的表示树木的种类，例如“松”“桃”等。有的表示物品的材料，例如“桌”“床”等。人居住的地方必然草木丰茂，所以“村”字中也有“木”。“集”字本义指群鸟栖息树上，引申为聚合之意。

Ancient form

木 is a pictograph. The ancient form of 木 looks like a tree. The top section is supposed to be tree branches, the middle section is the trunk, and the lower part represents the roots of the tree. Therefore, 木 means *tree or wood*. As a radical, 木 is often placed on the left side or other positions of a compound. Some characters with the 木 radical mean *the types of trees*, such as 松 (sōng; *pine tree*) and 桃 (táo; *peach tree*). Some have the meaning related to materials of the articles, such as 桌 (zhuō; *table*) and 床 (chuáng; *bed*). When we go to a village, we often see trees; therefore, the Chinese character for village is 村 (cūn). Further, trees are often full of birds who have gathered to rest. Thus, the character 集 (jí; *to gather or to collect*) has two radicals: the top one 隹 which means *bird* and the bottom 木.

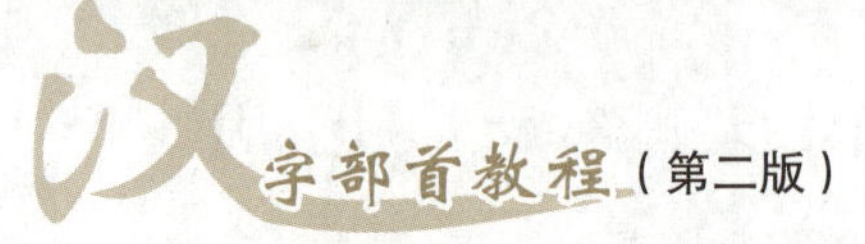

故事 Story

草木皆兵 (Cǎo mù jiē bīng)
草 grass 木 tree 皆 all 兵 soldier

草木皆兵 is a story from *The Life of Fu Jian* in the Records volume of *The History of the Jin Dynasty*. During the Eastern Jin Dynasty, King Fu Jian unified northern China as the Qin State. His plan was to take over southern China, which was unified under the Jin State. In 383, he led 900,000 infantry and cavalry troops to assault the Jin State, south of the Yangtze River. Unfortunately for Fu Jian, the first attack on the Jin troops was unexpectedly foiled and the Qin soldiers sustained heavy casualties. Many soldiers were in such a great panic that they ran away from the battlefield. Standing on the city wall of the Shouchun City, Fu Jian and his brother Fu Rong saw that, unlike their men, the Jin troops were gallantly arrayed and in high spirits. Even the bushes and trees that surrounded them seemed vibrant, as if they were armed soldiers too. Turning to his brother, Fu Jian sighed, “What a powerful enemy this is!” He deeply regretted that he had taken his enemy too lightly.

The idiom 草木皆兵 means every bush and tree looks like an enemy soldier. It is used to describe a person who is in a state of extreme agitation.

5. 手［龵 扌］(shǒu) 部 Hand

古字形

"手"是象形字，古文字像手指分开之形。从正面看，古文字的"手"恰好有五个指头。作为部首，"手"通常位于汉字的左侧，写作"扌"，俗称"提手旁"；有时位于汉字的上面，写作"龵"；有时位于汉字的下面，写作"手"。手部的字多和手或手的动作有关，例如"掌""打""拿"等字。"手"的另一个含义是指擅长某事的人，比如"歌手"。

Ancient form

手 is a pictograph. The ancient form of 手 looks like a hand with five fingers. As a radical, 手 is often placed on the left side of a compound, where it's written as 扌, which is called tí shǒu páng (lifted hand at the side). 手 also appears at the top of a compound written as 龵. When it appears at the bottom of a compound, it's written as 手. The 手 radical indicates that the character is about something related to hands, such as 掌 (zhǎng; *palm*) or actions done by hands such as 打 (dǎ; *to hit*) and 拿 (ná; *to fetch or to hold*). Hands also have connotations of "useful" and "capable." A person who can do a lot of things with their hands is competent. Therefore, another meaning of 手 is *a person who is good at a certain profession*. For example, 歌手 (gēshǒu) means *singer*.

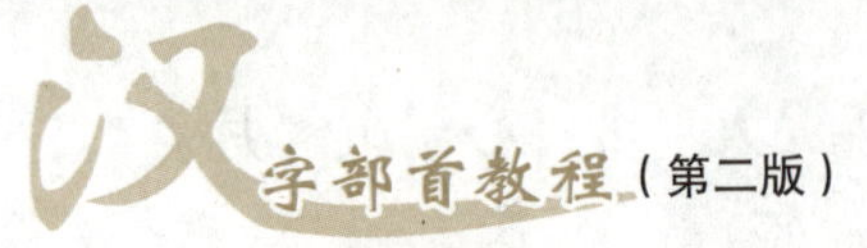

故事 Story

手舞足蹈 (Shǒu wǔ zú dǎo)

手 hands 舞 brandish 足 feet 蹈 tread

This idiom describes the situation when a person is so happy or excited, that he/she moves his/her hands and feet as in a dance.

A news article in the newspaper *East Net* on June 20, 2007 reported that a football fan Mr. Ge was watching a football game between the Netherlands and the Cote D'Ivoire. He could watch the game live by sitting on the railing of his balcony attached to his fourth-floor apartment. When the Dutch Team scored, he became so excited that he forgot where he was sitting. He became手舞足蹈. As a result, he fell off the railing, from the fourth floor to the ground level and fractured his body in four places. It seems too much excitement can occasionally be dangerous.

6. 人 [亻] (rén) 部 Person

古字形

“人”是象形字，古文字像一个侧身站立的人形，并突出了人的臂和腿。作为部首，“人”通常位于汉字的左侧，写作“亻”，俗称“单人旁”，如“他”“代”。“人”也出现在汉字的右边，如“从”，或汉字的上方和下方，如“众”。这个“众”字由三个“人”组合而成，表示人多的意思。

Ancient form

The pictograph 人 means *person*. The ancient form of 人 looks like a profile of a person. As a radical, it often stands on the left side of a compound, where it is written as 亻, which is called dān rén páng (one person at the side) such as in 他 (tā; *he*, *him*) and 代 (dài; *generation*). 人 can also be placed on the right side of a compound such as 从 (cóng; *to follow*), and at the top or bottom of a compound such as 众 (zhòng; *mass*). The character 众 consists of three people, to signify a lot of people.

故事 Story

郑人买履 (Zhèng rén mǎi lǚ)
郑 Zheng (State) 人 person 买 buy 履 shoes

This is a story about an ancient Chinese man in the Zheng State. The Zheng man wanted to buy a pair of shoes. He went to a shop and found a pair. He liked the color and style. Just as he was about to purchase the shoes, he realized that he had forgotten to bring the measurement he had taken of his feet, so he hurried home and got the measurement. Unfortunately, when he came back to the shop, it had already closed. His friend asked him, "Why did you need to go home to get the measurement? Why didn't you just try the shoes on with your own feet instead of going home?" The Zheng man answered, "I trust my measure before my feet." The idiom 郑人买履 ridicules those like the Zheng man who trust doctrine over reality.

7. 金［钅］(jīn) 部 Gold; Metals

古字形

有些学者认为“金”是形声字，从土，今声。金产生于土中，所以从土；土旁边的两点表示金属矿物埋藏于土。“金”的本义不是单指黄金，而是金属的通称。在所有的金属中，黄金是最珍贵的。今天我们也将货币称为金，如“现金”。作为部首，“金”通常位于汉字的左侧，写作“钅”，俗称“金字旁”，如“铜”；也可以位于汉字下面，如“錾”；上面，如“鑫”。金部的字，有的与金属的名称有关，如“铜”；有的是强调某些器物是由金属材料制作的，如“锅”。

Ancient form

Some Chinese scholars consider 金 (jīn; *gold*) a phonetic-semantic compound, because the ancient script of this character is formed with two characters: 今 (jīn) on the top represents the pronunciation of the character and 土 (tǔ; *earth*) at the bottom indicates its meaning—a precious metal (gold) that is excavated from the earth. The meaning of 金 is not limited to gold however. It refers to all metals and anything related to metal. In the past, gold was considered the most precious of all materials and was used as a standard of currency. As a result, 金 also means *money*, such as in the contemporary Chinese words 现金 (xiànjīn; *cash*). As a radical, when it stands on the left of a compound, it's written as 钅, called jīn zì páng (jin character at the side), such as in 铜 (tóng; *copper*). It can also be placed at the bottom 錾 (zàn; *chisel*), and on the top 鑫 (xīn; *prosperity*). The 金 radical indicates that the character signifies something related to metal such as 铜. It is also used to indicate an object that is typically made out of metal, such as 锅 (guō; *wok*).

故事 Story

拾金不昧 (Shí jīn bú mèi)

拾 pick up 金 gold 不 not 昧 put in a pocket; hide

拾金不昧 means one does not pocket the money one picks up.

This was a true story happened recently in a city in China. When leaving a taxi one day a company manager left his cell phone in the car. When the taxi driver discovered the cell phone he knew that the phone's owner must be very worried about his lost phone, so he tried to find him. However, the manager had not left his name and address with the driver, so it was only after great effort that the driver finally found him. When the manager saw his lost cell phone, he was touched by the driver's noble efforts and asked for the driver's home address. That weekend, the manager visited the driver and presented him with an envelope saying that there was just a thank-you note inside. After the manager left, the driver opened the envelope. To his surprise, in addition to the thank-you note there was also one thousand yuan! This situation generates an ethical question: If the driver accepts the money, can we still consider him to have 拾金不昧? If you were the driver, would you accept the reward money or not?

8. 心 [忄 ⺗] (xīn) 部
Heart

古字形

“心”是象形字，古文字像人体心脏之形：中间像心脏，外面像心的包络。心脏是人体最为重要的器官，心脏停止跳动意味着生命的结束。作为部首，“心”通常位于汉字的左侧，写作“忄”，俗称“竖心旁”；有时位于汉字下面，写作“心”或“⺗”。心部的字大多与人的思想感情有关。在中国古代，人们认为“心”是思考的器官，所以，像“思想”“意念”“感情”“思慕”等表示思维和情绪意义的汉字中都有“心”。

Ancient form

心 is a pictograph. The ancient form of it looks like a picture of the heart with its four chambers. The heart is one of the most vital organs in the human body. When the heart stops we die. When 心 is used as a radical on the left side of a compound, it is written as 忄 and called shù xīn páng (vertical heart at the side). 心 also occurs at the bottom of a compound, where it is written either as 心 or ⺗. In ancient China, people thought the heart was the source of all mental activity. Therefore, characters with the 心 radical tend to relate to thoughts and feelings such as 思想 (sīxiǎng; *thinking*), 意念 (yìniàn; *idea*), 感情 (gǎnqíng; *feeling*), and 思慕 (sīmù; *to admire*).

故事 Story

做贼心虚 (Zuò zéi xīn xū)

做 be 贼 thief 心 heart; mind 虚 uneasy

It was a dark night. A head thief led his three henchmen to a household. He climbed over the rear courtyard wall and approached the window of a bedroom. There he overheard a couple conversing within. The husband said: "Is it here yet?" The wife said: "Yes, but only the head is in." The head thief was astonished! How did the couple know that he was the head thief ? He beckoned his three lackeys into the yard with a wave of his hand. One of the thieves slipped around to the backyard. The husband asked: "How many now?" The wife said: "About half." The husband asked: "Shall we catch them now?" The wife said: "Definitely." This conversation scared the thieves away. They thought the couple was talking about them. Actually the couple were talking about the cockroaches inside of the room.

做贼心虚 is used to describe the paranoia of people who have a guilty conscience.

9. 土（tǔ）部 Soil; Earth

古字形

“土”是象形字，从古文字的构形来看，古人描摹的是一种特定意义的“土”：被竖立起来的土块。作为部首，“土”通常位于汉字的左侧或下面。土部的字可以表示土地的种类、地形、建筑物以及与土有关的事物，例如“地”“坡”“疆”等汉字中都有“土”。“堂”本来指高大的房子，所以“堂”从土。在中国古代，“堂”并不是一般人能进入的地方，因为国君经常在“堂”上举行祭祀、庆典等重要活动。由于“堂”在建筑上的非同一般，所以“堂”引申指盛大的样子。成语“堂堂正正”，原形容强大整齐的样子，后来也形容身材威武，仪表出众。“堂”又引申指同祖父的亲属关系，如“堂兄”。

Ancient form

土 is a pictograph. The ancient form of 土 indicates a small lump of clay. As a radical, it often appears either on the left or at the bottom of a compound. The meanings of characters containing 土 are often related to land, topography, the earth, or architecture. Here are some examples: 地 (dì; *land*), 坡 (pō; *slope*), and 疆 (jiāng; *border*). The original meaning of 堂 is *big building*, thus, 土 appears at the bottom of the character 堂. In ancient China, 堂 was a place where formal religious activities were held. Thus, 堂 often refers to a type of formal and magnificent building. The original meaning of the idiom 堂堂正正 is *powerful and well structured*. Its extended meaning refers to a person with outstanding character or handsome appearance. The extended meaning of 堂 also

refers to the relatives having kinship with grandfather (father's father), such as 堂兄 (tángxiōng; *cousin*).

故事 Story

安土乐业 (Ān tǔ lè yè)
安 peace 土 homeland 乐 happy 业 career

安土乐业 means living and working in peace and contentment.

During the Spring and Autumn Period, there was a man named Li Er. It was said that he had had grey hair and a long beard from the day he was born, therefore people called him Laozi (old man). Actually, this story is not true. Laozi is simply an honorific title the people of that time gave Li Er, because of their great respect for him. Laozi was a great scholar. He was dissatisfied with the society in which he lived because it was rife with war and poverty. He was nostalgic for the golden age of the Sage Kings. He proposed the "small country lower population" idea. He thought if the population of a small country is small, the society will have sufficient resources to support its people, and there would be no need to fight for resources and food. Then people can 安土乐业 —live a prosperous and contented life.

10. 月 [⺝] (yuè) 部 Moon; Flesh

古字形

“月”是象形字，古文字像上弦月或下弦月之形。本义指月亮，后又引申指时间，例如“年月”之“月”。月亮圆缺变化的一个周期，恰恰就是“月”表示时间的长短，所以人们根据月亮的圆缺变化周期确定了“月”这个时间单位。作为部首，“月”有时位于汉字的左侧，如“服”；有时位于汉字的右侧，如“期”；有时位于下面，如“背”。月部的字多与时间和光明有关系，例如“期”“明”等字。汉字经过隶变后，“月”和“肉”作为部首用于构字时，合并成一个形体，都写作“月”，所以月部的字又与人体有关，例如“胃”“腰”等都和人体有关，因此，在学习汉字时，我们要对“月”部字进行意义上的区分。

Ancient form

The original meaning of the pictograph 月 is *moon*. Its ancient form looks like a crescent moon. Because the waxing and waning of the moon divides the year into natural cycles, 月 also means *month*. As a radical, it can appear on the left 服 (fú; *clothes*), right 期 (qī; *period*), or at the bottom of a compound 背 (bèi; *back*).月 often indicates the meanings of the compound characters related to time and light, such as 期 and 明 (míng; *bright*). After the simplification of Seal Script in the Qin Dynasty, the character 肉 (ròu; *flesh*) was simplified to 月, the exact same character as moon. Therefore, in modern script we see characters such as 胃 (wèi; *stomach*), and 腰 (yāo; *waist*) written with 月. In these characters 月 means *flesh* rather than moon.

故事 Story

月下老人 (Yuè xià lǎo rén)
月 moon 下 under 老 old 人 man

This story took place in the Tang Dynasty. One day, a man named Weigu got up very early in the morning. As he stepped out the door to his house, he saw that the moon was still in the sky. He also saw an old man sitting on the stairway that led up to his house reading a book. When he asked the old man what he was reading, the old man replied that it was a book from the immortal realm. Shocked, Weigu asked what kind of job the old man held in the immortal world. The old man replied that he was in charge of human beings' marriages. Weigu was happy to hear this because he was very poor and had thus far been unable to find a beautiful girl to marry him. So Weigu asked the old man where he could find a girl to marry. The old man took him to a market and pointed to a three-year-old girl in a shabby dress in the distance, "She will be your future bride." Weigu was very disappointed and doubted the old man's words. But 14 years later, Weigu had become a government official and married a beautiful young girl. Curiously, he made inquiries and discovered that his bride was indeed the three-year-old girl he saw in the market 14 years ago. As Weigu's story spread, people began to believe that there was a supernatural matchmaker 月下老人 who arranged everyone's marriage.

第三课　糸、虫、言、女、竹、火、王、日、石、鱼

11. 糸 [糹 纟] (mì) 部 Silk

古字形

“糸”是象形字，古文字像一束细丝之形，本义指细丝。“糸”在现代汉语中只用作部首，不单独成字。作为部首，“糸”通常位于汉字的左侧，写作“纟”（繁体作“糹”），俗称“绞丝旁”；有时位于汉字的下面，写作“糸”。糸部的字多与服装、服饰质料有关，比如“线”“纱”，也与颜色等意义有关，比如“红”“绿”“紫”。“糸”显然不是一种颜料，为什么表示颜色的汉字中有“糸”呢？这是因为“糸”可以被染成不同的颜色。

Ancient form

糸 is a pictograph. Its original meaning is *silk*. The ancient form of 糸 looks like twisted strands of silk yarn. In modern Chinese, 糸 is no longer an independent character. It was replaced by another character 丝. 糸 is now used only as a radical. As a radical, when 糸 appears on the left of a character, it is written as 纟(糹 in traditional characters) and named as jiǎo sī páng (twisted

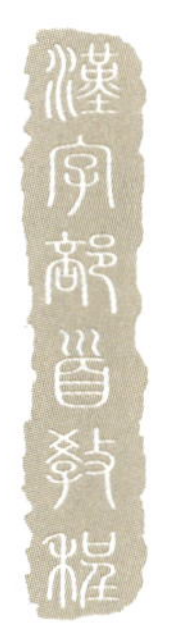

silk at the side). Characters with the 糸 radical have meanings related to making clothes or cloth materials such as 线 (xiàn; *thread*), and 纱 (shā; *gauze*). 糸 is also used for color words such as 红 (hóng; *red*), 绿 (lǜ; *green*), and 紫 (zǐ; *purple*). Why is 糸 used for color words? Because silk is dyed into different colors.

故事 Story

丝绸之路 (Sī chóu zhī lù)
丝绸 silk 之 of 路 road

According to archaeological research, China has been producing silk for about four thousand years. In the Han Dynasty, a diplomat named Zhang Qian opened a land trading route from Asia to Europe. This road started from Xi'an in China and went through Gansu, Xinjiang, West Asia, and ended in the Mediterranean countries. This route later was named as 丝绸之路— the Silk Road. According to legend, in the first century, an emperor of Rome wore a gown made of Chinese silk to watch an opera in a theater. Everyone in the theater was amazed by his luxurious gown. From then on, Chinese silk was a popular commodity among the Roman elite.

12. 虫（huǐ; chóng）部 Insect

古字形

“虫”是象形字，古文字像一条盘曲的蛇形：上面是蛇头，下面是蛇的身子。本读 huǐ，即“虺”，是一种毒蛇，后作为“蟲”的简体字。本义是昆虫的通称，引申指动物。作为部首，“虫”通常位于汉字的左侧或下面。虫部的字多与昆虫或动物有关，例如“蜜蜂”“蝴蝶”以及水生动物“虾”“蟹”等。

Ancient form

虫 is a pictograph. Its ancient form looks like a coiled snake with its head sticking out. The ancient pronunciation of 虫 is huǐ in the character 虺 (huǐ; *a venomous snake*). In modern Chinese, 虫 is the simplified form of 蟲 (chóng), which means *insect* and its pronunciation is chóng. The original meaning of 虫 refers to all kinds of insects. Its extended meaning also refers to animals. As a radical, 虫 often appears on the left side or at the bottom of a compound character. Characters with the 虫 radical usually have meaning related to insects such as 蜜蜂 (mìfēng; *bee*) and 蝴蝶 (húdié; *butterfly*). 虫 is also used for characters signifying small water animals, such as 虾 (xiā; *shrimp*) and 蟹 (xiè; *crab*).

故事 Story

冬虫夏草 (Dōng chóng xià cǎo)
冬 winter 虫 insect 夏 summer 草 grass

冬虫夏草 is the name of a precious traditional Chinese medicine which grows in the area of Tibet. It cures kidney and lung diseases. As its name suggests, this special medicine is a combination of insects and fungus. The formation of this medicine begins in winter, when a certain kind of fungus invades the body of an insect. The fungus grows and absorbs all of the insect's nutrients, eventually killing the bug. During the summer, the fungus grows out from the dead body of the insect into the ground. The medicine is then ready to be harvested. The harvesting period of 冬虫夏草 is only about 15 to 20 days. The complex development and short harvest period of this plant make this medicine rare and precious.

13. 言［讠］（yán）部 Speech

古字形

“言”是指事字，古文字像口中伸出舌头之形，表示有所言语，本义指说话，例如“发言”“言论”之“言”。作为部首，“言”通常位于汉字的左侧，写作“讠”，俗称“言字旁”；有时位于汉字的右侧或下面，写作“言”。言部的字多与言语有关，例如“评论”“谈话”等。“诚信”两个字中都有“言”。“诚”的本义为真实，不说假话。“信”的本义指作为一个人，言语应当真实，引申为信任、相信等意义。

Ancient form

言 is an indicative character. That is, the ancient script of 言 is not a pictograph—a picture of an object or event. Rather it uses symbols to suggest an abstract concept. The ancient form of 言 indicates a tongue sticking out of a mouth. It means *to speak.* As a radical, 言 is often placed on the left side, right side or at the bottom of a compound. Its simplified form is 讠, and it's called yán zì páng (yan character at the side). The 言 radical is used for words related to verbal behaviors, such as 评论 (pínglùn; *to comment*) and 谈话 (tánhuà; *to talk*). It is also used for words related to integrity, such as 诚 (chéng; *honest*) and 信 (xìn; *trust*), because integrity is established by keeping your word.

汉字部首教程

故事 Story

言归于好 (Yán guī yú hǎo)

言 talking (here 言 used as an auxiliary word) 归 restore 于 to 好 good relations

During the Spring and Autumn Period the feudal princes competed to expand their territories and authority, which caused many wars. To stop the endless violence, in 651 BC, Emperor Qi held a meeting in a city called Kuiqiu to discuss forming alliances among the princes. As a result of this meeting, the princes agreed to three things: There would be no more obstructing water resources, no more impeding food circulation, and no more hereditary officials. The princes put aside their past hostilities and became reconciled. Later, people use 言归于好 to describe any situation in which people stop fighting each other and become friends again.

14. 女（nǚ）部 Female

古字形 𠂉

“女”是象形字，古文字像一个敛手跪着的女人的形象。“女”的本义是女性、女人。作为部首，“女”通常位于汉字的左侧，如“姐”；有时位于汉字的下面，如“婆”。女部的字多和女性有关。“姓”是形声字，其中的“女”旁强调了女性在家族中的地位。传说中的“五帝”姓各不相同，黄帝姓姬，神农（即炎帝）姓姜，少昊姓嬴，虞舜姓姚，夏禹姓姒。“姬”“姜”“嬴”“姚”“姒”都是从“女”旁的，这说明在远古时代，中国历经过母系社会。不仅如此，而且那个时代，妇女处于被保护和受尊敬的地位，例如“安”字由“女”和“宀”（房子）组成。

Ancient form

女 is a pictograph. The ancient form of 女 looks like a female in a kneeling position with her two hands resting on her knees. The original meaning of 女 is *female*. As a radical, it usually appears on the left or at the bottom of a compound, such as in the character 姐 (jiě; *elder sister*) and 婆 (pó; *old woman*). Characters with the 女 radical usually have the meaning related to female. The character 姓 (xìng; *surname*) also has the 女 radical, which emphasizes the importance of the female. This is because a female gives a birth to her child. In prehistoric China, the legendary rulers the Five Lords, all had the 女 radical in their surnames. Their names were 姬 (Jī), 姜 (Jiāng), 嬴 (Yíng), 姚 (Yáo), and 姒 (Sì). This may indicate that, for a time, China was a matrilineal society—a society that traces heritage through mothers rather than fathers. It seemed that at that time,

females were protected and respected, which is reflected in the character 安 (ān; *peace or safe*). The top part of 安 is the radical 宀 (*house*) and the bottom part is 女. This could indicate the belief that a family is safe when it is run by a female.

故事 Story

女娲补天 (Nǚ wā bǔ tiān)
女娲 name of a goddess 补 patch 天 sky

In remote antiquity, there was a goddess named 女娲 . It is said that she had a human head and a snake body. She did many great things for mankind. Her most impressive gift to humanity was to patch up the sky. The sky was damaged when the God of Water had a fight with the God of Fire. In the course of their fight, one of four pillars holding up the sky was broken. Unsupported, half the sky collapsed. Then a huge crack appeared in the earth causing a big forest fire that spread across the world. The people's lives were in danger. In order to save them, 女娲 melted Five-Colored Rock and used the rock liquid to fill the hole in the sky. Then she took a huge tortoise, cut off all four feet and used them as four pillars to hold up the sky. Further catastrophe was averted and humans were able to resume normal life. However, the sky still tilted a bit towards the west and the earth tipped a bit towards the east. This is why today the sun and the moon travel towards the west, and the water in the rivers flows towards the east.

15. 竹 [⺮]（zhú）部 Bamboo

古字形

“竹”是象形字，古文字像竹之形：竹枝挺拔，竹叶下垂。作为部首，“竹”通常位于汉字的上面，写作“⺮”，俗称“竹字头”。竹部的字多与竹质材料有关系。例如“筷”，即筷子，一般是用竹子制作的，是中国人的主要餐具之一；“笛”是用竹子制作的乐器，有上千年的历史，是中国的一种民族乐器；“筏”是用竹、木等平摆着编扎成的一种水上交通工具；“簿”“篇”“笺”等字中“竹”都是表义符号，在纸发明以前，竹子曾被中国人用来制作成主要的书写材料。

Ancient form

竹 is a pictograph. The ancient form of 竹 depicts two upright bamboo poles with their leaves stretching out. When 竹 is used as a radical it often stands on the top of a compound and is written as ⺮, which is called zhú zì tóu (zhu character on the top). When it appears as a radical, it indicates that the thing the character represents is made out of bamboo. For example, 筷 (kuài) means *bamboo-made chopsticks*; 笛 (dí) means *bamboo flute*; and 筏 (fá) is a type of raft that is made of bamboo. The characters 簿 (bù; *notebook*), 篇 (piān; *a piece of writing*), and 笺 (jiān; *writing paper*) all contain ⺮. This is because before the invention of paper Chinese people wrote on slats of bamboo.

故事 Story

胸有成竹 (Xiōng yǒu chéng zhú)

胸 chest 有 have 成 mature 竹 bamboo

In the Northern Song Dynasty, a painter named Wen Tong was famous for his paintings of bamboos. Why was he so good at painting bamboos? His secret was that he planted all kinds of bamboos around his house, so he could observe these bamboos growing and changing in different seasons and in different weather conditions. Gradually, the varied images of these bamboos were imprinted in his mind, and appeared vividly before his eyes whenever he began to paint. A poet described Wen Tong's great skill in painting bamboos as 胸有成竹 —the concept of bamboo exists in painter's mind before painting. Later, people used this idiom to describe the situation of having a well-thought-out plan beforehand.

16. 火 [灬] (huǒ) 部 Fire

古字形

“火”是象形字，古文字像火苗上蹿之状。“火”的本义指火焰。作为部首，“火”有时位于汉字的左侧，写作“火”；有时位于汉字的下面，常写作“灬”，俗称“四点底”，例如“煮”指用火做饭，“热”指温度高。可想而知，火部的字大都与火、热或光等意义有关。例如“灭”，是新造会意字，上“一”下“火”，表示把火压住并使之熄灭。又如“灰烬”即物质燃烧后剩下的粉末状的东西。

Ancient form

火 is a pictograph. The ancient form looks like a burning campfire. Its original meaning is *fire*. As a radical, it is often placed on the left or at the bottom of a compound. When placed at the bottom of a character, 火 is sometimes written as 灬 and called sì diǎn dǐ (four drops at the bottom), as in the characters 煮 (zhǔ; *to cook*) and 热 (rè; *hot*). Obviously, if a character has 火 as a radical, its meaning probably relates to fire. For example, 灭 (miè) is formed by placing 一 (*a cover*) over 火 (*fire*), and so it means *to extinguish*. In the two-character word 灰烬 (huījìn) both characters have the 火 radical to indicate the meaning *ash*—the product left after a fire.

故事 Story

火烧赤壁 (Huǒ shāo chì bì)

火 fire 烧 burn 赤 red 壁 cliff

This is another story from the novel *Three Kingdoms*. In 208, Cao Cao, Liu Bei, and Sun Quan, were still competing to become the emperor of all of China. One day Cao Cao led 200 thousand soldiers in an attack on Liu's southern territory. He intended to defeat Liu and then conquer Sun. Liu and Sun, however, finally formed an alliance to stand against Cao at Red Cliff (a town in the south side of Yangtze River. Today the town is called Chibi City in Hubei Province). Zhou Yu—the General of Sun's army, and Zhuge Liang—the Military Councilor of Liu Bei, got together to prepare for this military assault. They knew that they had much fewer soldiers than Cao Cao. It would not be wise to engage in one-to-one direct combat. However, the battle was fought on the river beside Red Cliff. Cao's soldiers were all from dry northern China, and therefore most of them did not know how to swim. For this reason, Cao Cao had ordered his troops to connect their war boats with iron chains and also to pave the spaces between the ships with wood boards, so that the soldiers could engage in combat in the boats as if they were on land. Knowing this, Zhou and Zhuge decided to attack with fire. Pretending that they were going to capitulate to Cao, they prepared more than 10 small boats and sailed towards Cao's war boats. Cao was tricked and pleased to see his enemy with intention of surrendering. Then suddenly, each

small boat burst into flames! The strong southeast wind caught the fire and quickly spread it into Cao's battleships. Soon all of Cao's boats were burned to ash and most of his soldiers were dead by burning or drowning. All Cao could do was to collect his surviving soldiers and to withdraw to the north.

17. 王（玉）（wáng）部 King; Jade

古字形

“王”是象形字，古文字一说像斧头之形。斧头代表着杀伐之权，这样就很自然地引申为统治与权力。在中国古代，“王”专指最高统治者，即指统治天下的君主。作为部首，“王”有时位于汉字的下面，有时位于汉字里面，多与帝王等意义有关，例如“皇”。汉字经隶变之后，“王”和“玉”作为部首时，往往混同为一个形体，所以现代汉字中许多带有“王”部首的字，其意义往往和玉有关。例如“玲”指玉的声音，“理”本指对玉石加工或雕琢。

Ancient form

王is a pictograph. Some Chinese scholars believe the ancient form of 王 is a picture of an axe. An axe could represent the right to kill which extended only to the emperor. Therefore its extended meaning is *ruler*. As a radical, it sometimes appears at the bottom of a compound and sometimes inside a compound. Characters containing the 王 radical have meanings related to rulers or ruling such as皇 (huáng; *emperor*). After the simplification of Seal Script in the Qin Dynasty, 玉 (yù) was simplified to share the character as 王. 玉 means *jade*, as in 玲 (líng; *the clinking sound of jade pieces colliding*) and 理 (lǐ; *jade processing and carving*; *to handle*). Therefore, when you see a character with the 王 radical, bear in mind it could mean something related to jade rather than ruling.

故事 Story

抛砖引玉 (Pāo zhuān yǐn yù)
抛 cast 砖 brick 引 attract 玉 jade

In ancient China there lived a man named Zhao Gu, who wrote very good poems. Another man—Chang Jian—also wrote poems, but he thought his poetry was not as good as Zhao Gu's. Chang decided to surreptitiously solicit a poem from Zhao to keep it as a piece of collection. One day, Chang learned that Zhao would visit Lingyan Temple. So he wrote a few verses on the wall of the temple, but left the poem incomplete. He hoped that Zhao would see his half-done poem and would not be able to resist adding a second half. Sure enough, Zhao completed the poem. Later people started to refer to Chang's clever scheme as 抛砖引玉, because he used his mediocre verses (bricks) as bait to get excellent verses (jade) from Zhao Gu.

Today 抛砖引玉 means to initiate a discussion with simple remarks so that others may come up with valuable ideas. This is also a self-deprecating remark used when modestly referring to one's contribution in a group effort.

18. 日 [日] (rì) 部 Sun

古字形

“日”是象形字，古文字像太阳之形：轮廓像圆形的太阳，一横或一点表示太阳的光。“日”的本义指太阳，引申指白天，又引申为计算时间的单位，例如“十日”，即十天。作为部首，“日”通常位于汉字的左侧、上面或下面。日部的字多与太阳、时间等意义有关。“时”指一切事物不断发展变化所经历的过程，即时间。“早”本指早晨，即太阳升起的时候，引申指时间，与“晚”相对，例如“早起晚睡”。一年之计在于春，春为四季之始，阳光灿烂，万物复苏，生气勃勃，所以“春”字中也有日。

Ancient form 

日 is a pictograph. The ancient form of 日 is a picture of sun. The stroke inside the circle symbolizes the rays of sun. The original meaning of 日 is *sun*. Its extended meanings are *day and time*. For example, 时 (shí) means *time*; 早 (zǎo) means *morning* (the character suggests that the sun is rising over the horizon); 晚 (wǎn) means *night* (the character suggests that the sun is setting in the west); and 春 (chūn) means *spring* (the character suggests that the sunshine is now reaching the new spring grass). As you can see from the examples above, the 日 radical can occur on the left, top, or bottom of a compound.

故事 Story

夸父追日 (Kuā fù zhuī rì)
夸父 name of a giant 追 chase 日 sun

In remote antiquity, a group of giants lived deep in the mountains of northern China. The Head of the group was named 夸父. He had a pair of gold snakes hanging from his ears and had another two wrapped around his wrists. One year, the weather was extremely hot and dry. Every day the sun shone hotter than before. The trees all died and the rivers all dried out. 夸父 decided that to save themselves mankind needed to control of the sunshine, so he set out to capture the sun. After many days of chasing, he saw the sun was just in front of him. So he opened his arms to grab it, but the hot, bright sun slowly roasted him. He dehydrated and died. While dying, he lamented his failure and threw away his walking stick in grief. Suddenly, the ground where the walking stick fell erupted into a vast forest of peach trees. The peaches from these trees quenched the thirst of weary travelers throughout history.

19. 石（shí）部 Stone; Rock

古字形

“石”是象形字，古文字像岩角下一石块之形。“石”的本义指山石，后引申指坚定和牢固。作为部首，“石”通常位于汉字的左侧，有时位于汉字的上面或下面。石部的字多与山石或石制材料有关，如“础”本指柱脚石，引申指事物的基底或根基，如“基础”。“碗”是形声字，从石宛声。

Ancient form

石 is a pictograph. Its ancient form looks like a rock falling from a cliff. The original meaning of 石 is *mountain rock or stone*. The extended meaning is *strong and stable* (*as a rock*). As a radical, it can be placed on the left, top, or bottom of a compound. Characters with the 石 radical are often related to rock or things made from stone. For example, 础 (chǔ) means *foundation*, which is one of stone's primary functions. The character 碗 (wǎn; *bowl*) is a phonetic-semantic compound. The 石 radical on the left suggests that the bowl is made of stone. The right part 宛 is a phonetic radical to indicate that the pronunciation of this character is wǎn.

点石成金 (Diǎn shí chéng jīn)
点 touch 石 stone 成 become 金 gold

It is said that in the Jin Dynasty, there was a magistrate of Jingyang County, named Xu Xun, who could do magic. One year, due to terrible weather conditions, there was no harvest of grain. Peasants were not able to pay their taxes. Xu Xun then used his magic to help the people. He touched a stone and immediately it turned into a piece of gold. He distributed the gold to all the peasants so that they could use it to pay their taxes. Now the idiom 点石成金 also means to turn a crude essay into a literary gem.

20. 鱼［魚］（yú）部 Fish

古字形

“鱼”是象形字，古文字像鱼之形。“鱼”和“余”谐音，因此在中国的民俗文化中，“鱼”是富足、吉祥、有余的象征，所以中国人设宴庆祝节日时一定要吃鱼。作为部首，“鱼”通常位于汉字的左侧，有时位于汉字的下面。鱼部的字多和鱼有关，例如“鲤”，即“鲤鱼”，是中国常见的一种鱼。“鲜”字最早指活鱼、鲜鱼，引申指味道鲜美。“鲠”指鱼骨头。

Ancient form 

鱼 is a pictograph. The ancient form of 鱼 is a drawing of a fish. Because the pronunciation of fish 鱼 (yú) is the same as the pronunciation for 余 (yú; *surplus*), so Chinese people always eat a fish on major holidays to bring good luck and plenty. As a radical, 鱼 often appears on the left or at the bottom of a compound. The meanings of characters with the 鱼 radical often connect fish or fish related things, such as 鲤 (lǐ; *carp*), 鲜 (xiān; *fresh as fish*), and 鲠 (gěng; *fishbone*).

故事 Story

缘木求鱼 (Yuán mù qiú yú)
缘 climb 木 tree 求 catch 鱼 fish

In the Warring States Period, the King of Qi intended to rule his state with force. However, Mencius offered the King a piece of advice: "Your Majesty, using force to control your people would be just like climbing a tree to catch a fish. You're making a futile effort." The King accepted Mencius' advice and ruled his country with benevolence.

缘木求鱼 is used to describe working in a wrong direction or striving in opposition to natural laws. When a person works in this way it is impossible to achieve his goals.

第四课　山、足、鸟、疒、辵、衣、犬、目、刀、邑

21. 山（shān）部 Mountain

古字形

“山”是象形字，古文字像山峰并立之形。本义指地面上由土石构成的高出地面的部分。作为部首，“山”通常位于汉字的左侧，有时位于汉字的上面或下面。山部的字，一般都与山岭或山的形状有关系。“峰”指高而尖的山头，“岩”指高峻的山崖或构成地壳的石头，“岳”指高大的山。“五岳”指中国的五大名山：东岳泰山、南岳衡山、西岳华山、北岳恒山、中岳嵩山，其中泰山为五岳之尊。

Ancient form

山 is a pictograph. The ancient form of 山 depicts three distant mountain peaks. Therefore, the original meaning of 山 is *mountain*. As a radical, it sometimes appears on the left side of a compound and sometimes on the top or bottom of a compound. Characters containing the 山 radical have meanings related to mountain. For example, the character 峰 (fēng) means *peak*; 岩 (yán) means *crag or rock in a mountain*; and 岳 (yuè) means *magnificent mountains*.

In China, there are five 岳: 东岳 the Eastern Mountain (Mount Tai, 泰山), 南岳 the Southern Mountain (Mount Heng, 衡山), 西岳 the Western Mountain (Mount Hua, 华山), 北岳 the Northern Mountain (Mount Heng, 恒山), and 中岳 the Central Mountain (Mount Song, 嵩山). Among them, Mount Tai is the most famous.

故事 Story

愚公移山 (Yú gōng yí shān)

愚 foolish 公 old man 移 move 山 mountain

Once upon a time, there was an old man. People called him Yugong (foolish man). He was about 90 years old. In front of his home there were two mountains that caused great inconvenience to his family. To go anywhere they had to climb over the mountains. Yugong decided to remove the two mountains. Another old man called Zhisou (wise man) lived near the Yellow River. When he heard of Yugong's plan he laughed, saying, "Yugong is foolish. He is so old and the mountains are so big. How can he remove them?" But Yugong replied: "If I cannot finish my work, my children, grand-children and their descendants will continue my efforts. Eventually, we will move the mountains." Yugong's determination impressed the Lord of Heaven, so he sent two supernatural beings to help move the two mountains away.

This story shows that with dogged perseverance everything is possible.

22. 足［⻊］（zú）部 Foot

古字形

“足”是会意字，古文字下部是“止”，即脚的象形，上面的形状一说是膝盖的象形，两部分合起来正好是古代“足”所指的部位：自膝盖到足趾的部分，也就是今天我们所说的“小腿”。后来，“足”表示人和某些动物身体最下部接触地面的部分，也就是我们今天所称的“脚”。作为部首，“足”通常位于汉字的左侧，写作“⻊”。足部的字大多与脚有关。“跟”指脚的后部，“趾”指脚趾，“踢”指用脚触击，“跑”指两脚交互向前迅速前进，例如“跑步”，“路”指往来通行的地方。

Ancient form

足 is an ideograph. The top part of the ancient form indicates the knee, and the bottom part is the lower leg and foot. Afterwards, 足 came to be used to refer exclusively to feet. As a radical, 足 often appears on the left side of a compound, which is written as ⻊. Characters that contain 足 often have meanings related to parts of the foot or actions that use the feet. For example, 跟 (gēn) means *heel*; 趾 (zhǐ) means *toe*; 踢 (tī) means *to kick*; 跑 (pǎo) means *to run*; and 路 (lù) means *road* (*amenity for walking*).

故事 Story

画蛇添足 (Huà shé tiān zú)

画 draw 蛇 snake 添 add 足 feet

A long time ago, a family gave their God an offering of a jar of wine. After the ceremony, the host of the family gave the wine to his servants. There were several servants and all of them wanted the whole jar. One servant came up with an idea to decide the issue. He suggested that they hold a drawing contest. They would each draw a snake. The person who finished drawing the snake first would get the wine. Everyone agreed to this plan and started drawing. One person drew very fast. He finished the snake and grabbed the wine jar with one hand. Noticing the others were still working, he used his other hand to continue drawing and adding feet to his snake. When he was doing so, another person finished drawing and grabbed the jar of wine from his hand saying, "Snakes don't have feet, so what you drew is not a snake! I finished drawing a snake first so I am the winner."

This story is a warning not to ruin the effect by adding something unnecessary.

23. 鸟［鳥］(niǎo) 部 Bird

古字形

“鸟”是象形字，古文字像一只长尾长羽的飞禽之形。本义指鸟，引申指飞禽的总称。作为部首，“鸟”通常位于汉字的右侧，有时位于汉字的左侧或下面。鸟部的字多与飞禽及其习性有关。“鸡”“鸭”“鹅”之所以都从鸟部，是因为它们都是鸟类。“鸣”本来指鸟的叫声，引申指飞禽或昆虫的叫声。

Ancient form

鸟 is a pictograph. Its ancient form is a vivid portrayal of a bird with a long tail and long feathers. Therefore, its original meaning is *bird*. Later 鸟 was used to refer to any kind of birds. As a radical, 鸟 is often placed on the right side of a compound. Sometimes it is placed on the left side or at the bottom of a compound. The meanings of characters with the 鸟 radical are often associated with birds, such as 鸡 (jī; *chicken*), 鸭 (yā; *duck*), and 鹅 (é; *goose*). This radical can also signify birds' behaviors, such as 鸣 (míng; *birdsong*).

故事 Story

百鸟朝凤 (Bǎi niǎo cháo fèng)
百 hundred 鸟 birds 朝 follow 凤 phoenix

Long time ago, the phoenix was just one of hundreds of ordinary birds. The phoenix, however, was a very diligent bird. While the other birds were playing and sleeping, she worked everyday from morning till night collecting food and storing it in a cave, until she had amassed a huge store. One year, there was a huge drought. There was no food in woods and the other birds were starving. When seeing the other birds suffering, the phoenix opened her cave and let the others share her food so that no bird died. In order to thank the phoenix for her generosity, each bird pulled one feather from their body and made a beautiful robe. They presented it to the phoenix as a birthday gift. They also elected the phoenix Queen of the Birds.

This is why phoenixes are the most beautiful birds in the world.

24. 疒（nè）部 Sickness

古字形

“疒”是象形字，古文字描摹的是病人卧床之形。“疒”在现代汉语中只用作部首，不单独成字。作为部首，“疒”总是位于汉字的左上侧，俗称“病字旁”。疒部的字多与疾病或治疗等意义有关，如“癌”“痛”“疗”。“病”是形声字，从疒丙声，本义指疾病。

Ancient form

疒 is a pictograph. The ancient script of 疒 shows a sick person lying down in a bed. 疒 is no longer an independent character in modern Chinese. It is only used as radical. As a radical, it is often placed on the upper left of a compound, which is called bìng zì páng (sickness at the side). Characters containing the 疒 radical often have meanings related to disease, discomfort, and treatment, such as in the characters 癌 (ái; *cancer*), 痛 (tòng; *pain*), and 疗 (liáo; *cure*). The character 病 (bìng; *sickness*) is a phonetic-semantic compound. The 疒 radical signifies its meaning of sickness, 丙 (bǐng) hints at the sound of the character, which is bìng.

故事 Story

病入膏肓 (Bìng rù gāo huāng)

病 disease 入 attack 膏肓 vitals

The King of the Jin State was very ill. He had seen many doctors in the State, but his symptoms did not get any better. One day, he dreamed a dialog of two persons. The content of the dialog was "Even though the King of Jin is powerful, if we two get into his heart and destroy the vital parts of his organs, he would die." The King was very worried. Thus, he quickly sent his servant for a famous doctor in the Qin State. The doctor came to Jin and visited the King. He examined him carefully. After the examination, the doctor told the King that his illness was incurable because the disease had already attacked his vital organs. It was too late to do anything.

The idiom 病入膏肓 describes a problem or calamity that is already beyond repair.

25. 辵［⻌］（chuò）部 Walking; Movement

古字形

“辵”是会意字，古文字形像一个十字路口，上面有脚印。本义指走走停停。作为部首，“辵”通常位于汉字左下侧，写作“⻌”，俗称“走之底”。辵部的字大多与行走等意义有关，如“逃”“追”“迁”。再如，“进”的本义是向前移动；“造”的本义是到达，在现代汉语中“造”的另一个常用义是创造或制造。

Ancient form

辵 is an ideograph. The ancient form of 辵 looks like a picture of a crossroads tracked with footprints—to symbolize that people are walking in the streets. The original meaning of 辵 is *intermittent walking*. As a radical, when 辵 is placed on the lower-left of a compound, it is written as ⻌ and called zǒu zhī dǐ (walking at the bottom). The characters containing the 辵 radical often have meanings related to movement. For example, 逃 (táo) means *to run*; 追 (zhuī) means *to chase*; and 迁 (qiān) means *to move*. The character 进 (jìn; *to enter*) originally meant *to move forward*. In modern Chinese, however, some characters with the 辵 radical have more than one meaning. Consider, for example, the character 造 (zào), while its original meaning is *to reach,* in modern Chinese 造 also means *to make or to create*.

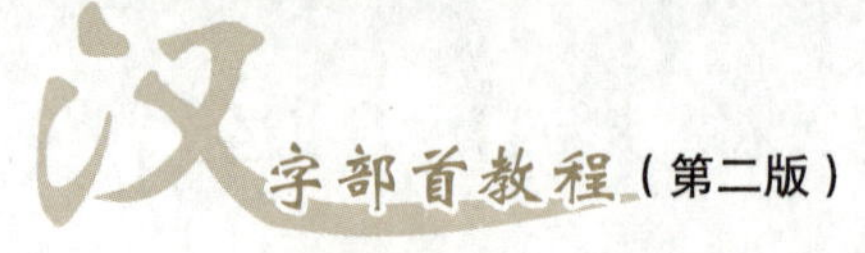

故事 Story

随与隋朝 (Suí yǔ Suí cháo)
随 sui 与 and 隋 Sui 朝 Dynasty

Character 随 originally was used for the Sui Dynasty because the surname of the first Emperor in the Sui Dynasty was 随. However, later the Emperor changed the character from 随 to 隋 for his Dynasty, because 随 has the 辶 radical which implies motion. The Emperor considered motion a sign of turbulence and instability, something he did not want for his country.

26. 衣［衤］(yī) 部
Clothes; Clothing

古字形

“衣”是象形字，古文字像上衣之形：上面像领口，两旁像袖筒，下面像两襟左右相覆。“衣”的本义指上衣，引申指衣服的通称。作为部首，“衣”通常位于汉字的左侧，写作“衤”，俗称“斜衣旁”；有时位于汉字下面，写作“衣”。衣部的字多与衣服有关。“装”本指行装，引申指“服装”“装饰”等意义。“衫”指上衣，如“衬衫”。“裁”本指剪裁衣服，引申指剪裁其他事物。

Ancient form 𧘇

衣 is a pictograph. The ancient form of this character depicts the top part of a Chinese gown with a low-cut collar and two loose sleeves. Originally, 衣 referred only to the clothes worn on the torso—coats and shirts. Later, 衣 came to be used to refer to all types of clothing. When the 衣 radical stands on the left side of a compound it is written as 衤 and called xié yī páng (cloth at the side). It sometimes appears at the bottom of a compound and is written as 衣. Characters containing 衣 are usually related to clothing and cloth. The character 装, its original meaning is *luggage* (*packed with clothes*). It also means clothes and adornment. 衫 usually refers to *clothes* for upper body such as 衬衫 (chènshān; *shirt or blouse*). The original meaning of 裁 is *to cut a piece of cloth*. Later, it also means *to cut any object*.

故事 Story

一衣带水 (Yī yī dài shuǐ)

一 one 衣 clothing 带 strip 水 water

At the end of the Southern Dynasties, there was a State located in south of the Yangtze River known as Chen. The Emperor Sui Wendi decided to conquer Chen in order to unify all of China. He led his army to the northern side of the Yangtze River, but due to the Yangtze River's raging current his army was not able to cross. However, the Emperor Sui did not give up. He said: “My goal of unifying the country will not be ruined by a strip of water.” So he ordered his

army to build ships. In the end he successfully conquered Chen and established the Sui Dynasty.

Today, Chinese people use 一衣带水 to describe two places are close but separated by a river.

27. 犬［犭］（quǎn）部 Dog; Animal

古字形

“犬”是象形字，古文字像犬之形。“犬”的本义指狗。古人多称“狗”为“犬”，犬是人类亲密接触的动物之一。“犬”还是动物类汉字的主要标志之一，例如“狼”“猴”“猫”等字中都有“犬”。作为部首，“犬”通常位于汉字的左侧，写作“犭”，俗称“反犬旁”；有时位于汉字的右侧和下面，写作“犬”。犬部的字多与狗或动物的名称、习性等意义有关。“吠”指狗的叫声。“嗅”本指狗的嗅觉灵敏。“猛”本指健壮的狗，引申指行动迅捷，力量强大。“狠”本指狗争斗时发出的声音，后引申指凶恶。“状”本指狗之形状，引申指各种事物的形状、形态。

Ancient form

犬 is a pictograph. Its ancient form looks like a dog in an upright position. According to historical chronicles, the Chinese people have always had a close relationship with dogs. This could be the reason that people use 犬 as a basic radical to create many new characters for animals such as 狼 (láng; *wolf*), 猴 (hóu; *monkey*), and 猫 (māo; *cat*). Please note that as a radical standing on the left side of a compound 犬 is written as 犭, which is called fǎn quǎn páng (dog at the side). It sometimes appears on the right or bottom of a compound and is written as 犬. The meaning of characters that contain 犬 are usually related to dogs, animals, or animal behaviors, such as 吠 (fèi; *to bark*). The character 嗅 (xiù; *to smell*) uses an allusion to dog's acute sense of smell to suggest its meaning. 猛 (měng; *fierce*) originally meant a strong dog; and the original meaning of 狠 (hěn; *ruthless*) is *the growl* produced by dogs when they are fighting. The character 状 (zhuàng; *shape*) originally referred to *the shape of a dog*.

故事 Story

蜀犬吠日 (Shǔ quǎn fèi rì)

蜀 short for Sichuan Province 犬 dog 吠 bark 日 sun

Surrounded by high mountains, the Sichuan Basin is humid, and it rains often. It is often foggy. The mist in the middle plain does not evaporate easily. Because of seldom seeing sunny days in that area, when dogs see the sun in the sky, they feel novel and start to bark. Thus, 蜀犬吠日 means having seen little, one gets excited easily.

28. 目（mù）部 Eye

古字形

“目”是象形字，古文字描摹的是眼睛的形状：外边轮廓像眼眶，里面像瞳孔。“目”的本义就是指人的眼睛。作为部首，“目”通常位于汉字的左侧，有时位于汉字的下面。目部的字多与眼睛有关。“眉”指眼睛上面的眉毛。“盼”本指眼睛黑白分明，引申指希望、向往。“睡”指闭目休息。“看”字由“目”和“手”组成，表示一个人把手放在眼睛上方正在看什么。

Ancient form

目 is a pictograph. The ancient form of this character is a picture of eye.

The original meaning of 目 is *eye*. As a radical, it often stands on the left side of a compound. It also sometimes appears at the bottom of a compound. Characters containing 目 have meanings related to eyes, the area of the face around the eye, or eye-related activities. For examples, 眉 (méi) means *eyebrow*. The character 盼 (pàn) originally referred to the bright colors in the eye—white and black. The extended meaning of 盼 is *to look forward*. 睡 (shuì) means *to sleep with eyes closed*. 看 (kàn) means *to see*. This character consists 手 and 目 indicating a hand is placed above an eye to see something.

故事 Story

刮目相看 (Guā mù xiāng kàn)
刮 rub 目 eye 相 to 看 look

During the Three Kingdoms Period, there was a General in the Wu State named Lü. Lü came from a poor family and had no opportunity for formal education. People said the only thing he knew how to do was to fight. Later, he took the King's advice and decided to teach himself reading and military knowledge. He studied diligently. After a few days he met with General Lu. They discussed military affairs together. Lu found that Lü had learned a lot. He praised him and said that although General Lü had studied only for three days, he must be considered with new eyes.

刮目相看 is used to describe the situation when a person must be treated with increased respect.

29. 刀［刂⺈］（dāo）部 Knife

古字形

“刀”是象形字，古文字像一把刀的形状。刀的历史十分悠久，据考古学家考证，在中国的史前时期已有许多石刀。作为部首，“刀”通常位于汉字的右侧，大多写作“刂”，俗称“立刀旁”，有时写作“刀”；位于汉字上面时写作“⺈”；位于汉字下面时写作“刀”。刀部的字大都与刀或刻划等意义有关。“利”是会意字，从刀从禾，表示以刀断禾的意思，本义指刀口快，锋利，例如“利刃”。“绝”也是会意字，从糸，表示与丝线有关，从刀，从卩（人），表示人用刀断丝，本义指把丝弄断，引申指断绝，例如“绝交”。“切”是形声字，从刀七声，意思是用刀把物品分成若干部分。“分”是以刀剖物，使之分开。

Ancient form

刀 is a pictograph. The ancient form of this character looks like a knife. According to archaeological studies, during the prehistoric age the Chinese people had already invented several types of stone knives. As a radical, when 刀 is placed on the right side of a compound, it is written as 刂 which is called lì dāo páng (erected knife at the side) and sometimes written as 刀. When 刀 is placed on the top of a compound, it is written as ⺈; at the bottom of a compound is written as刀. Characters that contain 刀 often have meanings related to using knife to do something. 利 (lì) is an ideograph. It is a combination of the 禾 (hé) radical for grain and the 刂 radical for knife. The original meaning of 利 is *to use a knife to cut grain*. The extended meanings of 利 are *benefits and sharp*.

绝 (jué) is also an ideograph. There is a 糸 (mì; *silk*) radical on the left. So the character means *to cut silk with a knife*. The extended meaning of 绝 is *to cut off*. 切 (qiē) is a phonetic-semantic compound. The left part, 七 (qī), indicates the pronunciation of the character. The right part 刀 indicates the meaning of this character—*to cut*. The character 分 (fēn) means *to separate*. The original meaning of it is *to cut an object into two pieces with a knife*.

故事 Story

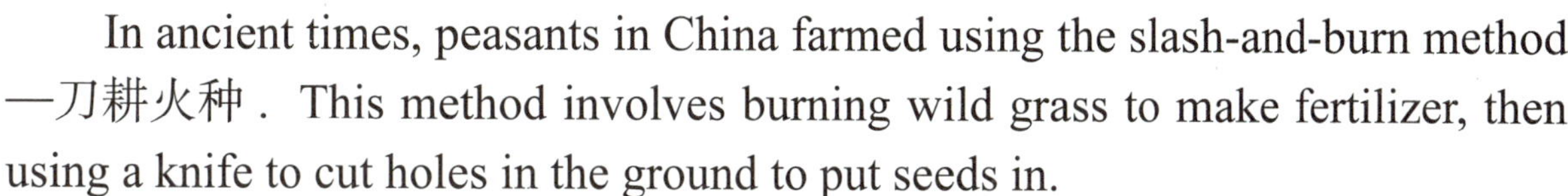

刀耕火种 (Dāo gēng huǒ zhòng)
刀 knife 耕 plough 火 fire 种 plant

In ancient times, peasants in China farmed using the slash-and-burn method —刀耕火种. This method involves burning wild grass to make fertilizer, then using a knife to cut holes in the ground to put seeds in.

刀耕火种 sometimes is used to describe something that is in a primitive or underdeveloped stage.

30. 邑［阝在右］（yì）部 City

古字形 𨸏

“邑”是会意字，古文字上面是“囗（wéi）”，表示疆域，下面是跪着的人形，表示人口，合起来的意思是城邑。作为部首，“邑”通常位于汉字的右侧，写作“阝”，俗称“右耳旁”。邑部的字多和地名、城郊等意义有关。“都（dū）”指大都市，“通都大邑”是指四通八达的大都会、大城市；又引申指某一国家最高的行政机关所在地，例如“首都”。“郊”指城市之外的区域。

Ancient form

邑 is an ideograph. In the ancient script it consists of two parts: the top part 囗 (wéi; *to encircle*) indicating the boundary of a city and the bottom part representing a kneeling person, which in this character signifies the populace. Together, 邑 means *city or town*. As a radical, 邑 is often placed on the right side of a compound, where it is written as 阝 and called yòu ěr páng (right ear at the side). Characters with 阝 often have meanings related to places, cities, or towns. For example, 都 (dū) means *metropolis*, and 通都大邑 refers to the convenience of road and transportation systems in metropolises and big cities. 都 also means *capital*. 郊 (jiāo) means *suburbs*.

故事 Story

五邑侨乡 (Wǔ yì qiáo xiāng)
五 five 邑 city 侨 overseas 乡 town

五邑 is located in the Jiangmen City in the west of Zhujiang Delta of Guangdong Province. Because Jiangmen City consists of five small towns, throughout history Jiangmen has been called 五邑 (the five cities). People also refer to 五邑 as 侨乡 (the town of overseas Chinese). This is because 57% of the population is composed of "overseas Chinese" —Chinese who were foreign born or spent some time abroad. People of 五邑 have been immigrating to foreign countries for over a thousand years. Immigrants from 五邑 are distributed over 107 countries in the world. Most of them reside in the United States and Canada. The younger generations of these immigrants also come back and reside in 五邑. This is the major reason that 五邑 becomes a 侨乡.

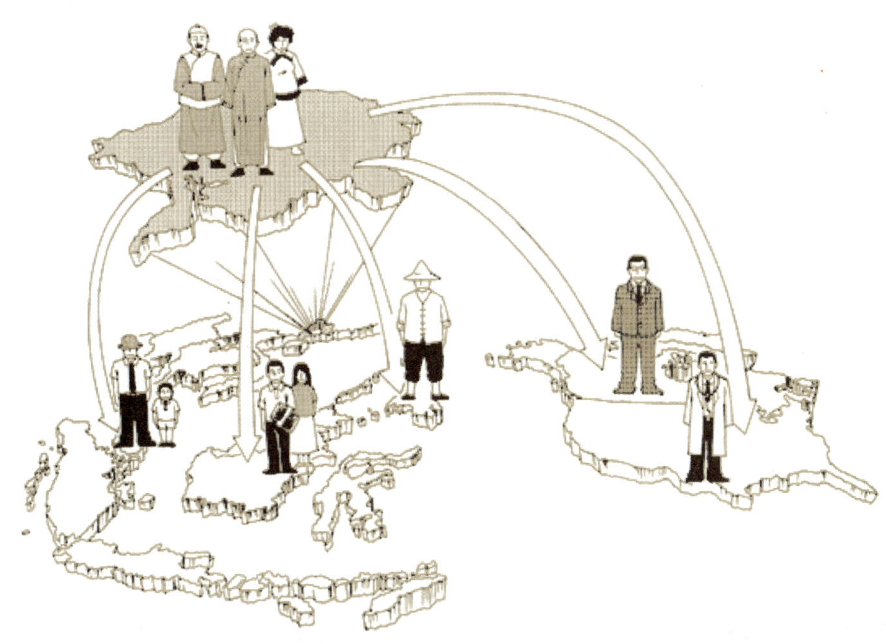

第五课 宀、禾、马、贝、车、阜、示、食、酉、八

31. 宀（mián）部 House

古字形 ⌒

"宀"是象形字，古文字像房屋之形。"宀"在现代汉语中只用作部首，不单独成字。作为部首，"宀"总是位于汉字的上面，俗称"宝盖头"。宀部的字多和房屋或居住有关。"家"指家庭，由"宀"和"豕"组成，"宀"表示房屋，是家的空间建筑形式；而"豕"则是一头猪。为什么让"豕"居于"宀"中才是"家"呢？从考古发现来看，新石器时代文化遗址中出土的家畜骨骸中猪骨最多。由此可以推断，先民饲养的家畜中，"豕"是最多的一类。"室"则指房间。

Ancient form ⌒

宀 is a pictograph. The ancient script of 宀 looks like an outline of a house. In modern Chinese 宀 is no longer an independent character. Rather, it is used only as a radical placed on the top of a compound, which is called bǎo gài tóu (roof on the top). The meanings of characters containing this radical relate to houses or rooms. The character 家 (jiā) means *home*. It consists of two radicals:

the 宀 radical indicating a dwelling and 豕 referring to a pig. Why did the ancient Chinese use a pig under a roof to indicate "home?" Archaeological studies show that pigs were the most common domestic animal during the Neolithic Age. This is probably the reason that 豕 was used to create the character 家. Another character 室 (shì), means *room*.

故事 Story

引狼入室 (Yǐn láng rù shì)

引 invite 狼 wolf 入 enter 室 house

Once upon a time, there was a shepherd who was tending to sheep. One day he realized there was a wolf following his flock. At first, he was very cautious, afraid the wolf would attack the sheep. The wolf, however, did not hurt the sheep. The next day, when the shepherd drove his sheep back into the mountains, the same wolf appeared. Again he did not attack the sheep but just followed quietly. After a month, the shepherd came to believe that the wolf was quite friendly, and so he began treating the wolf as if he were a shepherd dog. One evening, when it was time to herd the sheep home, he allowed the wolf to return together with his sheep, and stay overnight in the sheepfold. The next day, the shepherd discovered to his horror that the wolf had eaten a lamb and wounded several sheep!

We use 引狼入室 to describe the situation in which one trusts an enemy and as a result hurts oneself.

32. 禾（hé）部 Grain

古字形

“禾”是象形字，古文字像谷子的形状：上面是穗，下面是叶子和秸秆。“禾”的本义指谷子。在中国古代，禾是粟谷的专称，后来成为粮食作物的统称。作为部首，“禾”通常位于汉字的左侧，有时位于汉字的上面。禾部的字多与谷物、庄稼有关。“秋”字以禾谷成熟作为“秋”这一季节的特征，秋季是谷熟收获的季节，农作物呈金黄或火红色，这也是“秋”字以“禾”和“火”作为构字理据的原因。“香”的本义指谷物散发出的香甜的气味。“秧”是形声字，它的意思是农作物的幼苗。

Ancient form

禾 is a pictograph. The ancient symbol is a picture of mature grains that are ready to harvest. The original meaning of 禾 is *millet*. Later, 禾 was used to refer to all kinds of grains. As a radical, 禾 is usually placed on the left side of a compound. It sometimes also appears on the top of a compound. Characters with the 禾 radical often have meanings related to cereal or crops. The character 秋 (qiū) means *autumn*. This character has two radicals: 禾, which indicates the mature grains that we harvest in the fall, and 火 (huǒ; *fire*) which recalls the fiery colors ripe grains take on in the fall. The character 香 (xiāng) has 禾 on its top. The original meaning of 香 is *the rich aroma of maturing grains*. Later 香 came to be used to refer to all kinds of good smells. The character 秧 (yāng) is a phonetic-semantic compound which means *crop seeding*. 央 (yāng) on the right side indicates the pronunciation of the character.

故事 Story

锄禾 (Chú hé)
锄 weed and plow 禾 grain

悯农 is a Tang Dynasty poem widely known to the Chinese people.

悯农	Saluting the Farmer
锄禾日当午，	Weeding in the grain field under the midday sun,
汗滴禾下土。	Sweat rolling down to the earth.
谁知盘中餐，	Who realizes that the food on the plates,
粒粒皆辛苦。	Each grain comes from hard plowing.

33. 马[馬]（mǎ）部 Horse

古字形

“马”是象形字，古文字像一匹马的形状。马在中国古代是最重要的战争工具之一，古代打仗时经常用马拉战车。“马路”本指马行走的路，今天在城市的马路上已经很难看到马了，但是我们仍然用“马路”来指称交通道路。作为部首，“马”通常位于汉字的左侧，有时位于汉字的下面。马部的字多与马或驾驶等意义有关。“骄”本指健壮异常的马，而这种马是比较难驯服和控制的，由此引申为骄傲、骄纵等意思。“驾”本指把车套在马身上，使之拉车，引申指使开动或操纵。

Ancient form

马 is a pictograph. The ancient script depicts a standing horse. According to Chinese military history, horses were the most important assets in war. Horses were not only used by the cavalry, they also pulled the war chariots. The word 马路 (mǎlù; *highway*) originally meant *road for horses to go through*. As a radical, 马 is usually placed on the left side or bottom of a compound. Characters containing the 马 radical often have meanings related to horses or to drive. The original meaning of 骄 (jiāo) is *healthy and strong horses*. Because strong horses are sometimes willful, so 骄 also means *proud or arrogant*. The character 驾 (jià) means *to drive*. Its original meaning is *to have the horse pull a war chariot.*

故事 Story

指鹿为马 (Zhǐ lù wéi mǎ)
指 call 鹿 stag 为 as 马 horse

In the Qin Dynasty, a Prime Minister named Zhao Gao was very ambitious. Unsatisfied with his position as a Prime Minister he began plotting to usurp the throne. He was not sure, however, how many people in the court would support him. So, he devised a way to test the court officials to find out who were his supporters and who were his opponents.

One day, when all court officials were assembled to discuss court affairs, Zhao brought a stag in and said to the Emperor, "I present this excellent horse to your majesty." The Emperor was confused because he could see it was a stag. But Zhao insisted that it was a horse and asked the court officials to express their opinion on whether it was a stag or a horse. Some of the officials were afraid of being persecuted by Zhao if they told truth, so they agreed with Zhao and called the stag a horse.

指鹿为马 is used to describe willful misrepresentation, such as saying that black is white.

34. 贝［貝］（bèi）部 Seashell

古字形

“贝”是象形字，古文字描摹的是一枚贝壳的形状。“贝”通常位于汉字的左侧，有时位于汉字的下面。在中国的远古时代，“贝”曾被用作货币，所以贝部的字大多与钱财或价格有关。“账”指货币、货物出入的记载，“赔”是由于某种原因亏损了钱，而“赚”则是由于某种原因得到了钱。“贵”“贱”等字既表示物品价格的高低，又表示人之地位或身份的等级优越或低下。“贤”指多才多德；“责”本指索取借出去的财物，引申指责任。

Ancient form

贝 is a pictograph. The ancient symbol is a picture of seashell. When 贝 is used as a radical, it is placed either on the left side or at the bottom of a compound. In ancient China, 贝 was used as currency. Therefore, characters containing 贝 are mostly related to money, price, and valuables. 账 (zhàng) means *account*; 赔 (péi) means *to compensate* (a type of monetary transaction); 赚 (zhuàn) means *to earn money*; 贵 (guì) means *expensive* and 贱 (jiàn) means *cheap*. Both 贵 and 贱 are used to indicate the value of goods, and both have extended meanings that refer to an individual's social status. 贤 means *talented* (*with valuable skills*). The original meaning of 责 (zé) is *to ask for money back*. Its extended meaning is *responsibility*.

故事 Story

成语拾贝 (Chéng yǔ shí bèi)

成语 idiom 拾 pick up 贝 seashell

It is common knowledge that Chinese idioms usually consist of four or more characters. To give a few examples, the commonly used idioms such as 一不压众 (One person cannot beat a critical mass), 不破不立 (There is no construction without destruction), 无可奈何 (There is no help for it) are formed with four characters. 贝 was used as currency in a certain period of Chinese history; therefore, 贝also means something valuable or priceless. 成语拾贝 means to collect a few pieces of valuable information about Chinese idioms.

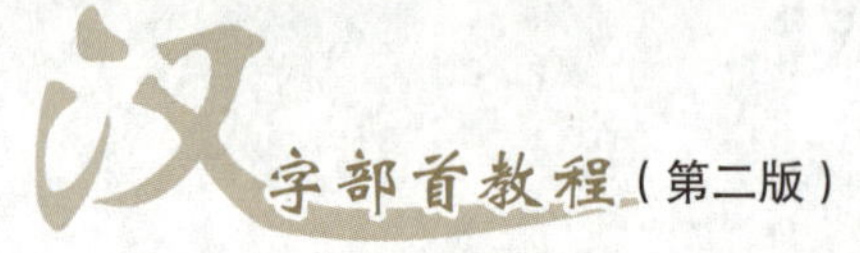

35. 车 [車 车]（chē）部 Cart; Vehicle

古字形

“车”是象形字，古文字描摹的是古代使用的两轮带架的车形。“车”的本义指陆地上有轮子的运输工具。作为部首，“车”通常位于汉字的左侧，写作“车”。车部的字多与交通工具或运输有关。“轨”本指车辙，即车子两轮之间的距离，引申指火车、电车等行驶的路轨。“辇”的上部是两个人，下部是车，意思是一种人拉的车，多用于宫廷、皇室。

Ancient form

车 is a pictograph. The ancient form of it depicts a type of two-wheeled cart that was used in ancient times. The original meaning of 车 refers to any wheeled form of transportation. As a radical, it often appears on the left side of the character and is written as 车. Character containing the 车 radical mostly have meanings related to vehicles or transportation. The original meaning of 轨 is *the distance between two wheels of a cart*. Now it also means *track*. 辇 (niǎn) has 车 underneath and two persons on the top. Together, it means *rickshaw*—a man-drawn carriage, which was a type of carriage often used in the royal palace and families.

故事 Story

杯水车薪 (Bēi shuǐ chē xīn)
杯 cup 水 water 车 cartload 薪 faggots

杯水车薪 means to extinguish a burning cartload of faggots with a cup of water. Here it is the story:

One day, a woodman cut and gathered several faggots in the mountain. Before dark, he loaded all the faggots onto his horse-drawn cart, then climbed up on the horse's back and drove the cart home. On the way, he stopped in front of a tea house and went to drink tea. After a while, he heard someone shouting outside: "The faggots are burning!" The woodman stood up at once and ran out grabbing a cup. He poured the tea onto the faggots. The fire, however, got stronger and stronger. Eventually, all the sticks were burnt to ashes.

This idiom describes situations in which people try to solve serious problems with utterly inadequate measures.

36. 阜［阝在左］（fù）部 Hill

古字形

“阜”是象形字，古文字像阶梯状的山坡，本义指土山。作为部首，“阜”通常位于汉字的左侧，写作“阝”，俗称“左耳旁”。阜部的字多与地势或升降等意义有关。“阳”的本义指山的南面水的北面，由于南面光线充足，所以“阳”的常用义为太阳、阳光，例如“向阳”“阳台”；再引申为明亮、温暖等意义。“阴”的本义指山的北面水的南面，由于北面光线不充足，所以“阴”的常用义为阴凉、黑暗等。“阳”与“阴”是一对相反的概念，中国古代的哲学家用以表示事物的两个对立面。“降”是形声字，原义指从高处（山上）下来，右边的“夅”是声旁。

Ancient form

阜 is a pictograph. The ancient form of 阜 looks like a terraced hillside. Its original meaning is *hill*. As a radical, 阜 usually stands on the left side of a compound and is written as 阝. So it is also called zuǒ ěr páng (left ear at the side). The extended meaning of 阜 relates to topography. The original meaning of 阳 (yáng) is *the south slope of a hill*. The south slope of a hill gets the most sunshine, so 阳 also refers to the sun and sunshine. 阴 (yīn) refers to the north slope of a hill, which often does not get enough sunshine. Therefore it also means *cool and dark*. The two characters 阴 and 阳 together refer to the opposites in nature—a key principle in traditional Chinese philosophy. Another character that uses the 阜 radical is 降 (jiàng). 降 is a phonetic-semantic compound, in which 夅 (jiàng) indicates the pronunciation. 降 means *to descend from a hill*.

故事 Story

曲阜 (Qū fù)
曲 zigzag 阜 hill

曲阜 is located in the southwest of Shandong Province. After the Chu State conquered the Lu State in 249 BC, the Lu State was reduced into Lu County. In 596, Lu County was renamed 曲阜, a name which has stuck until today. 曲阜 was so named because inside of Lu County there was a mountain ridge that zigzagged for about two miles. 曲阜 is the hometown of the great ancient scholar—Confucius. The two core philosophies of Confucious' thought are the maintenance of social hierarchies and the principle of benevolent rule. If you ever have a chance to visit 曲阜, there are three places you should visit: The former residence of Confucius, the Confucian Temple, and the Forest of Confucius (the Confucius Family Cemetery). 曲阜 is one of the World's Great Historical and Cultural Relics as designated by UNISCO.

37. 示［礻］（shì）部 To show

古字形

“示”是象形字，古文字描摹的是祭坛的形状。“示”的本义是祭祀，这一本义仅保留在部首意义中。“示”在现代汉语中的常用义是指让人看见或显现。作为部首，“示”通常位于汉字的左侧，写作“礻”，俗称“示字旁”；有时位于汉字的下面，写作“示”。示部的字多与祭祀、礼仪等意义有关。“祭”是会意字，由“肉”“又”“示”三个义符组成。“肉”表示牲肉，“又”表示手，“示”表示祭祀的地方，“祭”的意思是以手持牲肉在祭坛上祭祀神灵，向神灵祈福。“福”也是个会意字，本义指祭祀求福。另一个会意字“视”由“示”和“见”组成，意思是看见。

Ancient form

示 is a pictograph. Its ancient form looks like a stone table with food on top, which depicts a sacrificial altar. The original meaning of 示 is *to offer sacrifices to gods or ancestors*. People make offerings to demonstrate or show our reverence to the gods and the ancestors. Therefore, in modern Chinese, 示 means *to show or display*. As a radical 示 can be placed on the left side of a compound, where it is written as 礻 which is also called shì zì páng (shi character at the side). It is also placed at the bottom of compound characters. Most of characters with the 示 radical are related to religious ceremonies or ritual activities. The character 祭 (jì; *to sacrifice*) is an ideograph with three radicals: 肉 (*meat*), 又 (*hand*), and 示 (*to show*). Together they mean that people use their hands to sacrifice animals as offerings. The character 福 (fú) is also an ideograph. The left part is 示 and the right part is a wine jar. People also offer wine to the gods to pray for happiness. Therefore, 福 means *happiness*. Another character 视 (shì) combines the radical "to show" with the radical "to see" to form the meaning *to see*.

故事 Story

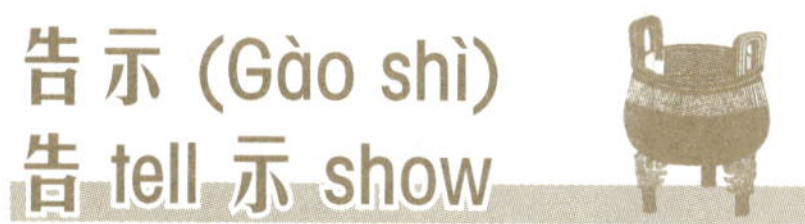

告示 (Gào shì)
告 tell 示 show

In the Tang Dynasty, a court officer named Zhou Xing was assigned to control of all prison affairs. He was an extremely brutal person and often created ruthless rules to mistreat his prisoners. Once, he posted a notice in front of the Court saying: "When they are summoned to court, all defendants claim that they are treated unjustly, but once their heads are cut off, they will all keep quiet." The purpose of this bulletin was to intimidate the defendants to make them plead guilty even if they were innocent.

38. 食 [飠 饣]（shí）部 

Food

古字形

“食”是象形字，古文字描摹的是一个带盖子的食器形状：上部为三角形，像个食器的盖子，下部像是一只盛着食品的食器。“食”的本义指供食用的物品。作为部首，“食”通常位于汉字的左侧，写作“飠”，简化作“饣”，俗称“食字旁”；有时位于汉字的下面，写作“食”。食部的字一般都与食品或吃有关系。例如“饿”和“饱”指吃东西前后的状态，“饺”和“饼”都是食品的名称。饺子和煎饼都是中国人最喜爱的食品。

Ancient form

食 is a pictograph. In the ancient script 食 looks like a bowl (the 𠮛 part), with a cover (the ∧ part), holding food (the middle section). The original meaning of 食 is *food*. As a radical, 食 is often placed on the left side of a compound, which is written as 飠 or 饣 (simplified version) and called shí zì páng (food at the side). 食 can also appear at the bottom of a compound. Characters with the 食 radical usually have meanings related to food or eating. For example, 饱 (bǎo; *full*) and 饿 (è; *hungry*) both refer to whether or not you have eaten; 饺 (jiǎo; *dumpling*) and 饼 (bǐng; *pancake*) are names for different types of food. Dumplings and fried thin pancakes are two of Chinese people's favorite foods.

故事 Story

东食西宿 (Dōng shí xī sù)
东 east 食 eat 西 west 宿 sleep

Once upon a time, there was a beautiful young maiden of marriageable age. One day, a rich couple in the east side of town proposed that she marry their son. They said that although their son was quite plain, if she would marry him, she could enjoy endless wealth. The next day a poor couple from the west side of town proposed that she marry their son. They argued that their son was very generous and handsome. If she married their son, she would enjoy endless marital happiness. The girl accepted both proposals and said that she would eat with the wealthy Eastside family and sleep with the poor Westside family. As a result, she was rejected by both young men.

This story tells us that there is nothing perfect in this world. If one is too greedy and tries to get everything, then he/she may end up with nothing.

39. 酉（yǒu）部 Alcohol

古字形

"酉"是象形字，古文字描摹的是酒器的形状，本义指酒。作为部首，"酉"通常位于汉字的左侧，也位于汉字的右侧和下面。酉部的字多与酒或发酵制成的食品有关。与酒有关的字如"醒""醉"。"醒"字从酉，本义指人酒醒。表示发酵制成的食品有"酱""醋"等。

Ancient form

酉 is a pictograph. The ancient form of 酉 indicates a wine jar. Therefore, the original meaning of 酉 is *alcohol*. As a radical, 酉 often appears either on the left side, right side or at the bottom of a compound. Characters that contain the 酉 radical are usually associated with alcohol, fermented foods, and drinking. For example, 酒 (jiǔ) means *wine*; 醉 (zuì) means *drunk*; and 醒 (xǐng) means *to wake up* (from a drunken sleep). 酱（jiàng; *soy sauce*）and 醋 (cù; *vinegar*) are both made through a process of fermentation, and so also contain the 酉 radical.

故事 Story

酒仙李白 (Jiǔ xiān Lǐ Bái)
酒 wine 仙 god 李白 name of a famous poet

李白 was a famous romantic poet in the Tang Dynasty, who was also referred to as a Wine Spirit. He himself claimed that, "There are 360 days in a year, and one should drink 300 glasses of wine each day." Unlike most other poets, Li Bai produced even better poems after drinking. One day, Emperor Tang invited Li Bai to create a few new poems for the Peony Party the Emperor was holding to enhance the Emperor and Empress' enjoyment of the beautiful peonies. Li Bai told the Emperor that producing a few poems was not difficult as long as the Emperor could provide him with enough wine. After a few cups of wine, Li Bai quickly dashed off three beautiful poems. The Emperor was very pleased with Li Bai's work, and ordered his servants to bring Li Bai a seven-treasure cup, which the Emperor himself filled with grape wine.

40. 八［丷］（bā）部 To divide; To separate

古字形)(

“八”是指事字，古文字像两条相背的弧线。这个形象表示的意义是分开、分别。“八”假借表示数字。作为部首，“八”通常位于汉字的上面，写作“八”，也作“丷”；有时位于汉字的下面，写作“八”。八部的字多和切分、分别有关。“分”字上面是“八”，下面是“刀”，表示用刀分物的意思，引申指分别，例如“分离”。“半”字上面是“八”，意思是把物体一分为二，例如“一半”“半百”；引申指事物的中间，例如“半夜”“半山腰”。

Ancient form)(

八 is an indicative character which refers to the way of forming abstract characters using indicative symbols. The ancient form of it indicates two items that are separated—so it means *separate or apart*. 八 also means *eight*. This is a phonetic borrowing and has nothing to do with the original meaning of 八. As a radical, 八 can be placed on the top of a compound, either in its original form or upside down as 丷. Sometimes it is also placed at the bottom of a compound. Characters containing 八 usually relate to separation or a part of a whole. The character 分 (fēn) has two radicals. The top is 八 and the bottom is 刀. It suggests using a knife to cut something into pieces. Therefore, the character means “separation.” 半 (bàn; *half*) has 丷 on the top. It means *to separate things into two equal halves*. It appears in words such as 半夜 (bànyè; *midnight*)—half way through the whole night, and 半山腰 (bànshānyāo)—midpoint to the mountain top.

故事 Story

八仙过海 (Bā xiān guò hǎi)
八 eight 仙 immortals 过 cross 海 sea

The eight immortals are legendary figures in Chinese folk stories. 八仙过海 is one story about the eight immortals recorded in a Ming Dynasty Chinese novel *Journey to the East*. According to the story the eight immortals arrived at the Eastern Sea and needed to cross, but all they could see were turbulent waves surging and crashing. One of the eight immortals suggested that each of them throw a magic weapon into the sea to demonstrate their magic powers. They all agreed and each used their magic powers to cross the sea. Later, people began to use 八仙过海 to describe when individuals try to outshine each other in a display of talents.

第六课　页、巾、门、广、大、米、田、十、彳、革

41. 页［頁］(xié; yè) 部 Head

古字形

“页”是象形字，古文字描摹了一个人的形状，突出了头部的细节。“页”本读xié，本义是人头，“页”的本义仅保留在部首意义中。在现代汉语中，“页”读作yè，表示“篇”或“张”的意思，例如“活页”；用作量词时，如“一页纸”。作为部首，“页”通常位于汉字的右侧。页部的字多与人的头部、面部、颈部等意义有关。“顶”本指头顶，“额”本指额头，“领”本指脖子。颐和园是北京著名的旅游景点。“颐”字现在常用其调养、保养之意，之所以有“页”符，是因为“颐”本指人的腮颊或下巴，而一个人保养得好坏，是可以从这些部位上看出来的。

Ancient form

页 is a pictograph. The ancient form of 页 (pronounced as xié) depicts a kneeling person with a huge head. Therefore 页 means *head*. In traditional characters 页 is written as 頁. In modern Chinese, 页 as an independent character has lost its meaning as head. It now is pronounced as yè and refers to "pages" (of a book), such as 活页 (huóyè; *loose-leaf*). It can also be used as a measure word, such as 一页纸 (yí yè zhǐ; *a piece of paper*). As a radical, 页 still retains the meaning of head. It often appears on the right side of a compound. Characters containing 页 often have meanings associated with the head, face, neck or prominent things (things situated at "the head"). For example, the original meaning of 顶 (dǐng) is *the crown of head*, now it also means *peak*; 额 (é) means *forehead*; and 领 (lǐng) means *neck*. There is a famous imperial garden called 颐和园 (Yíhé Yuán) in Beijing, China. It is known in English as "the Summer Palace." The original meaning of 颐 is *cheek*. Its extended meaning is *taking good care of one's health*, because a healthy person has bright cheeks.

故事 Story

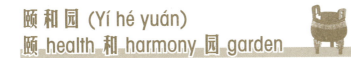

颐和园 (Yí hé yuán)
颐 health 和 harmony 园 garden

The Summer Palace is one of Beijing's famous historical sites. Constructed in 1750, its original name was Qingyi Yuan (Garden of Clear Ripples). In 1860 Anglo-French Allied Forces razed the palace to the ground. The Qing Government started to rebuild the park in 1886. Two years later the reconstruction was complete and the garden was renamed as Yihe Yuan (the Summer Palace). This Yihe Yuan at that time was served as a summer resort for the Empress Dowager Cixi, and so came to be known as the Summer Palace. The palace was again ravaged by the Allied Forces of the Eight Powers, which invaded China in 1900, and new repairs were made in 1902.

The palace covers an area of 2.9 square kilometers, three quarters of which is under water. The landscape is dominated primarily by Longevity Hill and Kunming Lake. The park's 70,000 square meters of ground space features a variety of palaces, gardens, and other fine examples of traditional Chinese architecture and landscape design. It is also well known for its large, priceless collection of cultural relics. In December 1998, UNESCO added the Summer

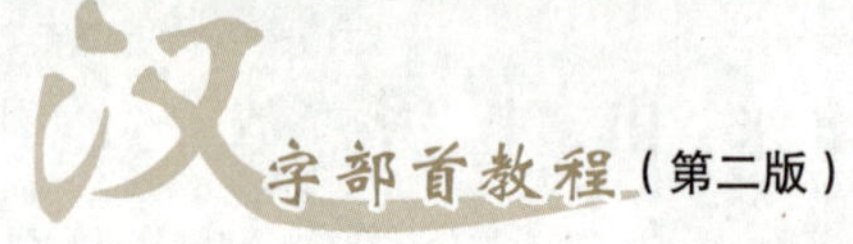

Palace to its World Heritage List. If you are interested in the past 500 years of Chinese history, then the Summer Palace is a must-see!

42. 巾（jīn）部 Towel; Cloth

古字形

“巾”是象形字，古文字像一条下垂的毛巾之形，本义是用于擦拭的毛巾。作为部首，“巾”有时位于汉字的左侧；有时位于汉字的下面；偶尔位于汉字的右侧，例如“帅”。巾部的字多与丝麻布等各类织品以及交换活动有关。“币”的本义指一种丝织品，引申指钱币。在古代男耕女织的社会中，“币”可能是因其便于携带而充当了商品交换的一般等价物，也是最早的货币之一。“幅”本指布帛等织物的宽度，引申作量词，例如“一幅画”，因为丝织品是用来画中国画的主要材料。

Ancient form 巾

巾 is a pictograph. In the ancient script it looks like a hanging towel. The original meaning of 巾 is *towel or cloth*. As a radical, 巾 can appear on the left, or bottom of a compound character, sometimes on the right side, such as 帅 (shuài; *handsome*). Characters with the 巾 radical often have meanings related to silk or trading. The character 币 (bì) has 巾 on the bottom. Its original meaning is *a kind of silk*. Since 币 was easy to carry, it was often used for trading. Therefore, 币 later evolved to mean "currency." Another character that uses 巾 is 幅 (fú). Its original meaning is *the width of a piece of silk*. It later came to be used as a measure word for paintings, such as 一幅画 (yì fú huà), because in ancient China paintings were primarily done on silk.

故事 Story

巾帼英雄 (Jīn guó yīng xióng)

巾帼 ancient woman's headdress 英雄 heroine

巾帼英雄 means a heroic woman. This saying comes from a story that took place in the Northern Song Period. The Central Plains Area was invaded by the Liao army. The Song General sent two strong soldiers to steal a special wood called Subduing-Dragon Wood from the Muke Stockade to make shafts for axes. When they reached the stockade, the soldiers were captured by Mu Guiying, the

daughter of the Chief of the Stockade. The Song General came to rescue his men, but he too was defeated by Mu Guiying. Later, when Mu Guiying learned that the Song army needed the Subduing-Dragon Wood to make weapons, she presented the wood to the General and also requested to join the army. Her request was approved. Mu Guiying led the army to fight against the invaders. Soon, the Song army returned in triumph. Mu Guiying was regarded as 巾帼英雄.

43. 门［門］（mén）部 Gate; Door

古字形 𠁣

“门”是象形字，古文字像两扇门对开之形。作为部首，“门”通常位于汉字的外围，俗称“门字框”。门部的字多与门、门径、方法等意义有关。“阅”指在门内清点东西，引申指考查、视察；“阔”指房间宽大，引申为面积宽。

Ancient form 𠁣

门 is a pictograph. The ancient form of 门 is a picture of a two-leaf door. As a radical, it often appears on the outside of a compound called mén zì kuàng (door on the outside). The original meaning of this radical is *gate or door*. Therefore as a radical, it usually refers to doors. But it also can refer to “methods of access”—the function that doors provide, and by extension “methods.” The character 阅 (yuè) means *to take stock and organize stuff inside a room*. Its extended meaning is *to examine or to read*. 阔 means *spacious room*. Its extended meaning is *broad or wide*.

故事 Story

门神 (Mén shén)
门 door 神 god

In ancient China, on the evening of December 30 in Chinese Lunar Calendar, people placed two carved peach-wood gods on either side of their front door. They hoped that these two wooden gods would help to keep disasters away from the family. These two gods came to be known as the Door-Gods.

Why do Chinese ancestors use peach wood to carve the Door-Gods? It is said that the two gods were brothers who lived on a mountain that had a giant peach tree growing on its peak. Every morning, the two brothers would check on the hundreds of ghosts and evils in the world to see if they had done anything harmful to mankind. If they did, then the two brothers would punish them.

44. 广（yǎn; guǎng）部
Big house

古字形 广

“广”是象形字，古文字像依山崖建造的房屋之形。“广”读作yǎn，其本义指宽大的房屋。现代汉语中读音为guǎng的“广”字，是“廣”的简化字，所以和用作部首的“广”字不属于同一个字。作为部首，“广”通常位于汉字的左上侧。广部的字多与房屋的种类或结构有关。“府”最早是指储藏文书的地方；引申指“官府”（官员办理公事的地方）。“库”字原本指储存武器的地方；引申指储存物品的地方，例如“仓库”。在古代，“庙”是祭祀祖先的处所，例如“宗庙”；后来引申指供神佛的地方，例如“寺庙”；由此再引申指为纪念历史上著名人物而建造的庙宇，例如“孔庙”。

Ancient form 广

广 is a pictograph. The ancient form of 广 looks like a house built against hill, which is why we do not see a wall on the right side. As a radical, its pronunciation is yǎn. Its basic meaning is *spacious house*. In modern Chinese, there is a character 广 (read as guǎng) which is the simplification of 廣 (*broad*). While they are written the same way, the character 广 and the radical 广 are different in terms of pronunciation and meaning. The characters with the 广 radical often have meanings related to types of houses or buildings and their structures. 府 (fǔ) is a place to store documents. It is also used to refer to government buildings. 库 (kù) is a place to store weapons; now it also refers to all storage places such as 仓库 (cāngkù). 庙 (miào) is a place to worship ancestry. It also refers to all temples, such as China's many Buddhist temples and memorial temples, such as the Temple of Confucius located in Shandong.

故事 Story

广厦千万间 (Guǎng shà qiān wàn jiān)

广厦 mansions 千万 thousands 间 measure word for room

The famous Chinese Poet, Du Fu was born in Gong County of Henan Province during the Tang Dynasty. His poetry expressed his deep sympathy for the poor and his great dissatisfaction with the problematic society of his time. One of his poems titled *Song of My Cottage Unroofed by Autumn Gales* (《茅屋为秋风所破歌》) described his poor living conditions and his wish for a better life for scholars like him. Here are a few lines from his poem:

安得广厦千万间，
If I could get mansions covering ten thousand miles,
大庇天下寒士俱欢颜，
I could host all the poor scholars and make them smile,
风雨不动安如山。
In the wind and rain these mansions would stand like mountains high.
呜呼！何时眼前突兀见此屋，
Alas! Should these houses appear before my eye,
吾庐独破受冻死亦足！
Frozen in my unroofed cot, content I would die!

45. 大（dà）部 Man; Big

古字形 大

“大”是象形字，古文字像伸开双臂的正面人形，本义指大人，引申指在体积、面积、数量、力量、规模、程度等方面超过一般或超过所比较的对象，与“小”相对。作为部首，“大”有时位于汉字的下面，有时位于汉字的上面或中间。大部的字多与人类或人事有关。“夫”由“大”和“一”构成，上面的“一”表示头发上插一根簪（zān）。在中国古代，男子成年时要行“冠礼”，之后要束发，故加“一”做标记，合起来的意思是成年男子。“天”古文字下面是大，上面是人头，小篆变成一横，本义指人头，引申指天空或位于顶端的。

Ancient form 大

大 is a pictograph. Its ancient form looks like a man with his arms stretching out side to side. The original meaning of 大 is *big man*. Its extended meaning is *big*, which is opposite to small. As a radical, it can be placed on the bottom or top, or in the middle of a compound. Characters with the 大 radical often have meanings related to people. The character 夫 (fū) consists of 大 and 一; 一 indicates a hairpin 簪 (zān). In ancient China, when a man was fully grown he attended a ceremony that marked his becoming an adult. After this ceremony he would bind his hair in a bun with a hairpin as a mark of adulthood. Therefore, 夫 means *mature male*. The character 天 is different from the character 夫. In the character 天, 一 is on the top of 大. Here, 一 means *the head of a person*. Above a person's head is sky, so 天 means *sky*.

故事 Story

雷声大，雨点小 (Léi shēng dà, yǔ diǎn xiǎo)
雷 thunder 声 sound 大 loud，雨 rain 点 drops 小 small

The thunder is loud but the raindrops are small. This idiom can be used to describe a situation in which much is said but little is done. This is similar to the English expression: great boast, small roast.

46. 米（mǐ）部 Rice

古字形

“米”是象形字，古文字像细碎的米粒之形。“米”的本义指谷物或其他植物去壳之后的籽实。作为部首，“米”通常位于汉字的左侧，俗称“米字旁”，有时位于汉字的下面。米部的字多与米或粮食的种类有关。“粟”是中国北方的一种主要粮食作物，通称“谷子”。“粽”是用苇叶包裹糯米做成的一种多角形的食品。

Ancient form

米 is a pictograph. The ancient form of 米 depicts small grains scattered on the ground. The meaning of 米 is *unshelled grains*. As a radical, 米 appears on the left called mǐ zì páng (rice at the side) or bottom of a compound. Characters with the 米 radical often have meanings related to kinds of food or grains. For example, 粟 (sù; *millet*) is a common crop in northern China. 粽 (zòng) is a kind of snack made from sweet rice.

故事 Story

鱼米之乡 (Yú mǐ zhī xiāng)

鱼 fish 米 rice 之 of 乡 town

鱼米之乡 means a land of fish and rice. It is used to describe a place that is rich in agricultural and fishing products, and the citizens do not need to worry about life's basic necessities. In China, the Yangtze River divides the land into two regions: Jiangbei (North of the River) and Jiangnan (South of the River). Jiangnan is a region in the lower Yangtze Valley, where the weather is mild and there is plenty of rain. Many small rivers are scattered over these vast plains, creating an excellent environment for agriculture and aquiculture. Chinese people refer to Jiangnan as 鱼米之乡 .

47. 田（tián）部 Land; Field

古字形 田

“田”是象形字，古文字像一块块的农田。“田”的本义是耕种用的土地，引申指田野。作为部首，“田”通常位于汉字的左侧和上面，有时位于汉字的下面。田部的字多与耕种、界线、田猎等意义有关。“苗”指田里生长的、未吐穗的庄稼，形状像草，即禾苗。“界”是形声字，从田介声，本义指地界。“男”字由田和力构成，“田”就是田地，“力”即“耒”，是一种农具，用使用农具耕作于农田的形象来表示男子。

Ancient form 田

田 is a pictograph. The ancient form of this character looks like a tract of divided land. The basic meaning of 田 is *land*. It also refers to fields. As a radical, it appears either on the left, top, or bottom of a compound. The meanings of characters with the 田 radical often relate to farming, land boundaries, or field activities. For example, the character 苗 (miáo) refers to an immature crop and 界 (jiè) means *land boundaries*. The character 男 (nán) means *male*. It consists of two radicals 田 and 力 . 力 stands for a tool that was used to plough the land. In ancient times, men worked in the field pushing the plough.

故事 Story

井田制 (Jǐng tián zhì)

井 well 田 land 制 system

During the Western Zhou Dynasty, all lands were owned by the emperor's family. In order to make it easy to loan the land to the Nobility, the land was divided into thousands of square pieces. Nine plots of land together were referred to as "one well" because they looked like the shape of a square Chinese well (井). The Nobility had the right to use the land, but not to sell or transfer it to others. They also had to pay a tax to the imperial family for using the land. The Nobility, of course, forced their peasant slaves to work in the fields. The well-field system has become a symbol of the oppressive feudal system in Chinese history.

48. 十（shí）部 Perfect; Many

古字形

“十”是指事字，古文字用一竖画代表数字“10”，后在竖画中部加圆点，圆点后来又演变成一横。“十”的本义是九加一之和。“十”虽然是一个实指的数字，但也可以虚指，有“多”或“全”的意思，如“十全十美”。作为部首，“十”位于汉字的左侧、上面、下面或右侧。十部的字多与十足、多、全等意义有关。“协”字繁体作“協”，“十”表示众多，“力”表示一种农具，合起来表示众人同力耕田劳动，引申指合作、共同、和谐等义。

Ancient form

十 is an indicative character. It uses a vertical line to represent the number 10, and then adds a dot in the middle of the vertical line. Later it evolves into a horizontal line. The original meaning of 十 is *the sum of nine plus one*, which means *ten*. Although 10 is a real number, it can also be referred to fullest, such as 十全十美 which means *100 percent completion and perfection*. As a radical, 十 is placed on the left, top, bottom or right side of a compound character. Characters with 十 as their radical are often related to full, many, or congruent. The traditional form of 协 (xié) is 協, which is formed by combining 十 (many) with 劦 (力refers to a kind of farming tool). Together, it means that many people work together in the farming land. Its extended meaning is *cooperation, commonness, or harmony*.

故事 Story

十全十美 (Shí quán shí měi)

十 ten 全 complete 十 ten 美 perfect

In the Zhou Dynasty, a doctor's payment was based on the cure rate of his patients. If ten of his patients all recovered from their illnesses, then the doctor would get level-one payment. If, however, only nine or eight out of ten were cured, then the doctor would receive a level-two payment, and so on. Later, 十全十美 began to be used to describe a perfect situation. It is similar to the English expression: the peak of perfection.

49. 彳（chì）部 Small steps

古字形

“彳”来源于“行”（ ）的左半， 像四通八达的道路。“彳”在现代汉语中一般只用作部首。作为部首，“彳”通常位于汉字的左侧，俗称“双人旁”。彳部的字多与走、道路等意义有关。“行”在现代汉语中是走的意思，也有流通、流行的意思。“得”字的本义是得到、获得，从古文字字形来看，“得”（ ）由“彳”“贝”“手”构成，古代的“贝”曾用作货币，人在路上捡到贝也就是得到了钱财，所以“得”有获得的意思。

Ancient form

彳 originated from . It is the left part of this pictography. looks like the roads leading to all directions. In modern Chinese, 彳 appears only as a radical in compounds. It is often placed on the left side of a compound, which is called shuāng rén páng (double persons at the side). Characters that contain the 彳 radical often have meanings related to walking or roads. 行 (xíng) means *to walk*. Its extended meanings are *to become popular and circulation*. The character 得 (dé) is formed by combining three radicals: 彳, 贝, and 手. As mentioned earlier, 贝 (*seashell*) was used as currency at one point in Chinese history. 得 represents that a person who was walking on the road picked up a seashell with his hand. Therefore, the meaning of 得 is *to gain*.

故事 Story

彳和亍 (Chì hé chù)

彳 walk in small steps 和 and 亍 stop walking

The commonly accepted meanings of the characters 彳 and 亍 are "small steps" and "stop walking" respectively. Another translation for 彳 is "to step forward with left foot" and 亍 is "to step forward with right foot." These two characters are seldom used in modern Chinese. The combination of these two characters forms a new character 行. This character means "to walk."

50. 革（gé）部 Leather

古字形 𩊿

“革”是象形字，古文字描摹的是被剥下的兽皮之象：中间的圆形物，是被剥下的兽身皮，余下的部分是兽的头、身和尾。“革”的本义指去毛的兽皮，引申指改变。作为部首，“革”通常位于汉字的左侧。革部的字多与皮革制品有关，例如“鞋”“靶”“鞍”“鞭”等字，其制作材料都和皮革有关系，虽然今天这些物品的制作材料已经不仅仅限于皮革了，但是“革”作为物质文化发展进程中的遗存却依然保留在汉字中。

Ancient form 𩊿

革 is a pictograph. The ancient form of 革 depicts an animal hide as it is peeled off the carcass. The top part is the head of the animal, the middle section is the body, and the bottom part is the tail. The basic meaning of 革 is *leather.* Its extended meaning is *to change or to transform*. As a radical, 革 stands on the left side of a compound to indicate the object represented by the character is made of leather. Some examples are: 鞋 (xié; *shoe*), 靶 (bǎ; *leather target*), 鞍 (ān; *saddle*), and 鞭 (biān; *leather whip*). Although in modern times, the materials used for making those objects are no longer limited to leather, the legacy of 革 as part of material culture remains in the Chinese characters.

故事 Story

马革裹尸 (Mǎ gé guǒ shī)

马 horse 革 hide 裹 wrap 尸 corpse

马革裹尸 literally means to be wrapped in a horse hide after death (figuratively to die on the battle field). In the Eastern Han Dynasty, there was a great General named Ma Yuan. At that time the Han Nationality was frequently invaded by the Huns. Ma Yuan was not afraid of death and he asked the Emperor to assign him an expedition. He said "A good man should go out to battle for his country. The best end is to be wrapped in horse hide after death." He was a hero in his time. Later he died of illness in the battlefield.

Now we use 马革裹尸 to describe a soldier's heroic and fearless spirit on the battlefield.

第七课 攴、戈、尸、穴、力、舟、口、雨、厂、又

51. 攴 [攵] (pū) 部 Action by using hands

古字形

“攴”的古文字形是会意字，像手持棍棒。“攴”的本义指敲击，击打。“攴”在现代汉语中只用作部首，不单独成字。作为部首，“攴”通常位于汉字的右侧，常写作“攵”，俗称“反文旁”。攴部的字多与敲击或手的动作有关系。“敲”有打、击等意义。“牧”字的本义是放牧牲畜。

Ancient form

The ancient form of 攴 is an ideograph. It looks like a hand is holding a stick. Its original meaning is *to hit or to beat*. In modern Chinese, however, 攴 is no longer an independent character but serves only as a radical in compounds. 攴 usually stands on the right side of a compound and it is often written as 攵, which is called fǎn wén páng (article at the side). The meanings of characters containing 攴 are often related to actions that use the hands. For example, 敲 (qiāo) means *to knock*, *to beat*, *or to strike*; 牧 (mù) means *to tend or herd*.

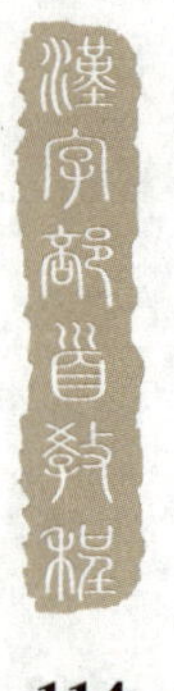

故事 Story

推敲 (Tuī qiāo)
推 push 敲 knock

Jia Dao was a great poet who lived in the Tang Dynasty. One day, he wrote a poem that began: 鸟宿池边树，僧敲月下门 (birds are resting on the tree by the pond, the monk is knocking on the door in the moonlight). At first, he was not quite sure whether he should use the character 推 or 敲 for the second line. He was so focused on his lines as he was riding down the street, that he accidently ran into an official's carriage. During that era this was a horrible offense. Fortunately, the official in the carriage was Han Yu, one of the great scholars of the Tang Dynasty. After Jia Dao explained the reason he had walked into the carriage, Han Yu not only forgave Jia Dao but also helped him figure out which word, 推 or 敲, was better for the poem. After some thought Han Yu suggested using 敲, because 敲 could evoke an aural image of sound, which could emphasize the silence of the night by contrast. Now we use 推敲 to describe weighing one's words or doing things after careful deliberation.

52. 戈（gē）部 Weapon

古字形

“戈”是象形字，古文字像长柄横刃的兵器之形。“戈”的本义是一种兵器，后泛指武器，成语“反戈一击”是说掉转武器向自己原来所属的阵营进行攻击。作为部首，“戈”通常位于汉字右侧。戈部的字多与兵器或战事有关。“戟”是古代的一种兵器，是由戈和矛组合而成的；“战”指作战、打仗；“戒”像两手持戈形，表示戒备森严，引申指防备、警惕；“武”是会意字，从止从戈，表示拿着武器去打仗，又引申指干戈军旅之事。

Ancient form

戈 is a pictograph. The ancient form of 戈 is a picture of an ancient spear which was a sharp knife installed on the top of a long shaft. The original meaning of 戈 is *dagger-axe*. Its extended meaning refers to weapon. The idiom 反戈一击 means to turn back to hit those who have misled you. As a radical, it often appears on the right of a compound. The meaning of characters containing 戈 are often connected to weapons and war. 戟 (jǐ) is another type of long-handled ancient weapon. It consists of a spear at the point with a battle-axe: affixed to the side. 战 (zhàn) means *fighting or battle*. The ancient form of the character 戒 (jiè) looks like two hands holding a 戈, which indicates its meaning—*to guard or take precautions*. The character 武 (wǔ) means *forces or to arm with weapons*.

故事 Story

同室操戈 (Tóng shì cāo gē)
同 same 室 room 操 operate 戈 dagger-axe (an ancient weapon)

This idiom is used to describe internal strife, such as when family members fight, or when members in a collective work to further their own interests rather than cooperating for the benefit of the group. This is similar to the English expression: A house divided against itself cannot stand. A Chinese poem titled *The Seven-Pace Poem* (《七步诗》) from the novel *Three Kingdoms* offers a vivid example of 同室操戈. The story behind the poem's creation, and its curious name, appears in book *A New Account of Tales of the World* in the Southern Dynasties. The story goes that Cao Pi, the King of the Wei State, was jealous of his younger brother Cao Zhi's talent and therefore ordered him to compose a poem within the time it takes to walk seven steps. If Cao Zhi could not complete the poem within that time, the King would kill him. Not only did Cao Zhi successfully complete his poem, he actually had finished it before the seven steps were completed. The poem presented below is not the same poem composed by Cao Zhi, but it expresses Cao Zhi's feelings on being forced to perform by his brother. It reads:

煮豆燃豆萁，Beanstalks are burned to cook beans,
豆在釜中泣。But in the pot the beans are weeping.
本是同根生，Beans and beanstalks are from the same root,
相煎何太急？ Why are they so urgent to kill each other?

53. 尸（shī）部 House; Corpse

古字形

“尸”是象形字，古文字像人俯身屈膝之形。从出土文献的用字情况来看，“尸”是“夷”的早期字形。作为部首，“尸”通常位于汉字的左上侧。尸部的字多与人体或动物等意义有关，例如“尾”本义指人或动物的尾巴，又引申指事物主要部分以外的部分，例如“尾声”“尾数”之“尾”。尸部的字还与居住有关，例如“居”指人居住的地方，“屋”则指人居住的处所。

Ancient form

尸 is a pictograph. The ancient script looks like a person who is bending over. The archeological studies show that 尸 is the early form of the character 夷 (yí). As a radical, it often appears at the upper left of a compound. Characters containing the 尸 radical often have meanings related to human or animal bodies. For example, 尾 (wěi) means *tail* which refers to the tail of human beings or animals. Its extended meaning also refers to the ending part of an object or event such as in the word 尾声 (*the end of...*) and 尾数 (*the ending number*). Characters containg the 尸 radical also related to dwelling. The word 居 (jū) means *a place that people live in*；屋 (wū) means *house or cottage.*

故事 Story

碎尸万段 (Suì shī wàn duàn)

碎 break 尸 corpse 万 ten thousand 段 piece

This idiom is used to express feelings of extreme hatred towards an enemy. It means you want to tear their corpse into thousands of pieces.

部首 Radical

54. 穴（xué）部

Hole; Cave; Den

古字形

“穴”是象形字，像挖地建造的居室，本义是洞穴。作为部首，“穴”

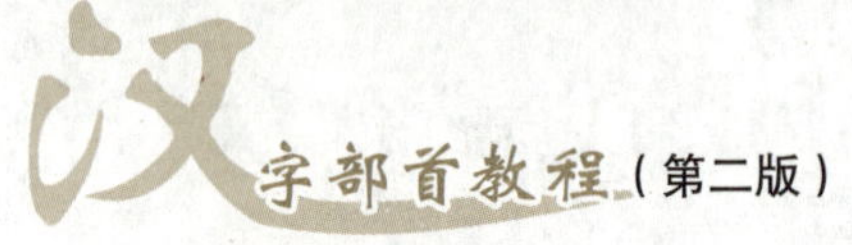

通常位于汉字的上面。穴部的字多与洞穴、房屋等意义有关。"突"是会意字，从穴从犬，犬从洞穴中蹿出，这种情景给人的感觉显然有些"突然"。"窗"指房间里用来换气透光的装置，"同窗"指在一起读书的同学。穴部的字还与窘迫有关。"穷"由"窮"简化而来。"窮"是形声字，本义指极尽、完结，引申义指缺乏财物。

Ancient form

穴 is a pictograph, which depicts a cave welling. The original meaning of this radical is *hole, cave, or den* within a house. As a radical, 穴 stands on the top of a compound. Characters with 穴 have meanings related to houses or holes. The character 突 (tū; *sudden*) is an ideograph consisting of 穴 and 犬. It depicts a dog darting *suddenly* out from a cave. The character 窗 means *window* (*a hole in the wall of a room*). Characters with 穴 also refers to poor. The character 穷 is simplified version of 窮. 窮 is a phonetic-semantic compound. The original meaning is *to exhaust*, *to end.* Its extended meaning is *poverty.*

故事 Story

千里之堤，溃于蚁穴 (Qiān lǐ zhī dī, kuì yú yǐ xué)
千 thousand 里 mile 之 of 堤 dyke,
溃 collapse 于 from 蚁 ant 穴 hole

千里之堤，溃于蚁穴 means that one ant hole may cause the collapse of a thousand miles of dyke. This idiom is a warning that a slight negligence can lead to a great disaster. It is similar to the English expression: a small leak will sink a great ship.

55. 力（lì）部 Strength

古字形 

“力”是象形字，古文字像耒的形状，耒是古代用于耕田的农具。用耒耕种需用力气，所以“力”的基本义是体力、气力。作为部首，“力”通常位于汉字的右侧或下面，例如“功”“努”。力部的字多与力气和力量有关系。“劳动”都是“力”部字。“劣”是会意字，由“力”和“少”构成，意思是弱小，引申指不好的事物。

Ancient form

力 is a pictograph. The ancient form of 力 looks like a ploughshare. Peasants needed to use their own strength to plough the land. Therefore, 力 means *strength*. As a radical, 力 is often placed either on the right side or at the bottom of a compound, such as 功 (gōng; *achievement*), and 努 (nǔ; *to put forth one's strength*). Characters containing the 力 radical often have meanings related to strength. Both characters in the word 劳动 (láodòng; *to work*) have the 力 radical. 劣 (liè) is an ideograph which consists of 力 and 少 (shǎo; *few or lack*). Its original meaning is *weak*. Its extended meaning is *inferior or low quality*.

故事 Story

手无缚鸡之力 (Shǒu wú fù jī zhī lì)
手 hand 无 no 缚 truss up 鸡 chicken 之 of 力 strength

手无缚鸡之力 literally means "He/she lacks the strength to truss a chicken." This idiom is used to express that a person is very weak, either physically or psychologically, and that he/she is unable to get things done.

56. 舟（zhōu）部 Boat

古字形

“舟”是象形字，古文字描摹的是一只船的形状：两边像船帮，中间的线条代表船头、船舱和船尾。作为部首，“舟”通常位于汉字的左侧，有时位于汉字的上侧。舟部的字多与船或航行有关。“船”是重要的水上交通运输工具，“舵”指船上控制方向的设备。“航”原来指行船，后来也用来指飞行。

Ancient form

舟 is a pictograph. Its ancient form looks like a boat with two hollow sections—representing the hold. As a radical, it often stands on the left side or top of a compound. Characters containing 舟 tend to have meanings related to water transportation or transportation in general. 船 (chuán) means *boat or ship*; 舵 (duò) means *helm*. The original meaning of 航 (háng) is *to sail*. In modern Chinese, it also means *to fly* (sail in the sky).

故事 Story

刻舟求剑 (Kè zhōu qiú jiàn)
刻 mark 舟 boat 求 seek 剑 sword

Once upon a time, a gentleman with a sword rode a ferry across a river. Unfortunately, when they reached the middle of the river his sword unexpectedly fell into the water. This gentleman immediately made a mark on the edge of the moving boat and said "This is where my sword fell in." After the ferry reached the far bank of the river, he jumped into the river to look for his sword under the spot where he made the mark earlier. Of course, he was unable to find the sword.

This idiom is used to describe a person who is ridiculously rigid and takes measures without regard to changes in circumstance.

57. 囗（wéi）部 To enclose

古字形 ▢

“囗”是象形字，古文字像回环之形。“囗”的本义是将四周拦挡起来。作为部首，“囗”通常位于汉字的外围，写作“囗”，俗称“国字框”。囗部的字多与包围等意义有关。“围”是形声字，从囗韦声，意思是环绕。“囚”是会意字，从人在囗中，用作名词时，指被拘禁的人，例如“囚犯”；用作动词时，指拘禁、囚禁，例如“被囚”。“困”也是会意字，从木在囗中，指处于艰难痛苦或无法摆脱的环境中。

Ancient form ▢

囗 is a pictograph. The ancient script of 囗 looks like an encircling wall. Its original meaning is *to enclose*. As a radical, it often appears at the outside of a compound written as 囗, which is called guó zì kuàng (guo character around). Characters with the 囗 radical often have meanings related to enclosure. 围 (wéi) is a phonetic-semantic compound. 韦 (wéi) inside 囗 indicates the pronunciation of the character, which is “wéi.” The meaning of this character is *to enclose or surround*. 囚 (qiú) is an ideograph meaning *to imprison* as a verb, and meaning *prisoner* as a noun. Another ideograph character 困 (kùn) means *to be stranded*.

故事 Story

围城打援 (Wéi chéng dǎ yuán)
围 besiege 城 city 打 attack 援 relief troops

In Chinese military history, there was a classic battle named 虎牢之战—the Battle of Hulao.

It was in the third year of the Emperor Tang Wude's reign. The Emperor was still new and the Central Government was not very strong. There were frequent uprisings. Li Shimin, the King of the Qin State (who later became the second emperor of the Tang Dynasty) directed his army to attack the rebels in the City of Luoyang. But Luoyang's fortifications were very strong. Li's soldiers were not able to get into the city. So he put the city under siege so that the enemy's food and supplies would be cut off. In the meantime, another uprising had taken place in the city of Hulao. The rebels there intended to storm in and rescue Luoyang. King Li decided to leave a small portion of his army in Luoyang to continue the siege and take the rest of his soldiers to fight the would-be relief troops in Hulao. After a few months of stalemate, Li Shimin devised a trick to lure the relief troops from the city of Hulao. His trick worked, and he destroyed them. Soon, the starving enemy in Luoyang also surrendered.

The Battle of Hulao is a heroic story of the 24-year-old Li Shimin defeating two sets of rebels with one battle. He is remembered for his strategy of besieging the left and attacking the right.

58. 雨 [⻗] (yǔ) 部 Rain

古字形

“雨”是象形字，古文字描摹的是天上落雨的情景。作为部首，“雨”通常位于汉字的上面。雨部的字多与天气或自然现象有关。下雨时，天空中伴随着闪电而传来的强大声音叫作“雷”；深秋季节，附着在地面或植物上面的微细的白色结晶称为“霜”；冬季摄氏零度以下时，由空中降下的冰晶叫作“雪”。雪洁白而光亮，因此，“雪”又引申指像雪一样白或像雪一样亮的东西。“零”是形声字，从雨令声，本义指雨徐徐而下，引申指草木花叶的凋谢。“零”还有两个十分常用的义项：一是零碎，一是数学上的零数。

Ancient form

雨 is a pictograph. The ancient form of 雨 depicts falling rain. The meaning of 雨 is *rain or to rain*. As a radical, 雨 often appears on the top of a compound character. Characters with the 雨 radical often have meanings related to weather and meteorological phenomena such as 雷 (léi; *thunder*), 霜 (shuāng; *frost*), and 雪 (xuě; *snow*). The character 零 (líng) is a phonetic-semantic compound. The bottom part 令 indicates its pronunciation. The original meaning of this character is *to rain continuously*. The character 零 has been borrowed to indicate other meanings such as *withered*, *fragmentary*, *or zero*.

故事 Story

呼风唤雨 (Hū fēng huàn yǔ)
呼 summon 风 wind 唤 call for 雨 rain

In the Ya'an area of Sichuan Province there is a mountain with an ancient well at its peak. According to the local chronicles, this well could summon the wind and call forth the rain whenever people removed its cover. Local people considered the well to be a magical gift from the gods. Because of this, the well has become the subject of national legend.

Modern scientific study has provided a possible explanation to this ancient myth. Due to geographic location, the air in the area is very moist, and during most of the year, this area is quite rainy. So the well does not cause the rain, it is simply the local climate. It is possible that occasionally when local people removed the cover of the well, it coincidently started rain. This may be why the well is afforded magical powers in the local historical records.

Now we use 呼风唤雨 to describe mankind's ability to control the forces of nature. It is also used to describe someone who is very capable of stirring up trouble.

59. 厂（hǎn; chǎng）部 House; Shelter

古字形 厂

“厂”是象形字，古文字像山崖之形状，有人认为其本义是没有墙壁或只有一面墙壁的房屋。部首“厂”读作hǎn，现代汉语中读作chǎng的“厂”字，是“廠”的简化字，所以和用作部首的“厂”不属于同一个字。“厂”在现代汉语中只用作部首，不单独成字。作为部首，“厂”通常位于汉字的左上侧。厂部的字与房屋有关。“厢”指供人居住的地方，特指在正房前面东西两旁的房屋，又引申指具有房屋特征的地方，例如戏院或影院里特意隔开的座位叫“包厢”，车里容纳人或货的地方叫“车厢”。“厅”指聚会或招待客人用的大房间。“厦”是高大的屋子。

Ancient form 厂

厂 is a pictograph. Its ancient form looks like a cliff, though some scholars argue it represents a room with the right wall missing. As a radical it is pronounced as hǎn. In modern Chinese, the simplification of a different character, 廠 (chǎng; *factory*), is 厂 —identical in form to the radical 厂. However, the radical hǎn is different from the character chǎng in terms of both pronunciation and meaning. 厂 no longer appears as an independent character in modern Chinese. It is used only as a radical in compounds. As a radical, it is often placed on the upper left of a compound. Characters with the 厂 radical often have meanings related to housing. 厢 (xiāng) refers to the side rooms in a big house. 厅 (tīng) means *hall* and 厦 (shà) means *big building or house*.

故事 Story

高楼大厦 (Gāo lóu dà shà)
高 high 楼 building 大 large 厦 mansion

Which city holds the densest concentration of skyscrapers in the world? The answer is Hong Kong. Between Wan Chai (湾仔) and Central (中环), an area a little more than a mile wide, is regarded as the area with the greatest concentration of skyscrapers in the world. A few of them can be considered global landmarks and symbols of Hong Kong's development.

One of these buildings is the 汇丰银行 (HSBC). Built in the fifties, it was the first high building with a full-steel structure. It was very popular among the people of Hong Kong. Another building, the 合和大厦 (Hopewell Mansion), was built in the seventies. The round building is the first in Hong Kong to feature a revolving restaurant on top. It quickly became a must-see spot for Hong Kong tourists. In the eighties, because of its unique sword-shape design, 中银大厦 (the Bank of China Tower) became very popular. In the nineties, many new skyscrapers were built. Among them, 国际金融中心大厦 (the International Finance Centre), quickly replaced 新中银大厦 and became the tallest building in Hong Kong. This building has 88 stories and is 415meters (1362 feet) tall. If you have a chance to go to Hong Kong, do not forget to visit these skyscrapers.

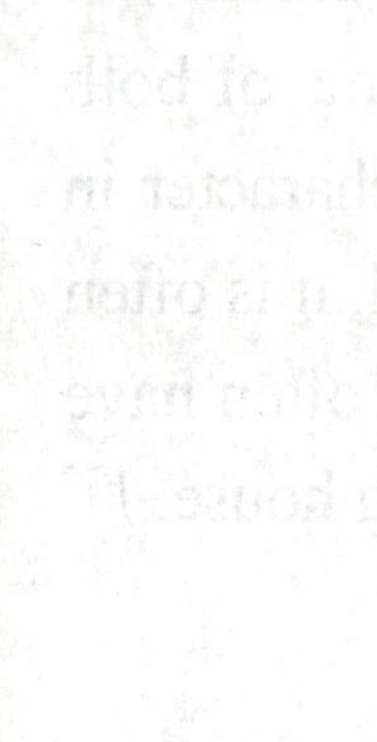

60. 又（yòu）部 Hand

古字形

“又”是象形字，古文字像右手的形状，表示“右手”的意思，后来写作“右”。“又”被借作副词，表示动作行为的重复或继续。作为部首，“又”有时位于汉字的下面或上面，有时位于汉字的左侧或右侧。又部的字多与手或手的动作有关。“反”是个会意字，从厂从又，“厂”表示山崖，“厂”和“又”放在一起，意思是用手攀登山崖，引申为翻转的意义；“取”指用手获取；“受”指用手交接。

Ancient form

又 is a pictograph. The ancient script of 又 looks like a hand. The original meaning is *right hand*. Later, the character 右 (yòu) was invented to represent *right*. 又 is used as adverb to indicate the repetition (of an action). This meaning has no connection with its original meaning as hand. As a radical, 又 may appear in any position of a compound. Characters containing 又 often have meanings related to hands or the action of hands. The character 反 (fǎn) is an ideograph consisting of 厂and 又. 厂 means *cliff*. Together, it is 反 which means *climbing a cliff*. Its extended meaning is *to turn over*. The character 取 (qǔ) means *to get things with hands*. The character 受 (shòu) means *to receive things with hands*.

故事 Story

无功不受禄 (Wú gōng bú shòu lù)

无 no 功 contribution 不 not 受 receive 禄 reward

Once, Confucius visited Emperor Qi. The Emperor wanted to bestow on Confucius a piece of land, but Confucius declined. When his students asked him why, he explained, "I heard that a gentleman receives rewards only if he has made a contribution. Today, I paid a visit to Emperor Qi to present my ideas. Emperor Qi did not accept my ideas, but granted me a piece of land. He really does not understand me." Later Confucius left the Qi State.

Now, we use 无功不受禄 to refer to a noble person who does not wish to receive an award without deserving it.

第八课　牛、皿、夂、羽、羊、弓、歹、小、欠、子

61. 牛［牜］(niú) 部 Cattle

古字形

“牛”是象形字，古文字像正面的牛头的形状，并突出了两只牛角翘起的特征。“牛”是六畜之一。中国古代，牛除了用作耕作之外，还有一个最重要的用途，就是作为祭品祭祀神灵。古人认为牛是所有祭品中的上品，因此，凡是隆重祭奠，牛是不可缺少的。古代祭牲的专用名称为“牢”，中间的“牛”字成为祭牲的代表。“牺”“牲”是祭神祀祖所用的祭品，也是以“牛”为代表。作为部首，“牛”通常位于汉字的左侧，写作“牜”，俗称“牛字旁”；位于汉字下面时写作“牛”。牛部的字多和牛或牲畜有关。“特”字从牛寺声，本义指雄性的牛，用作形容词，表示独特、突出的意思。“犊”本义就是指小牛。

Ancient form

牛 is a pictograph. The ancient form of 牛 outlines the head of a cattle. Therefore, the meaning of 牛 is *cattle*. In ancient China, cattle is one of the six domestic animals. The other five were pig, goat, horse, fowl, and dog. In addition to farming, 牛 was used for important sacrificial offerings in worship. The ancient Chinese people considered 牛 as the best animal for sacrifices. Therefore, the character 牢 (láo) which originally signified "animals used as sacrificial offerings," has 牛 as its radical. Later, 牢 began to be used to mean *fold*. As a radical, when 牛 stands on the left side of a character, it is written as 牜 and called niú zì páng (cattle at the side). When 牛 is placed at the bottom of a compound, it is written as 牛. Characters with the 牛 radical often relate to cattle or domestic animals. The character 特 originally meant *bull*. Now it means *special or unique*. The character 犊 originally meant *young cattle*.

故事 Story

归马放牛 (Guī mǎ fàng niú)
归 return 马 horse 放 release 牛 cattle

It was said that the last Emperor of Shang Dynasty led a life of shameless indulgence. His extravagance provoked voices of discontent throughout the empire. A person named Ji Fa mobilized the people and the army to rebel and overthrow the Shang Emperor. Soon the whole country was embroiled in war. Because the Emperor had already lost the confidence of the people, his army was quickly overcome. Defeated, the Emperor decided to commit suicide. With his death, the Shang Dynasty ended forever.

Ji Fa established the Zhou Dynasty and became the first Emperor of Zhou. He announced to his people that the war had come to an end and the country should restore its peace. In his announcement, he said "We should now lay down our arms and construct a civil administration. We should return the war horses to the south of Hua Mountain and release the war cattle into the Taolin field." This means that Emperor Ji wanted those horses and cattle recruited for the war to return to agricultural use in their original lands.

归马放牛 now is used to describe the situation in which war has ended and peace is being restored.

62. 皿（mǐn）部 Container

古字形

“皿”是象形字，古文字像一个圆足的大口容器，本义是盛饭食的器具的总称。作为部首，“皿”通常位于汉字的下面。皿部的字多与器具有关。“盘”本是盛水用的容器，后来泛指浅而开口很大的盛物的器具；“益”是会意字，从皿从水，本义指器皿中的水满后溢出、漫出，后引申用作名词，指好处、利益；“盗”是会意字，也写作“盜”，从次从皿，是说看见别人的好东西，羡慕得流口水，于是便生盗窃之心。

Ancient form

皿 is a pictograph. The ancient form of this character is a picture of utensil for storing or cooking food. As a radical, 皿 is often placed at the bottom of a

compound. Characters with the 皿 radical often relate to cooking or kitchen utensils. The character 盘 (pán) originally meant *vessel for water*. Now it can be used to refer to any type of kitchen utensil with a wide-open top. 益 (yì) is an ideograph consisting of 皿 and 水. Its basic meaning is *overflowing water.* Its extended meaning is *benefits*. 盗 (dào) which means *to steal or to rob* is also an ideograph, which can be also written as 盜. This suggests when people see the delicious food in others' plates, envy and desire may drive one to steal it.

故事 Story

杯盘狼藉 (Bēi pán láng jí)
杯 cup 盘 plate 狼 wolf 藉 clutter

This expression describes the scene after a feast, when the cups and plates are strewn half-hazard across the table. It looks as messy as in a wolf's den. It also suggests that the people who just ate there are ill-mannered and uncivilized.

63. 仌［冫］（bīng）部 Ice

古字形

“仌”是象形字，古文字描摹的是水凝结成冰以后的纹理。“仌”在现代汉语中只用作部首，不单独成字。作为部首，“仌”通常位于汉字的左侧，写作“冫”，俗称“两点水”，例如“冰”；有时位于汉字下面，例如“寒”。仌部的字多与冰或寒冷等意义有关。“冰”字最初写作“仌”，表示水凝结之义。后来出现了“凝”字，“冰”字就专门用来指零度以下水凝结成的固体。冰给人的感觉是凉爽或寒冷，所以有“冰凉”“冰冷”等词语。

Ancient form

仌 is a pictograph. The ancient form of it depicts the veins that appear in the ice of frozen bodies of water. However, 仌 is no longer an independent character in modern Chinese. As a radical, 仌 often stands on the left side of a compound and is written as 冫, which is called liǎng diǎn shuǐ (two drops of water), such as in 冰 (bīng; *ice*). Sometimes it appears at the bottom of a compound, such as in the character 寒 (hán; *cold*). It usually relates to icy and cold. The character 冰 orginally was written as 仌, which means that water is frozen, the shape 仌 looks like a frozen texture of water. Later, a character 凝 was created for the meaning of “congealing” due to coldness. So character 冰 is used to refer to ice. As 冰 gives a feeling of coldness, therefore, all the characters in the words 冰凉 (bīngliáng; *cold as ice*) and 冰冷 (bīnglěng; *frigid as ice*) have 冫.

故事 Story

冰灯 (Bīng dēng)
冰 ice 灯 lights/lanterns

If you travel to northern China during the winter, you can see a dazzling array of lighted ice sculptures. Local people call these sculptures 冰灯. Ice sculpture is a popular art form in the area. The city of Harbin holds a grand Ice Light Festival every year.

Harbin's Ice Light Festival originated in early sixteenth century, but it was not until 1985 that the city decided to hold an official Harbin International Ice Festival every year. Since then, the festival has grown into a massive event. Many teams from countries such as Canada, Japan, France, Russia, and South Africa come to the festival to demonstrate their exquisite ice-sculpting skills. The event draws millions of tourists from all over the world. The festival starts on January fifth and lasts until the end of February. During the festival, you can see lighted ice sculptures of all kinds, such as lions, tigers, eagles, dragons, Chinese lanterns, and sometimes European style churches and pavilions. Their colored lights are especially magnificent in the evening.

64. 羽（yǔ）部 Feather

古字形 𦏲

“羽”是象形字，古文字像羽毛的形状，特指鸟翅膀上的长毛，后来泛指鸟的羽毛。作为部首，“羽”位于汉字的右侧、上面或下面，例如“翻”“翼”“翁”。羽部的字有的与鸟的翅膀有关，有的与鸟飞行的动作有关。“翅”是形声字，从羽支声，本义为鸟类、昆虫的翅膀。“翻”是形声字，从羽番声，本义是指鸟儿飞，引申指位置变动、改变的意思。“翔”是形声字，从羽羊声，本义为鸟儿盘旋地飞而不扇动翅膀，后来则指鸟类或虫类等用翅膀在空中往来活动。

Ancient form 𦏲

羽 is a pictograph. Its ancient script looks like a feather. As a radical, 羽 can appear on the right, top, or bottom of a compound. Characters with the 羽 radical often have meanings related to birds, bird behaviors, or flying object. For example 翻 (fān; *to turn over*), 翼 (yì; *wing*) , 翁 (wēng; *neck feather of birds*) all contain the 羽 radical. The character 翅 (chì) originally meant *the wings of birds or flying insects*. The original meaning of 翻 (fān) refers to the change of body position when a bird is flying. Its extended meaning is *to turn over or to change*. The original meaning of 翔 (xiáng) is *a bird spreading its wings and circling in the sky*. It now also refers to any kind of flying position.

故事 Story

积羽沉舟 (Jī yǔ chén zhōu)
积 accumulate 羽 feather 沉 sink 舟 boat

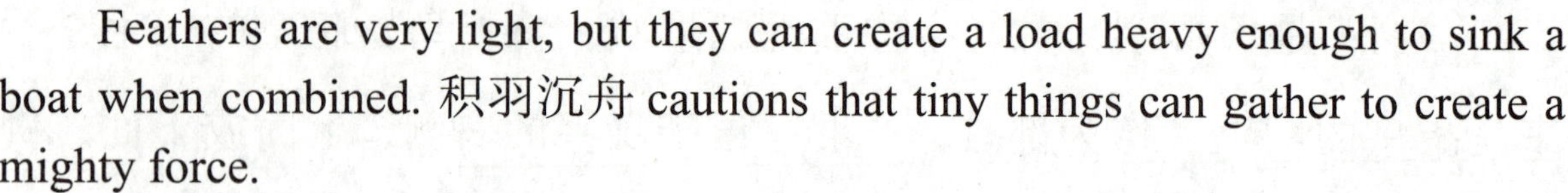

Feathers are very light, but they can create a load heavy enough to sink a boat when combined. 积羽沉舟 cautions that tiny things can gather to create a mighty force.

During the Warring States Period, there were seven states: Qin, Qi, Chu, Yan, Han, Wei, and Zhao. Among them, Qin was the strongest. The King of the Qin State was very ambitious and intended to conquer other states. To resist Qin's attack the other six states formed a strong alliance. After considering this situation, Zhang Yi, the Premier of the Qin State, resigned from his position and went to infiltrate the government of the Wei State. Zhang quickly gained trust of Wei Xiangwang—the King of Wei—and became the Premier of Wei. He then tried to convince Wei Xiangwang to unite with Qin, but Wei Xiangwang refused to do so. Upon hearing that his former premier was unsuccessful, the King of Qin was furious. He ordered his armies to attack Wei. After four years of confrontation, Wei Xiangwang passed away. His Son, Wei Aiwang, took the throne and became the new King of Wei. Like his father, he had no intention of

uniting with Qin. However, under the constant onslaught of Qin forces, Wei was beginning to collapse. In the following year, Qin also moved to attack the Han State. With one member of the six-state alliance down, and another under attack, the alliance was severely weakened. Zhang Yi took advantage of this situation to again push Wei Aiwang to unite with Qin. He pointed out that the power of the Wei State was being undermined both internally and externally. Those factors, though still minor, would eventually combine and destroy the Wei. He used the analogy 积羽沉舟 to persuade Wei Aiwang to unite with Qin before Wei's situation got any worse. Wei Aiwang was at last convinced. He decided to withdraw from the alliance and seek protection from Qin. Subsequently, the King of Qin conquered the six states and unified China.

65. 羊［⺶⺷］（yáng）部 Goat; Sheep

古字形

“羊”是象形字，古文字像羊头的正面形状，并突出了羊角的特征。作为部首，“羊”有时位于汉字的右侧或左侧，例如“群”“羚”；有时位于汉字的上面，例如“羔”。羊部的字多与羊、吉祥等意义有关。与羊有关的，例如“羔”，指未满一岁的小绵羊。而“吉祥”的意义，则突出反映在“祥”“美”“善”三个字中。“祥”字本义指好的或不好的预兆，后来则专门表示好的征兆，也就是“吉祥”之义。“美”是会意字，从羊从大，一个正面站立的人，头上用羊角作装饰，很美丽。“美”后引申指善、好。“善”是会意字，从言从羊。因为羊是吉祥的象征，所以“善”字本义就是指吉祥，引申指美好、善良的行为和品质。

Ancient form

羊 is a pictograph. The ancient script of 羊 outlines the head of a goat. As a radical, it appears on either the left or right side of a compound such as in the characters 群 (qún; *herd of sheep*) and 羚 (líng; *antelope*). It can also appear on the top of a compound, such as in 羔 (gāo; *lamb*). Characters containing 羊 refer to *goat/sheep or things associated with goodness*. For example, 羔 means *baby goat/sheep*. The original meaning of 祥 (xiáng) is *omen*. 吉祥 (jíxiáng) means *good omen*. 美 is an ideograph, which is formed by combining 羊 on the top and 大 on the bottom which represents a person. So, this ideograph shows a standing person with goat horns decoration on the head to beautify the outlook. Thus, 美 means *beautiful*. Its extended meanings are *kindness and goodness*. 羊 is also considered as an auspicious animal, thus 善 (shàn) as an ideograph means *kindness*. Its extended meaning relates to *a person's noble characters and behaviors*.

故事 Story

亡羊补牢 (Wáng yáng bǔ láo)
亡 lose 羊 sheep 补 repair 牢 fold

During the Warring States Period, there was a Minister of the Chu State named Zhuang Xin. He admonished the Emperor of the Chu State for his self-indulgence. He said that if the Emperor continued to sacrifice state business for personal enjoyment, then the country would soon be conquered by other states. The Emperor was not happy to hear this and considered Zhuang's words alarmist. Dismayed, Zhuang told the Emperor that he could not bear to watch the impending destruction of the Chu State, so he would have to leave immediately. Five months after Minister Zhuang left Chu, the Qin State attacked. With the state of Chu in dire peril, the Emperor of Chu sent for the Minister Zhuang to return and help save the country. Zhuang returned, saying, "It is not too late to mend the fold even after the sheep is lost..."

亡羊补牢 is used to indicate that although there are problems, it is not too late to take remedial measures.

66. 弓（gōng）部 Bow

古字形

“弓”是象形字，古文字像弓的形状。“弓”的本义指一种射箭或打弹丸用的武器，引申指形状或作用像弓一样的器具。作为部首，“弓”通常位于汉字的左侧或下面，如“张”“弩”。弓部的字多与弓有关，或用来表示弓的种类，例如“弧”“弩”；或表示弓的一部分，例如“弦”；或表示用弓的动作，例如“张”“弛”。其中，“弧”字是形声字，从弓瓜声，在古代指的是一种木弓，引申指圆或椭圆的一部分的形状，即“弧形”。“弦”左为“弓”，右为“玄”，本义指用丝做成的系在弓背两端的、能发箭的绳状物的“弓弦”。

Ancient form

弓 is a pictograph. The ancient script shows a bow. Its extended meaning relates to objects with a bow shape. As a radical, 弓 is often placed on the left side or the bottom of a compound. For example, in the character 张 (zhāng), 弓 appears on the left. The original meaning of 张 is *to draw a bow*; its extended meaning is *to open or expand*. Characters that contain the 弓 radical often signify types of bows, the parts of a bow, or how to use a bow. For instance, 弧 (hú) means *the curved part of a bow*; 弦 (xián) means *bowstring*; 弩 (nǔ) means *crossbow* and 弛 (chí) means *to release the tension of a bow*.

故事 Story

杯弓蛇影 (Bēi gōng shé yǐng)
杯 cup 弓 bow 蛇 snake 影 shadow

In the Jin Dynasty, a gentleman named Yue Guang invited a friend to come to have a drink at his home. After the first sip, when Yue Guang's friend replaced his wine cup on the table, he noticed a tiny little snake coiled in his cup. Although this made Yue's friend uneasy, he still finished the whole cup of wine. The next day, Yue Guang heard that his friend had become ill after drinking

wine with him. Yue Guang was horrified and went to see his friend and ask why he thought the wine had made him sick. After hearing his friend's story about the little snake in the wine cup, Yue Guang hurried home to investigate. After much searching, he realized that the bow hanging on his dining room wall, cast a shadow that reflected in the wine cup. The shadow looked just like a snake. He hastily invited his friend to his home again and explained the illusion. When his friend realized that there was no snake in the wine cup he was very relieved and his sickness disappeared.

Now, we use 杯弓蛇影 to describe a person who is very suspicious and over-sensitive.

67. 歹 [歺] (è; dǎi) 部
Remains; Skeleton

古字形

“歹”本写作“歺”，是象形字，古文字像剔去肉后残留的骨头的形状，本义指残骨，读作 è。后表示恶、坏的意思，读作 dǎi。作为部首，“歹”通常位于汉字的左侧，例如“殆”“殁”。歹部的字多与死亡、坏或不吉利等意义有关，例如“残”“死”。其中“死”是会意字，从人从歺，是说人死之后，魂魄就会脱离形体，全部器官也停止了活动，所以本义就是生命的终止。

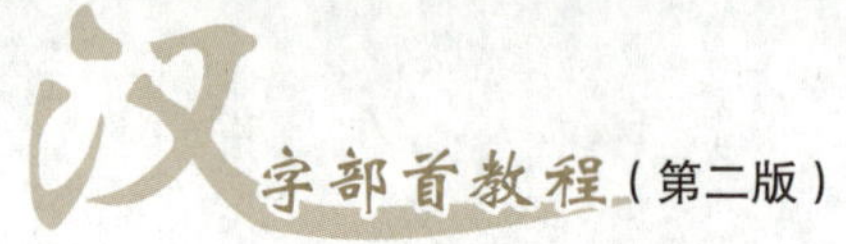

Ancient form

歹 is a pictograph. Its original pictograph form is 歺 —as depicted in the ancient script. It looks like a human skeleton. The pronunciation of 歺 is è, meaning *remains of dead bodies*. Later, it extends to the meaning of *evil behaviors* and is read as dǎi. As a radical, 歹 is often placed on the left side of compound characters, such as in 殆 (dài; *dangerous*), and 殁 (mò; *to die*). Characters with the 歹 radical often that have meanings associated with death and bad things, such as 残 (cán; *to injure, deficient*). The character 死 is an ideograph consisting of 人 and 歹. The image depicts a soul leaving a body. So the meaning of this character is *death*.

故事 Story

为非作歹 (Wéi fēi zuò dǎi)
为 commit 非 crime 作 do 歹 evil

Below is a story told by a Buddhist Master of the Law (a title of respect for a Buddhist priest).

There was a wealthy man who committed many crimes and did evil things in order to get more money. After a long life his death finally neared. From his

sickbed, he sent for a Master of the Law to chant Buddhist scriptures for him so that he could redeem his wayward soul and enjoy his afterlife in the Land of Ultimate Bliss. The Master came and prayed for him: Avalokiteshvara namo, please find a Buddha from afar to carry this rich man to the Land of Ultimate Bliss!" After hearing this, the rich man was very unhappy and cried out from his sickbed: "I am going to die very soon! Why don't you fetch a nearby Buddha instead of calling for one from a distance?" The Master replied: "The Bodhisattvas nearby all know that you got your riches through 为非作歹. None of them is willing to take you to the Land of Ultimate Bliss, so I have to pray hard and hopefully to find one from afar."

68. 小［⺌］（xiǎo）部 Small

古字形

“小”是象形字，古文字以沙粒表达“小”的意思。“小”本指面积、体积、容量、数量、强度、力量等不及一般或不及所比较的对象，与“大”相对。作为部首，“小”通常位于汉字的上面，写作“小”，例如“尖”“尘”；又可写作“⺌”，例如“光”“当”。小部的字多与微小等意义有关。“尘”是会意字，从土从小，指体积微小的尘土。此外，当说到“数量小”时，有时就用与“小”字形相似的“少”字来表示，例如“少量”。

Ancient form

小 is a pictograph. The ancient script of 小 represents three grains of sand, indicating its meaning—*small*. As a radical, 小 often appears on the top of compounds, such as in 尖 (jiān; *small sharp point*), and 尘 (chén; *dust*). 小 is sometimes written as ⺌, such as in the character 光 (guāng; *tiny rays*), and 当 (dāng; *when*). The similar character 少 (shǎo) can also refer to small amount.

故事 Story

小隙沉舟 (Xiǎo xì chén zhōu)

小 small 隙 crack 沉 sink 舟 ship

Once upon a time, a merchant purchased a beautiful ship from a shipbuilder. After several years of use, a member of the crew found a tiny crack in the ship's fore, just above the water level. He reported this problem to the merchant. The merchant knew that if he took the ship in for repairs it would take at least one month. He could not wait that long because he had urgent cargo that needed to be delivered. He told himself a small crack was not that critical; repairs could wait until after this shipment was delivered. The next day, the ship embarked as scheduled. The weather was favorable on the first day of travel, and the ship sailed smoothly. However, the next day the weather changed for the worst, and the ship was battered by a ferocious typhoon. The pounding waves tore at the small crack, which became larger and larger, until water started pouring into the cabin. The ship began

to sink and the crew had to abandon ship. Because he did not fix his problem immediately the merchant lost both his cargo and the ship.

This parable cautions us that small problems should be dealt with right away in order to avoid greater losses. It is similar to the English idiom: A stitch in time saves nine.

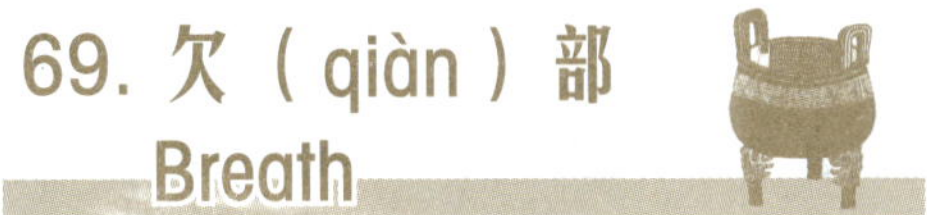

69. 欠（qiàn）部 Breath

古字形

“欠”是象形字，古文字像人张口呼吸的形状。“欠”的本义指张口呵气，打呵欠。人的呼吸有吸进空气和呼出空气两种情况，“欠”属于后者。因为“欠”只呼出而不吸进空气，所以引申为亏欠。作为部首，“欠”通常位于汉字的右侧。欠部的字多与口的动作有关系，例如“歌”“欢”，都是从“欠”得义。又如，“吹”是会意字，由“口”和“欠”组成，合拢嘴唇用力出气就叫作“吹”。

Ancient form

欠 is a pictograph. The ancient form of 欠 depicts a person with a large mouth (to indicate exhaling). 欠 means *exhale*, but not *inhale*. Because exhaling is an act of expelling and expending, it therefore has the extended meaning—*to owe*. As a radical, 欠 often appears on the right of a compound. Characters with the 欠 radical have meanings related to vocalizing or breathing. Some examples are: 歌 (gē; *to sing a song or a song*), 欢 (huān; *to cheer or hail*), and 吹 (chuī; *to blow*).

故事 Story

欢欣鼓舞 (Huān xīn gǔ wǔ)

欢欣 happy and joyful 鼓舞 upbeat

Many years ago, the Yellow River was like a wild horse. Unrestrained, it surged over its banks each year and caused huge floods to villages and surrounding farmlands. Every year the floods left thousands homeless and caused mass starvation. At that time, a man named Feng Yi heard that if a person drank the juice of the narcissus flower for one hundred days he or she would become immortal. Feng Yi decided to give it a try. For 99 days Feng Yi collected juice from narcissus flowers, crossing the Yellow River many times in his quest. He thereby became very familiar with the geographic configuration of the river. On the 100th day, when crossing the river for his final dose, the water level suddenly swelled and pulled him under. The terrified Feng Yi sank into the water and quickly drowned. After he died his spirit went before the Jade Emperor (the supreme deity of Taoism) to denounce the Yellow River's indiscriminate killing. Knowing Feng Yi's familiarity with the river, the Jade Emperor appointed Feng the River God and charged him with the task of taming the wild river. Feng agreed, and spent many days mapping the Yellow River. He gave this map to Da Yu (the founder of the Xia Dynasty) who had resolved to bring the Yellow River to heel. With the help of this important map together with two other treasures: a mountain axe and an anchor, Da Yu toiled on the river for thirteen years. Finally, the Yellow River was brought under control. Once this news was spread, people along the river were all 欢欣鼓舞 because they could finally live peaceful and prosperous lives, free from the floods.

70. 子（zǐ）部 Baby

古字形 孑

“子”是象形字，古文字像婴儿在襁褓中之形。“子”的本义指婴儿，引申为幼小、小的等意义。婴儿是血缘的传递者，因此，“子”又有了种子、卵子等意义。作为部首，“子”通常位于汉字的左侧或右侧，例如“孙”“仔”；有时位于汉字的上面或下面，例如“孕”。子部的字多与孩子或生育等意义有关系。例如“字”，由“宀”和“子”组成，本义为在屋内生孩子，孩子承继血脉，正如文字传承文明和文化一样，所以“字”又用来指记录语言的符号。

Ancient form 孑

子 is a pictograph. The ancient form of 子 looks like a baby in swaddling clothes. The original meaning of 子 is *infant*. 子 also means *young or the younger generation*. Because infants are human offspring, 子 also has meanings related to seeds and eggs. As a radical, 子 may appear in any position within a compound. Characters with the 子 radical often have meanings associated with procreation, pregnancy, children, and heritage. For example, 孙 (sūn) means *grandson*; 仔 (zǎi) means *son or young animal*; and 孕 (yùn) means *to be pregnant*. The character 字 (zì; *character or Chinese script*) consists of 宀 and 子. The original meaning of this character is *to give a birth to baby inside a house*. Giving birth ensures the succession of a family line, just as Chinese characters ensure the transmission of Chinese history and culture to future generations. Therefore 字 means *Chinese character*.

故事 Story

折箭教子 (Zhé jiàn jiào zǐ)

折 break off 箭 arrow 教 teach 子 children

折箭教子 is an ancient fable. Once upon a time, there was a man named A Chai who was a tribal leader and had 20 sons. A Chai was very ill, and he knew that he was going to die very soon. He didn't forget that his elder brother passed the throne to him after he died. So he would also pass the throne to his younger brother Muwei after he passed away. Thus, he called his sons and brothers to his bedside. He asked his sons to fetch his arrows. And then he told each of them to break an arrow in half. Needless to say, each broke their arrow easily. Then he asked his second younger brother Muliyan to break one arrow and then a bundle of nineteen arrows, respectively. Muliyan tried very hard but could not break the bundle of nineteen arrows. A Chai said to his brothers and sons that one arrow was easy to break but many arrows together were difficult to break. He hoped that they could understand a simple principium: As long as all of them could work together to form a joint force, the tribe would become stronger and would not be conquered by invaders. Then he died and Muwei inherited the throne.

第九课 隹、耳、白、骨、立、见、厶、毛、卜、齿

71. 隹（zhuī）部 Short-tailed bird

古字形

“隹”是象形字，古文字像鸟之形，为短尾鸟的总称。“隹”在现代汉语中只用作部首，不单独成字。作为部首，“隹”通常位于汉字的右侧，有时位于汉字的上面或下面，例如“集”“雀”。隹部的字多与鸟类有关。“雏”本指刚出生的小鸡，引申指其他幼小的鸟类。后来，“雏”字所指的范围进一步扩大，泛指幼小的动物或初涉社会的人，例如“雏虎”“雏儿”之“雏”。但凡鸟类，多喜欢成群结队地生活，这一现象从“集”的繁体“雧”字中就可以得到印证。“集”字本义是群鸟栖息于树木之上，引申有聚合、会合等意义。

Ancient form

隹 is a pictograph. The ancient form of 隹 is a picture of a short-tailed bird. In modern Chinese, 隹 is no longer an independent character. As a radical, it can appear on the right, top, or bottom of a compound. Characters with the 隹 radical are often associated with birds. For example, 雀 (què) means *sparrow.* 雏 (chú) originally meant *young bird*. Now it also refers to baby animals. Birds usually like to live in groups. 雧, the traditional version of the character 集 (jí) describes this phenomenon. 集 consists of two radicals 隹 and 木 indicating a flock of birds resting in a tree. The extended meaning of 集 is *collective or gathering.*

故事 Story

孔雀东南飞 (Kǒng què dōng nán fēi)
孔雀 peacock 东 east 南 south 飞 fly

孔雀东南飞 is a well-known poem from the Han Dynasty. The poem is a tragedy about a tragic marriage.

The story took place in Anhui Province sometime between the years 196 and 219. Liu Lanzhi, the wife of a county official, was forced to divorce her husband. Out of devotion to her former husband, Liu resolved to never marry again. Her parents wanted her to get remarried however, because a divorced woman staying with her parents was socially unacceptable at that time. With no way to escape a second marriage, Liu committed suicide. When Liu's former husband learned of her death he was overwhelmed by sadness and also committed suicide in their former home. To honor this couple's deep love, a poet wrote this poem, the first two lines of which read: *The peacock is flying towards the southeast, but it looks back every five li* (孔雀东南飞，五里一徘徊).

72. 耳（ěr）部 Ear

古字形

“耳”是象形字，古文字像耳朵的形状。本义指耳朵，引申指形状与耳朵相似的东西，例如“木耳”，是一种可以食用的真菌，由于其形状与耳朵相似，故有此称。作为部首，“耳”通常位于汉字的左侧；有时位于汉字的下面，例如“聋”。耳部的字多与耳朵或听觉有关。“取”是会意字，从耳从又，“又”表示手，合起来表示以手取耳。古人作战时往往用割下的敌方耳朵来计算俘虏的数量，耳朵割得越多，功劳就越大。“聪”本义指听觉灵敏。因为听觉灵敏是明辨是非的重要条件，所以“聪”又引申指聪明。

Ancient form

耳 is a pictograph. The ancient script of 耳 looks like an ear. Therefore, the meaning of 耳 is *ear*. It also refers to things that have a shape similar to an ear, such as 木耳 (mù'ěr; *an edible tree fungus*). As a radical, 耳 often appears on the left side of a compound character, as in the character 取 (qǔ). 耳 can also appear at the bottom of a compound, such as in the character 聋 (lóng; *deaf*). Characters with 耳 often have meanings related to ear or auditory sense. 取 is an ideograph consisting of 耳 and 又 (*hand*). Together, these radicals mean that a hand is fetching an ear. Why? On the ancient battlefield, the victors would cut off the ears of their enemies who were slain in battle. They did this not only to keep the ears as trophies, but also because warriors were paid by the number of enemies they killed. Ears were used as proof in order to claim rewards.

The original meaning of 聪 (cōng) is *keen hearing*. Because keen hearing can improve learning, the extended meaning of 聪 is *smart*.

故事 Story

掩耳盗铃 (Yǎn ěr dào líng)
掩 cover 耳 ear 盗 steal 铃 bell

Once upon a time, a person wandering on the street came across an exquisite doorbell hanging on the door of a rich family's house. The bell was very responsive: sounding a beautiful and resonant chime at the slightest touch. He fell in love with the bell right away and decided to steal it. He knew that if he touched the bell it would ring, and then he would be caught. He thought and thought, and finally devised a plan. He decided to cover his ears when stealing the bell. Of course, though he himself did not hear, the bell rang as soon as he touched it, and he was caught by the owner of the bell.

掩耳盗铃 describes a stupid self-deceptive behavior and is similar to the English expression: The cat shuts its eyes when stealing cream.

73. 白（bái）部 White

古字形

“白”是象形字，古文字像日光照射之形。有人认为“白”字的本义指太阳之明，引申指天亮。在现代汉语中，“白”字的常用义是“白色”，例如“白雪”。从某种意义上讲，白色近似于无色，于是“白”引申指一无所有，即不花一点儿代价的意思。从另一角度看，白色给人的感觉为明亮、干净，由此“白”又引申指清楚、明白等意义。作为部首，“白”有时位于汉字的左侧；有时位于汉字的上面，例如“泉”。白部的字多与白色、光亮有关，例如“皑”指洁白，“皎”指月光明亮。

Ancient form

白 is a pictograph. The ancient form of 白 looks like a sun with a shining ray. Some Chinese scholars believe the original meaning of 白 is actually *bright* with an extended meaning of *daytime*. In modern Chinese, 白 means *white*. Because white means the absence of color; therefore, 白 also has the negative extended meaning *to not own a thing or to pay no price*. Conversely, white also suggests cleanliness and brightness. Hence, 白 also means *clear*. As a radical, 白 sometimes appears on the left side of compounds, such as in the characters 皑 (ái; *very white*) and 皎 (jiǎo; *bright white*). 白 can also appear on the top of a compound such as in 泉 [quán; (*pure*) *spring water*].

故事 Story

《白蛇传》(Bái shé zhuàn)
白 white 蛇 snake 传 biography

The Story of White Snake is a legendary Chinese story from the Song Dynasty. The story tells of a white snake spirit that transformed herself into an enchanted lady named Bai Suzhen. Bai came to the human world to give her appreciation and love to a scholar named Xu Xian, who had saved her life in a previous incarnation. Bai finally found her beloved Xu Xian and married him. All was well until one day, the couple visited Jinshan Temple. The Great Master Fahai in the temple could see that Bai Suzhen was not a human being but a snake, and promptly warned Mr. Xu. Xu did not believe it at first, so Fahai gave him a magical wine that Xu could use to test whether Bai was a snake or not. On the Day of the Dragon Boat Festival, Xu took advantage of the holiday to invite Bai to drink the special wine. This wine transformed Bai back into a snake. Xu was so horrified that he dropped dead on the spot. In order to save her husband's life Bai raced up to heaven and stole a magical medicine. Bai forced the magical herb down Xu's throat and he recovered. But the Great Master Fahai was intent on separating Xu from Bai because a human coupled with a snake was

an abomination. So he lured Xu to the Jinshan Temple and put him under house arrest. When Bai came to the Temple looking for her husband Fahai attacked her with his magic power. The two fought hard. To win the fight Bai disobeyed the law of heaven and used a magic to flood the Jinshan Temple. After giving birth to a son, she was buried under the Leifeng Pagoda in Hangzhou.

74. 骨（gǔ）部 Bone

古字形

“骨”本写作“冎”，古文字形像骨架，后加“月”成为形声字“骨”。“骨”的本义即指骨头。骨头支撑了整个身体，正如在事物中起基本作用或主要作用的成分，所以“骨”引申指事物主要部分等意义，“骨干”指的就是在业务上起主要作用的人；由此再引申，“骨”还可表示人的品格以及文学或书法作品的风格，例如“骨气”是说高傲自尊、刚强不屈的人格，“风骨”则是指诗文雄健有力的风格。作为部首，“骨”通常位于汉字的左侧。骨部的字多与骨头或人体有关。“骼”是形声字，从骨各声，本指禽类或兽类之骨，引申指人或动物的骨骼。“骸”也是形声字，从骨亥声，本指胫骨或小腿骨，后来，所指的范围扩大，由指人体的部分骨骼，转而表示人或动物的整个躯体。

Ancient form

The original shape of 骨 was 冎 which looks like the bone structure of human body or animal. However, later 月 was added to it and has made this character as a phonetic-semantic compound. 冎 is also used to indicate the pronunciation of the character. Its original meaning is *bone*. The skeleton is the foundation of the body. Therefore, the extended meaning of 骨 is *to play an integral role*. The word 骨干 (gǔgàn) means *backbone or mainstay*. Another meaning of 骨 is *style or personality*, such as in the words 骨气 (gǔqì; *moral integrity*) and 风骨 (fēnggǔ; *vigor of style in writing or painting*). As a radical, 骨 often appears on the left side of a compound. Characters with 骨 often have meanings related to human or animal bodies, such as 骼 (gé; *bone structure*) and 骸 (hái; *remains*).

故事 Story

《三打白骨精》(Sān dǎ bái gǔ jīng)
三 three 打 fight 白 white 骨 bone 精 demon

《三打白骨精》is a story from the famous Chinese novel *Journey to the West*, written in the Ming Dynasty. *Journey to the West* tells us a story about four monks who went to the Western Heaven to acquire Buddhist scriptures. On their way they encountered many hardships. The four monks on the pilgrimage were Tripitaka, who was a master monk, Piggy Zhu, Sandy Sha, and Sun Wukong—the Monkey king. Sun Wukong was the main character of the novel. He had fiery eyes and diamond pupils, which enabled him to discern disguised demons and see through all kinds of tricks. In the story of《三打白骨精》, 白骨精—the White Bone Demon, wanted to capture Tripitaka and eat his flesh because this could make it immortal. The White Bone Demon attempted to trap Tripitaka by first disguising itself as a beautiful girl, later as an old lady, and finally as an old man. Unsuspecting Tripitaka almost fell into each of the snares set by

it. Fortunately, Monkey Sun was able to see through these snares and came to protect Tripitaka and fight with 白骨精. In the end, 白骨精 was defeated, and the four continued on their journey.

75. 立（lì）部 To stand

古字形

“立”是会意字，古文字像一人立于地上之形，上面的“大”表示人，下面的“一”表示人所立之处。“立”的本义指站立。此外，“立”还可用作副词，表示时间短暂，例如“立即”。作为部首，“立”有时位于汉字的左侧，有时位于汉字的右侧或下面，例如“位”“竖”。立部的字多与站立或位置等意义有关。“站”本义指直立，例如“站立”；直立之后，两腿并拢，因此无法行动，所以又引申指停止，例如“车站”之“站”。“端”本指站得直；身体直立就不会歪斜，所以又引申指端正，例如“端坐”。

Ancient form

立 is an ideograph. In the ancient script 立 looks like a person standing on the ground. The original meaning of 立 is *to stand up*. As an adverb, 立 also means *a very short time*. For example, 立即 (lìjí) means *right away*. As a radical, 立 is often associated with *standing or position*. It usually appears on the left side of compounds, such as in 站 (zhàn; *to stand or station*). Sometimes it appears on the right or at the bottom of a compound, such as in 位 (wèi; *location*), and 竖 (shù; *upright*). The character 端 (duān) means *standing upright*. Its extended meaning is *level or to hold something level*.

故事 Story

程门立雪 (Chéng mén lì xuě)

程门 the door of Cheng's house 立 stand 雪 snow

During the Northern Song Dynasty, there lived a man named Yang Shi. Although Yang passed the highest civil service examination, he was very modest and always willing to learn new things from other scholars and also his mentor,

the famous scholar Cheng Yi. One day Yang and his friend went to Cheng's home seeking advice. At the door, they were told that Cheng was taking a nap. Yang decided not to disturb his mentor. So he and his friend waited outside the door. Very soon it began to snow. The snow became heavier and heavier. When Cheng finally got up from his nap, he discovered two snowmen standing outside of his house. Cheng was very touched. He was honored Yang and his friend valued his opinion so highly, and he admired Yang and his friend's persistence and sincerity in the pursuit of knowledge.

Later, people use 程门立雪 to praise those who show great respect for their mentors and determinedly seek knowledge.

76. 见［見］（jiàn）部 To see

古字形

“见”是会意字，古文字上面是“目”，下面是“人”，在人的头上加只眼睛，是为了突出人的视觉器官。“见”的本义是看见、看到。作为部首，“见”通常位于汉字的右侧，有时位于汉字的下面。见部的字多与观看或观看的方式等意义有关，例如“观”是仔细地看，“览”是粗略地看。

Ancient form

见 is an ideograph. The ancient character consists of a giant eye atop a person's body. 见 means *to see*. As a radical, it often appears on the right side or at the bottom of a compound. Characters with the 见 radical have meanings associated with vision, viewing, or observation. For example, 观 (guān) means *to view carefully*, and 览 (lǎn) means *to view cursorily*.

故事 Story

见异思迁 (Jiàn yì sī qiān)

见 see 异 difference 思 think 迁 change

During the Spring and Autumn Period, the King of the Qi State asked his Prime Minister Guan Zhong: "How can we make people live and work in peace and contentment?" Guan answered: "First, we should classify people into four categories according to their occupations: scholars, farmers, workers, and merchants. Second, we should have people with same occupation live together, so that they can learn from each other and love their work. They will not often be exposed to new things and so they will not change their jobs too frequently. In this way, everyone can enjoy a good and prosperous life."

见异思迁 means a person's desire to change his or her work the moment he or she see something different. Now it is also used to describe people who are inconstant and always seek out change when they see something that seems better. This phrase belittles people who lack single-hearted devotion to their professions.

77. 厶（sī）部 Privacy

古字形

“厶”指个人的、自己的事情，即后来的“私”字。“厶”在现代汉语中只用作部首，不单独成字。作为部首，“厶”通常位于汉字的上面或下面。值得注意的是，许多字典或词典里所收的厶部字，已经很少有保留与“厶”的本义有关的汉字了。日常生活中我们常用的“私”字，许多字典将其归入禾部，而将“公”字归到八部。但这两个字，都与“厶”的本义有着密切的关系。“公”与“私”的意义相反，本指正直无私、大公无私，引申指公开等意义，所以“私”就有了不公开、秘密而又不合法等意义。

Ancient form

厶 refers to personal matters, same with the character 私 now, which means *privacy, or selfishness*. In modern Chinese, 厶 is no longer an independent character. It is used only as a radical in compounds. In many modern Chinese dictionaries, we see only a few characters listed under the 厶 radical. Many characters that contain 厶 are listed under other radicals. 私 (sī; *privacy or selfish*) is listed under the 禾 radical; 公 (gōng; *public or selfless*) is listed under the 八 radical. Though listed under other radicals it is clear just by looking at their meanings that these characters are all meaningfully associated with 厶.

故事 Story

公而忘私 (Gōng ér wàng sī)
公 public 而 as to 忘 forget 私 selfish

During the Spring and Autumn Period, there was a government official named Qi Huangyang. Once, the Emperor of the Jin State asked Qi to nominate a capable person to be the county magistrate. Unexpectedly, Qi nominated a person who had offended him before. Later, the Emperor asked him to nominate another person to be the commander-in-chief. Qi nominated his own son regardless of other people's disapproval. Qi always recommended people whom Qi considered would best serve the country rather than those who would advance his own interests. Confucius praised Qi as a 公而忘私 person. 公而忘私 means to put the interests of the public before personal advancement.

78. 毛（máo）部 Hair

古字形

"毛"是象形字，古文字像毛之形状。"毛"的本义指禽兽之类的毛，例如"兽毛""羽毛"，引申指形状似毛发的谷物或草木以及人的须发。尽管"毛"字有诸多引申意义，但其主导意义，仍是表示禽兽之毛。作为部首，"毛"有时位于汉字左下侧或右侧，偶尔位于汉字的下面。毛部的字多与皮毛等意义有关，例如"毯"指厚实有毛绒的成片织品，"毫"指细长而尖的毛。

Ancient form

毛 is a pictograph. The ancient form of 毛 depicts a tiny piece of down. The original meaning of 毛 is *animal fur or birds' feathers*. Later, 毛 also came to mean *human body hair and wispy hair-like grasses or plants*. As a radical, it appears on the lower-left, right, or bottom of compounds. Characters with the 毛 radical have meanings associated with any kind of hair. For example, 毯 (tǎn) means *blanket* and 毫 (háo) means *long, fine hair*.

故事 Story

九牛一毛 (Jiǔ niú yì máo)
九 nine 牛 ox 一 one 毛 hair

In the Han Dynasty, the great scholar and historian Sima Qian was persecuted by the government. Sima Qian offended the government by supporting General Li Ling who, when faced with an utterly hopeless situation on the battlefield, had surrendered to the Huns. To punish Sima Qian, the government had him castrated. Initially, Sima Qian was extremely humiliated and wanted to commit suicide. But later he became convinced that his humiliation and death were of little importance. His death would be like pulling a single hair from nine oxen 九牛亡一毛. He realized his death would not help to change the Emperor's mind and people's prejudice. So he decided to live and endure the humiliation in order to continue his important mission: to finish his great book, *Historical Records* (《史记》). Later, people derived 九牛一毛 from Sima Qian's poetic turn of phrase to describe a very small minority.

79. 卜[⺊](bǔ)部 Divination

古字形

“卜”是象形字，古文字像龟甲被烧灼后出现的裂纹形状。古人将甲骨进行处理后，放在火上灼烧，根据其裂纹形状判断吉凶。占卜完毕后，占卜之人还会将其姓名、占卜所问之事、占卜日期、占卜结果等内容刻在龟骨上，即我们通常所说的“卜辞”。“卜辞”因为是刻写在龟甲兽骨上的，所以这些文字被称为“甲骨文”。“甲骨文”是我们今天所看到的记录中国古代历史文献最早的文字形式。卜部的字多与占卜吉凶等意义有关。“卦”是古代占卜用的象征自然现象和人事变化的一套符号。“八卦”就是《周易》中的八种基本图形，象征天、地、雷、风、水、火、山、泽八种自然现象，这些图相互拼合得六十四卦，用来象征各种事物。

Ancient form

卜 is a pictograph. The ancient script of it depicts the cracks in an oracle bone. Ancient Chinese people used turtle shells for divination. They heated the turtle shell over a fire until it cracked, then they interpreted their fortunes according to the cracks. When the divination was complete, the bone-reader carved four things into the shell or bone: the names of those who had requested the divination, the content of the divination, the time and the result of the divination. These records are referred to as *oracle bone inscriptions* which are the earliest extant pieces of Chinese script, and are believed to be characters' origin. Characters that contain the 卜 radical often relate to fortune-telling. The character 卦 (guà) stands for a set of symbols representing changes within nature

and human society. These symbols were a tool in soothsaying. 八卦 is from the *Book of Changes* (commonly known as the *I Ching* or *Yì Jīng*. It consists of eight types of hexagrams which stand for the eight kinds of natural phenomena: heaven, earth, thunder, wind, water, fire, mountain, and marsh. These natural forces can combine in 64 different ways to create all things and events in the world. Each of these 64 combinations is represented in the 八卦.

故事 Story

中国古代占卜术 (Zhōng guó gǔ dài zhān bǔ shù)
中国 Chinese 古代 ancient 占卜术 divination

Divination (specifically: to divine by means of the Eight Diagrams as described in the *Book of Changes*) in Chinese history is a method of fortune-telling. Divination played an important role in people's lives during the pre-science era. While based in superstition, it gave rise to many of the rational mainstays of Chinese society, such as the early Chinese writing system, philosophies, mathematics, astronomy, geology, and archeology.

80. 齿 [齒] (chǐ) 部 Tooth

古字形

“齿”在甲骨文中是象形字，像口中有齿形，后添加“止”字为声符，成为形声字。“齿”本指人口中的上下两排牙齿。作为部首，“齿”通常位于汉字的左侧。齿部的字多与牙齿或年龄等意义有关。“龈”指围绕牙颈及覆盖上下颌牙槽的组织，泛指牙槽及其四周的软组织；“龄”字中之所以有“齿”，是因为从牙齿可以看出年龄的长幼。

Ancient form

齿 is a pictograph. The ancient script of 齿 looks like two teeth in a mouth. Later, 止 was added to the top of the pictograph to indicate the pronunciation. This created the modern character 齿 which is a phonetic-semantic compound. As a radical, 齿 often appears on the left side of a compound. Characters with 齿 often have meanings associated with teeth. For example, 龈 (yín) means *gum*. The 齿 radical also signifies age or aging. 龄 (líng) means *age*, because we can tell a person's age based on the condition of their teeth.

故事 Story

唇亡齿寒 (Chún wáng chǐ hán)

唇 lips 亡 gone 齿 teeth 寒 cold

During the Warring States Period, the King of the Jin State wanted to expand his territory. He decided to invade the Guo State. In order to reach the Guo State, Jin's army had to go through the Yu State. So the King of Jin sent his ambassador to Yu to get the King's permission to march an army through his lands. The ambassador presented two gifts—a priceless jade and a precious horse—to the King of Yu. Yu was very pleased with these gifts and wanted to let the Jin army through. However, a senior official advised the King of Yu that it was not a good idea to allow the Jin army to go through Yu's territory to attack Guo. He reminded the King that Guo and Yu had always had good relations, and had become interdependent. If the Guo State was conquered by Jin, then the State of Yu would be sandwiched between the Jin's two territories and the Jin would inevitably attack Yu. He likened the relationship of Guo and Yu to teeth and lips: When the lips were gone, the teeth would be exposed to the coldness.

The King of Yu, however, did not take this good advice. He let the Jin army go through his state to attack the State of Guo. After the Jin conquered Guo, they turned around and conquered Yu.

唇亡齿寒 describes an interdependent relationship between two things. It is a reminder that when your ally falls, you are in danger.

第十课　方、黑、殳、儿、彡、气、勹、爪、瓦、走

81. 方（fāng）部 Square

古字形

“方”是象形字，有人认为像两只船并立之形，本义指并立、并排。在现代汉语中“方”的本义已不再使用，而以其引申义通行。“方”用作名词，表示方形的东西，引申指空间位置或方位。作为部首，“方”位于汉字的左侧。由于现代的字典或词典都把表示旗帜的意义全部归入“方”部，所以方部的字还与旗帜等意义有关。中国清代满族实行军政合一的“八旗制度”，所以“旗”又特指满族，例如“旗人”即满族人。“旗袍”是一种富有中国民族风情特色的女性服装，由满族妇女的长袍演变而来。“旅”是军队的编制单位，“方”在“旅”字中表示旗帜，因为每个军队都有军旗；又因为军队经常行军打仗，所以“旅”的引申义是旅行。

Ancient form 㫃

方 is a pictograph. Some scholars think the ancient form of 方 looks like two parallel boats together. This meaning is no longer in use in modern Chinese, however. 方 now means *square*. Its extended meaning is *physical* space or position. In modern Chinese, the radical for *flag* or *banner* has been replaced by 方. Therefore, characters that contain 方 are usually related to either space or flags. 旗 (qí) means *flag*. In the Qing Dynasty, the Manchu Nationality adopted a military administrative system called 八旗 (bāqí; *Eight Banners*). Thus, another name for the Manchu Nationality was 旗人 (qírén; *flag people*). The 旗袍 (qípáo; *cheongsam*) is a dress that developed from the gown worn by Manchu women. 旅 (lǚ; *brigade*) is a military unit. Because each military unit has its own banner, so 方 is the radical for 旅. Because the army often travels to fight with enemies, thus, 旅 also means *to travel*.

故事 Story

右手画圆，左手画方
(Yòu shǒu huà yuán, zuǒ shǒu huà fāng)
右 right 手 hand 画 draw 圆 circle,
左 left 手 hand 画 draw 方 square

Once upon a time, a person thought that he was very smart. He bragged that he could simultaneously draw a circle with his right hand and a square with his

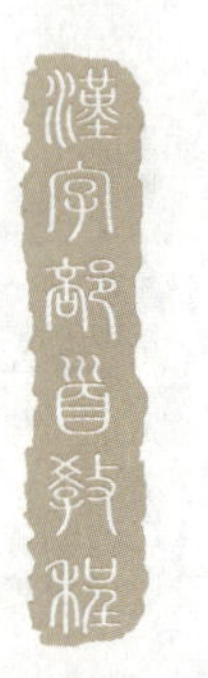

left. But when he tried he produced a deformed circle and a rounded square.

This story says that ordinary people can't do too many things at the same time without sacrificing quality. Those who can are geniuses. Therefore, 右手画圆，左手画方 is now used to describe one who tries to focus on too many things simultaneously and consequently produces poor results. But it can also be used to describe a person who possesses extraordinary abilities and can successfully handle many tasks simultaneously.

82. 黑（hēi）部 Black

古字形

“黑”是会意字，古文字下面像燃烧的火形，上面像窗子的形状，合起来表示烟火熏黑之意。“黑”的本义为黑色，引申为暗、光线不足等意义。暗处不易被看到，所以“黑”也指秘密的、不公开的或非法的。作为部首，“黑”通常位于汉字的左侧，有时位于汉字的上面或下面。黑部的字多与黑色等意义有关。“墨”本指书画所用的黑色颜料。“黛”指青黑色。

Ancient form

黑 is an ideograph. The bottom part of the ancient character looks like a wood-burning fire. The top part looks like a window with some black spots due to heavy smoke. Together, they mean *black*. The extended meaning of 黑 is *dark*. Because things are not easily observed under the cover of darkness, thus, 黑 also means *secretive or illegal*. As a radical, 黑 can appear on the left, top, bottom of a character. Characters with the 黑 radical have meanings related to black color. For example, 墨 (mò) means *ink* for writing calligraphy; 黛 (dài) is a greenish-black color.

故事 Story

近朱者赤，近墨者黑 (Jìn zhū zhě chì, jìn mò zhě hēi)

近 close to 朱 vermilion 者 person 赤 red,
近 close to 墨 ink 者 person 黑 black

Ouyang Xiu was a great scholar during the Northern Song Period. He was renowned as a noble-minded person and a great writer. One day, Ouyang Xiu's friend Fan Zhongyan came to visit him. Fan chatted with Ouyang's subordinate—a man named Lü. During their conversation, Fan told Lü about a Chinese saying: "Things that are close to vermilion are reddened and things that are close to ink are blackened." He thought Lü was such a lucky man to be able to work closely with a great scholar like Ouyang Xiu, because Lü would be reddened—his character would be bettered and he would learn a lot from Ouyang Xiu.

近朱者赤，近墨者黑 is similar to the English saying: He who keeps company with the wolf will learn to howl.

83. 殳（shū）部 Ancient weapon

古字形

“殳”的古文字形是会意字，像手持长柄器具之形。“殳”本指一种兵器，引申指以手持器械击打某物。作为部首，“殳”通常位于汉字的右侧。殳部的字大多与以手持械击打等意义有关。“段”字本义为用锤击打，后加金字旁，即“锻”。“毁”字的造字理据是以手持械破坏器物，由器物被损坏产生出引申义——毁坏。

Ancient form

The ancient form of 殳 is an ideograph. 殳 looks like a hand holding a weapon with a long shaft. The original meaning of 殳 is *a type of ancient weapon*. Its extended meaning is *holding an apparatus with which to strike*. As a radical, 殳 often appears on the right side of a compound character. Characters with the 殳 radical often have meanings related to hitting or striking. The original meaning of 段 was *to hit with a hammer*, later the radical 金 (钅) was added to form the character 锻 meaning (*an object is*) *beaten out or shaped by hammering*. The original meaning of 毁 (huǐ) is *to use apparatus to break pottery*. Its extended meaning is *to destroy*.

故事 Story

古代车战兵器——殳 (Gǔ dài chē zhàn bīng qì—shū)

古代 ancient 车 carriage 战 combat 兵器 weapon—殳 shu

The use of the weapon 殳 in chariot combat started in the Pre-Qin Dynasty Period. According to historical records, 殳 was created in the Shang Dynasty. However, its shape had been lost to history for more than two thousand years. It was not until the 1978 archaeological discovery in Sui County that the 殳 was revealed to the modern world. The shaft of a 殳 was about three-meter tall, made out of bamboo or wood. A bronze or iron pointed head was mounted at the top of the shaft. The 殳 was a very popular and effective weapon during the Warring States Period. That period saw near constant warfare as seven states contended for supremacy. After the Han Dynasty, chariot combat gradually lost its popularity. As such, use of the 殳 was also diminished.

84. 儿（rén; ér）部 Child

古字形

“儿”的古文字是象形字，即“人”字的另一种写法。作为部首，用在汉字的下面，读作rén。现代汉语中的“儿”读作ér，是“兒”的简化字。中国古代，“儿”专指男孩儿，例如“儿子”。作为部首，“儿”多位于汉字的下面，例如“兄”“允”。儿部的字多与男性等意义有关系。“兄”从传世文献的用法来看，指亲戚中同辈男性中年龄大的。后来，旁系亲属中同辈而长于自己的男性也可称为“兄”，如“堂兄”。

Ancient form

The ancient form of 儿 is a pictograph. It is another form of 人. As a radical, it is often placed at the bottom of a compound character and pronounced as rén. In modern Chinese, however, 儿 is pronounced as ér which is the simplified form of the character 兒 (ér; *children*). As a radical, 儿 usually appears at the bottom of compounds, such as in 兄 (xiōng) and 允 (yǔn). 兄 refers to elder males, especially elder brothers, such as 堂兄 (tángxiōng; *cousin*). 允 means *to trust* (*your elders*). Its extended meaning is *to allow or to permit*.

故事 Story

难兄难弟 (Nán xiōng nán dì)
难 difficult to be 兄 elder brother
难 difficult to be 弟 younger brother

This story took place during the Han Dynasty. A County Magistrate had two gifted sons—Chen Ji and Chen Chen. They both got married and had a child. One day, the two children began arguing over whose father was a better one. Unable to resolve the issue, they went to see their grandfather, the County Magistrate, and asked him to give a judgment. The grandfather smiled and said, "Chen Ji is the best elder brother and Chen Chen is the best younger brother. I cannot tell who is a better one. They both were excellent."

We use this idiom to describe two of a kind who are different but of equal worth. However, this idiom is seldom used in the modern Chinese. According to the *Modern Chinese Dictionary* (Commercial Press, 2005), most of time this idiom is used to describe two of a kind who are in equal bad situation. In this case 难兄难弟 is pronounced as nàn xiōng nàn dì.

85. 彡（shān）部 To embellish

古字形

“彡”是象形字，古文字像图画文饰之形。“彡”在现代汉语中只用作部首，不单独成字。作为部首，“彡”通常位于汉字的左侧或右侧，如“须”“彩”；有时位于汉字的下侧，例如“彦”。彡部的字多与色彩或修饰等意义有关系。“彩”是形声字，从彡采声，本指文章富有文采，引申指彩色，“五彩缤纷”是指色彩丰富多样，非常美丽。现代汉字“须”是会意字，从页（头）从彡，彡表示胡须。

Ancient form

彡 is a pictograph. The ancient script depicts decorative patterns. In modern Chinese, 彡 is no longer used as an independent character. As a radical, it often appears on the left or right side of a compound such as in 须 (xū; *moustache*) and 彩 (cǎi; *colorful*). Sometimes, 彡 appears at the bottom of a compound character, such as in 彦 (yàn; *a man of virtue and ability*). Characters with the 彡 radical have meanings related to color or embellishment. 彩 is a phonetic-semantic compound. 采 represents the pronunciation (cǎi) and 彡 hints at the meaning—*colorful* (*embellishment*). 五彩缤纷 describes rich and varied colors to make things visually very beautiful. The modern Chinese character 须 is an ideograph consisting of two radicals. 页means *head* and 彡 means *embellished.*

故事 Story

巾帼不让须眉 (Jīn guó bú ràng xū méi)
巾帼 ancient woman's head dress (women)
不 not 让 yield to 须眉 moustache (men)

Toward the end of the Northern Wei Dynasty, barbarians neighboring the Han Nationality became stronger. They often invaded the Central Plains of the Han Nationality. The court had to conscript an army.

A young woman named Hua Mulan had liked horseback riding and archery since she was a child. One day Mulan's aged and weak father was drafted into the defense militia. Worried her father couldn't handle military service, Mulan came up with a plan. She disguised herself as a young man and went to war in her father's place. She remained in the army for twelve years and won many military honors. Her fellow soldiers never knew that she was a woman. They greatly respected Mulan's courage. After the war, the Emperor summoned all the officers and soldiers who made great contributions in defeating the invaders and granted each of them a promotion. But Mulan told the Emperor that she did not want to be promoted. All she wanted was a good horse to carry her home immediately. The Emperor granted her request. When she reached her home, she took off her armor and put on her lady's dress. The fellow soldiers who had accompanied her home were shocked. They praised Mulan, saying "巾帼不让须眉—Women could do men's work just as well as men."

86. 气（qì）部 Air; Gas

古字形 气

“气”是象形字，古文字像云气蒸腾上升的样子，本义为云气。后来则用以指没有一定的形状或体积，能自由流动的物体。在中国古代的医学中，人们把能使人体器官发挥功能的动力称为“气”，例如“气功”之“气”。“气功”是中国特有的一种健身术，通过调心（调控心理活动）、调息（调控呼吸运动）、调身（调控身体的姿势和动作）等步骤，达到防病治病、健身延年、开发潜能的目的。作为部首，“气”通常位于汉字的右上侧，例如“氛”。气部的字多与云气或气体有关，大多为表示自然界中空气组成成分的后起字，例如“氢”“氧”等。

Ancient form 气

气 is a pictograph. The ancient form of 气 looks like rising air. 气 originally referred to clouds. Later, it became used to refer to any kind of air or gas. According to traditional Chinese medicine, there is a kind of air inside the body whose movement keeps one alive and maintains the body's vitality. The Chinese developed a set of exercises that help maintain the healthy flow of this air. These exercises are known as 气功 (qìgōng). The practice of 气功 involves three things: regulating thoughts and emotions, modulating the breathing, and coordinating breathing with physical movement. As a radical, 气 often appears on the upper right of a compound. Characters with the 气 radical often have meanings related to air, gas, or atmosphere—such as 氛 (fēn; *atmosphere*), 氢 (qīng; *hydrogen*), and 氧 (yǎng; *oxygen*).

故事 Story

紫气东来 (Zǐ qì dōng lái)

紫 purple 气 air 东 east 来 come

During the Eastern Zhou Dynasty, a man named Yin Xi worked as the Head of the Hangu Pass. One morning, as he left home, he saw the rosy rays of the rising sun in the east. As he admired the dawn, he noticed a huge purple cloud drifting towards the west. As the purple cloud drifted it became thicker and thicker. It made the mountain in the distance especially magnificent. He suddenly realized the cloud was a good omen that there would be a wise man coming to the Hangu Pass. Sure enough, shortly after he saw this omen, the great scholar—Laozi arrived. Yin Xi invited Laozi to stay in the Hangu Pass. Laozi agreed. During his stay, Laozi wrote his great work—*The Taoteching* (*The Classic of Virtue*), a splendid piece of literature whose influence on Chinese philosophy and culture is immeasurable and continues to today.

部首 Radical

87. 勹（bāo）部 To wrap up; To packet

古字形

“勹”是象形字，古文字像人身体弯曲之形，本义为包裹。“勹”只用作部首，不单独成字。作为部首“勹”通常位于汉字的右上侧，例如“包”“勾”。勹部的字多与包裹、弯曲等意义有关。“包”的本义就是包裹，又引申指容纳在内，例如“包括”“包含”。

Ancient form

勹 is a pictograph. The ancient form of 勹 looks like a person who is in a bending down position to hold something. The original meaning of 勹 is *to wrap up*. 勹 can not be an independent character. It is only used as a radical for compound characters，such as in 包 (bāo; *to wrap up*; *package*) and 勾 (gōu; *to hook up*; *hook*). The character with the 勹 radical usually relates to meanings *to wrap up*, *to crook or bend*. As we mentioned the character 包 means *package*. Its extended meaning relates to *inclusive* which is reflected in the words such as 包括 (*to include*) and 包含 (*to embody*).

故事 Story

包罗万象 (Bāo luó wàn xiàng)

包 wrap 罗 include 万 ten thousand 象 phenomenon

Pu Songling was one of the great authors of the Qing Dynasty. He wrote a collection of short stories named *Strange Stories from a Chinese Studio*. It had 12 volumes with 491 stories. Each story features some type of ghosts or spirits. The author used these fantastical figures to explore real social problems. The book has been wildly popular in China since its publication—both for its haunting stories and what it reveals about social life in the Qing Dynasty. Because the book created such a large number of rich and distinct characters, people used 包罗万象 to praise its comprehensiveness. 包罗万象 is now used to describe anything of an encyclopedic nature.

88. 爪［爫］（zhǎo）部 Claw

古字形

“爪”是象形字，古文字像鸟爪之形，本义为鸟类的爪子，引申指手。作为部首，“爪”有时位于汉字的上面，写作“爫”，俗称“爪字头”，例如“采”；有时位于汉字的左侧，例如“印”“爬”。爪部的字多与用手抓取等义有关。“采”字由“爪”和“木”组成，表示用手从树上摘取，引申指细心挑选、选取、搜集，例如“采访”“采购”。“印”字的左边是“爪”的变形，右边是“卩”（跪着的人形“”），合起来表示用手按着一个跪着的人，取“按压”之义。印章加盖到纸上需要按压，会留下“印记”，手的印记为“手印”。

Ancient form

爪 is a pictograph. In the ancient script it looks like a claw. Its orignal meanings are *claws of birds*. Its extended meaning are *hands*. As a radical, 爪 sometimes appears on the top of a compound, where it is written as 爫 and called zhǎo zì tóu (claw on the top), such as in the character 采 [cǎi; *to pick* (*by using fingers*)]. Sometimes it appears on the left side of a compound character, such as in the characters 印 (yìn) and 爬 (pá). Here the left part of 印 is the alternative version of 爪 and the right part is 卩 (*a kneeling person*). Together, they suggest using the fingers to press down a seal, or to stamp. 爬 means *to crawl*, to *creep or to climb*.

故事 Story

一鳞半爪 (Yì lín bàn zhǎo)

一 single 鳞 fish scale 半 half 爪 bird claw

This idiom describes a situation in which one sees only a small fraction of a whole, like seeing a single scale of a whole fish or half of a talon on a whole bird. It cautions that if we make a decision or judgment based on a partial understanding, we are likely to make mistakes.

89. 瓦（wǎ）部 Tile

古字形

“瓦”是象形字，古文字像屋瓦相接之形。“瓦”是烧制而成的土器的总称。作为部首，“瓦”通常位于汉字的右侧，例如“瓶”；有时位于汉字的下面，例如“瓷”。“瓷”是形声字，从瓦次声，现在多用以指瓷器。中国是瓷器的故乡，瓷器的发明是中华民族对世界文明的巨大贡献。被称为“瓷都”的江西景德镇，早在元代就已出产青花瓷，举世闻名。

Ancient form

瓦 is a pictograph. The ancient symbol for 瓦 looks like a roof tile. 瓦 refers to all kinds of things made from firing in a kiln. As a radical, 瓦 is often placed on the right or bottom of a compound character, such as in the characters 瓶 (píng; *bottle*) and 瓷 (cí; *porcelain*). China has a long history of producing porcelain. Jingde Zhen, a city located in Jiangxi Province, began producing a blue and white porcelain as early as the Yuan Dynasty. This porcelain became famous all over the world.

故事 Story

宁为玉碎，不为瓦全 (Nìng wéi yù suì, bù wéi wǎ quán)
宁 would rather 为 be 玉 jade 碎 broken,
不 not 为 be 瓦 tile 全 unbroken

In the year 550, Gao Yang, the General of the Eastern Wei in the Northern Dynasties, forced Emperor Xiaojing to resign and made himself the Emperor. The next year, fearful of losing his rule, he killed Xiaojing and his three sons. But eliminating these heirs was not enough to allay his fears, as he was afraid other members of the former Emperor's family would seek revenge. Soon, he slaughtered 44 entire families who were related to Xiaojing and shared the same surname. In a total, he killed more than 700 innocent people. When news of these massacres had spread, everyone who shared Xiaojing's surname was scared. Several decided to change their surname. One man however, was very brave. He decided he would not yield to Gao Yang. He said: "I would rather be a shattered jade than an unbroken piece of tile. I will never change my surname."

Today, 宁为玉碎，不为瓦全 means "It is better to die in glory than live with dishonor." A similar English expression is: Better to die on one's feet than live on one's knees.

90. 走（zǒu）部 To run; To walk

古字形

“走”是会意字，古文字上面为“夭”，像人摆开两臂跑步之形；下面为“止”，突出其为脚的动作。“走”本义指跑，例如“飞禽走兽”说的就是天上飞翔的鸟和地上奔跑的野兽。后来，本义不再单独使用，“走”专门用来表示行走之义。作为部首，“走”多位于汉字的左下侧。走部的字多与奔跑或行走的动作有关。“赶”是形声字，从走干声，表示追赶、驱赶之义，例如“赶鸭子上架”，人们用来比喻强人所难，迫使他人去做不能做的事。“越”本义为经过、超过。

Ancient form

走 is an ideograph. The top part of the ancient form looks like a walking person, while the bottom part is a foot to emphasize the action of walking. The original meaning of 走 is *to run*. In modern Chinese, 走 only means *to walk*. As a radical, it often appears on the lower-left side of a compound. Characters with the 走 radical often have meanings related to foot movement, such as 赶 (gǎn; *to catch up with*) and 越 (yuè; *to jump over*).

故事 Story

走马观花 (Zǒu mǎ guān huā)
走 run 马 horse 观 watch 花 flowers

走马观花—seeing flowers while riding on horseback—came from a poem written by a famous Tang poet, Meng Jiao. When Meng Jiao was young, he studied very hard but repeatedly failed the Civil Service Exam, which was the prerequisite to attaining a government post. However, at the age of 46, Meng Jiao finally passed the exam and became a successful candidate for government office. He wrote the two lines: *Flushed with success, the horse runs fast, seeing all the flowers of Chang'an city in just one day* (春风得意马蹄疾，一日看尽长安花). These lines expressed his unbridled elation at his accomplishment.

Now, the expression 走马观花 has come to describe that people gain only a superficial understanding of a situation only through a cursory observation or visit.

第十一课 匚、户、工、止、寸、夂、矢、斤、舌、身

91. 匚（fāng）部 Box; Container

古字形 匚

“匚”是象形字，古文字像受物之器，“匚”本指一种盛放物品的方形器具。“匚”在现代汉语中只用作部首，不单独成字。匚部的字多和箱子或类似箱子的器物有关，例如“匡”“匣”。“匡”是形声字，从匚王声，本是盛东西的器具，即“筐”，引申指纠正、匡正等意义。“匣”也是形声字，从匚甲声，是一种小型的、盖子可以开合的储物器。

Ancient form 匚

匚 is a pictograph. The ancient symbol for 匚 looks like a rectangular box with one side open. In modern Chinese, 匚 is no longer an independent character but appears only as a radical. Characters containing 匚 have meanings related to boxes or containers, such as 匡 and 匣. 匡 is a phonetic-semantic compound consisting of two radicals: 匚 indicating the meaning (*a container*), and 王 suggesting the sound (kuāng). The extended meaning of 匡 is *to correct*. 匣 is also a phonetic-semantic compound combining 匚 and 甲. It is pronounced as xiá and it means *small box*.

故事 Story

神医华佗 (Shén yī Huà Tuó)
神 magic 医 doctor 华佗 Hua Tuo

In the Eastern Han Dynasty, Hua Tuo was an accomplished doctor. His medical knowledge covered many fields, including contagious diseases, respiratory diseases, gynecology, dermatology, and pediatrics. In addition to herbal medicines, he was also adept at acupuncture. Because he could cure so many diseases many people of the time revered him as a magician. When he learned of Hua Tuo's great reputation, Cao Cao, forced Hua Tuo to be his personal doctor. Cao Cao suffered from chronic headaches. He hoped that Hua Tuo could help him. One day, at midnight, Cao Cao suffered a serious headache, so he called for Hua Tuo. Hua Tuo was now familiar with Cao Cao's medical situation. He believed Cao Cao had a brain tumor. He suggested that Cao Cao first drink some herbal soup that would dull the pain, then undergo surgery to get rid of the tumor. Cao Cao flew into a rage. He shouted at Hua Tuo: "How dare you try to kill me!" Then he had Hua Tuo imprisoned at once. Before long Hua Tuo died in prison. Before his death, he recorded all of his vast medical knowledge in a manuscript, and presented it to the prison guard. But the guard was terrified that Cao Cao would find out, so he burned the manuscript. Therefore, Hua Tuo's medical knowledge was lost to future generations.

92. 户（hù）部 Single-leaf door

古字形 ⾣

“户”是象形字，古文字像单扇门形。“户”本义是单扇门，后泛指门户、门第。户部的字多与门户有关。“房”指住人的建筑物。“扇”是个会意字，从户从羽，表示开门像鸟扇动翅膀。“扇”的本义指门扇，引申指扇子。

Ancient form ⾣

户 is a pictograph. In the ancient script it looks like a single-leaf door. This was the original meaning of 户. Its extended meaning is *household or family status*. Characters with the 户 radical have meanings related to housing or households. 房 (fáng) means *house*. 扇 is an ideograph. It consists of 户 (*house*) and 羽 which is the feather (of a bird). 扇 indicates that opening a door (of a house) is like a bird stretches its wings. Thus, the original meaning of 扇 is *a leaf of door*. Its extended meaning is *a fan*.

故事 Story

门当户对 (Mén dāng hù duì)
门当 door sleepers (underneath of the door)
户对 door pillars (on the top of doorframe)

In traditional Chinese architecture, door sleepers and door pillars were used as decorations for a traditional Chinese two-leaf door. In traditional China, rich families were very particular about the ornamentation on their doors, because they reflected the family's wealth and glory. Different designs and materials signified different economic condition, social status, and occupations. In fact, before betrothing their children, family members would send a servant to observe the quality of the prospective bride or groom's door decorations to determine whether the prospective family was rich or poor. Because of this, 门当户对 later came to be used to refer to an affianced couple who are well-matched in terms of social and economic condition.

93. 工（gōng）部 Ruler

古字形 工

“工”是象形字，古文字像曲尺之形。“工”本指工匠用的曲尺，引申作动词，指擅长、精于等意思。“工”用作形容词，有精巧、精致的意思，例如“工巧”。作为部首，“工”通常位于汉字的左侧，有时位于汉字的下面。工部的字多与擅长或不擅长等意义有关。“左”的本义是辅佐，帮助，即“佐”，引申义是左边。“巧”是形声字，从工丂声，常用来指某人技艺高明或某物工艺精巧。“差”是指做得不好。

Ancient form 工

工 is a pictograph. The ancient script depicts an ancient three-slatted carpenter's square. Thus, 工 means *an instrument used for measurement.* When 工 is used as a verb, it means *to be good at doing* (*something*). As a radical, it can appear on the left, or bottom of a compound. Characters with 工 often have meanings related to aptitude and specialization. The original meaning of 左 (zuǒ) is *to assist or to help*. 巧 (qiǎo) is a phonetic-semantic compound, which means *skillful*. The original meaning of 差 (chà) is *differing from or lacking in quality*.

故事 Story

良工巧匠 (Liáng gōng qiǎo jiàng)

良 good 工 worker 巧 skillful 匠 craftsman

Lu Ban was a carpenter in ancient times. He was regarded as a 良工巧匠—a highly skilled craftsman. When Lu Ban was very young, his family was very poor. He had to leave home and go to Zhongnan Mountain to be the apprentice of a master carpenter. His journey to Zhongnan Mountain was full of hardship, but he was not discouraged. When he finally reached his future master's home the carpenter seemed to have no intention of training him. He set Lu Ban to menial tasks, such as sharpening disused and rusty woodworking tools such as axes and planers. Lu Ban spent seven days and nights making them sharp and shining again. Then the master asked him to cut down a thousand-year-old tree and make it into a smooth helm with two thousand holes. Lu Ban did not complain. He worked steadily for twelve days and nights until he finally completed his task. His master was pleased by his diligence and finally revealed to Lu Ban his own exquisite woodworking models that were collected in a private showroom. He did not tell Lu Ban how to recreate these pieces, instead he instructed Lu Ban to figure out himself. Lu Ban was determined to learn his master's skills. He studied his master's woodwork. After three years of hard work, Lu Ban had become a master of his craft, and later, he became a well-known carpenter.

94. 止（zhǐ）部 Foot

古字形

“止”是象形字，古文字像人之脚形，本义指人的脚，引申指脚趾，即后来的“趾”。现代汉语“止”一般用作动词，表示停止、制止、阻止等意义。作为部首，止部的字多与行走等意义有关。例如“步”指行走时两脚间的距离，也指用脚走；“歧” 的本义是岔道，又引申为不一致。

Ancient form

止 is a pictograph. The ancient symbol for 止 looks like a foot. The original meaning of 止 is *foot*. Its extended meaning is *toe*. Now 止 is usually used as verb meaning *to stop or to halt*. Characters with 止 often have meanings related to walking. For example, 步 (bù) means *the distance between two feet while walking*. It also means *steps*. The original meaning of 歧 (qí) is *forked road*. Its extended meaning is *divergent or different.*

故事 Story

望梅止渴 (Wàng méi zhǐ kě)
望 watch 梅 plum 止 quench (stop) 渴 thirst

During the Eastern Han Dynasty, Cao Cao led his army on a march through a mountain ridge in order to attack their enemies on a steamy summer day. Their pace was greatly slowed by the humidity and high temperature. The soldiers had no water to drink and some of them were suffering from heatstroke. Cao Cao was very worried that the battle would be lost because the men were exhausted. He asked the guide if there was any water nearby. The guide told him, there was no water near. Cao Cao pondered for a few minutes, then he addressed his soldiers: "There is a forest of plum trees just ahead. I understand you are all thirsty and want to have some juicy plums. Let's move faster and get to the plum forest." The soldiers were immediately encouraged. Dreaming about the mouthwatering plums they felt they were not so thirsty, so they picked up their pace and reached the destination as scheduled. Although the troop did not see a plum forest during their marching, they quenched their thirst by just thinking of plums.

望梅止渴 describes a situation of imagined satisfaction.

95. 寸（cùn）部 Chinese unit of length

古字形 ⺕

“寸”是指事字，古文字强调了“寸”在人之手臂上的位置。“寸”的本义是“寸口”，即手腕上可以触摸到脉搏的部位，“寸口”是中医切脉常取的穴位。“寸”引申指长度单位。作为部首，“寸”通常位于汉字的下面或右侧，例如“寻”“导”“射”。寸部的字多与手及手的动作或法度有关。“寻”是古代的长度单位（一寻等于八尺），后来被引申指寻找等意义。“导”是指引或带领。“射”是会意字，古文字从弓从又（手），或从寸，像箭在弓上，以手（寸）发出，后来“弓”讹写成“身”，所以有了今天的“射”字，“射”的本义是用手发箭。

Ancient form ⺕

寸 is an indicative character, or a character that symbolically suggests its meaning rather than being purely pictographic. The ancient form shows a hand. The horizontal stroke on the left indicates the acupuncture point on the wrist, which is about one inch below the end of the palm. The extended meaning of 寸 is *a Chinese unit of length* (about 1.094 inch). As a radical, 寸 often appears at the bottom or on the right of a compound, such as in the characters 寻, 导, and 射. Characters with the 寸 radical tend to have meanings related to hands, action executed with the hands, or the direction of an action. 寻 (xún) is an ancient unit of length, which is about eight Chinese feet. Its extended meaning is *to look for*. 导 (dǎo) means *to guide*. 射 (shè) is an ideograph. The left part of 射 was initially 弓 (*bow*) and the character indicated a hand 寸 pulling the bow

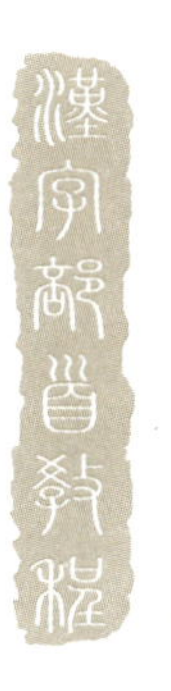

string. With the development of Small Seal Script, 弓 later was modified into 身. 射 means *to shoot*.

故事 Story

尺短寸长 (Chǐ duǎn cùn cháng)
尺 foot 短 short 寸 inch 长 long

尺短寸长 means sometimes a foot may be too short and an inch may be too long or everyone has his or her strong and weak points. Below is a Chinese fable *The Camel and the Goat.* It conveys a similar moral.

A camel and a goat were standing outside of a garden. They were engaged in a heated debate over the advantages and disadvantages of their heights. The camel was tall, so he argued that being tall was much better than being short. To prove his statement, he immediately stretched his neck and reached the tree leaves growing over the garden fence. "You see I can reach the tree leaves effortlessly," he said to the goat. Of course the goat could not reach the tree leaves because he was short. The goat however, was able to steal inside of the garden between two upright poles of the garden fence. He started munching on the garden's delicious grass. "See, I could get through the fence effortlessly but you cannot," the goat said to the camel. They both insisted they were right, and neither would admit the merits of the other parties' height.

96. 夂（zhǐ）部 Arriving

古字形 ᚠ

“夂”是象形字，本义指人从后面走来。“夂”在现代汉语中只用作部首，不单独成字。作为部首，“夂”通常位于汉字的上面，例如“冬”；有时位于汉字的下面或左下侧，例如“复”“处”。“夏”本义指“中国之人”，即夏朝、夏族，也指“华夏”。据说“夏禹”是夏代的开国之君。后多用“华夏”代指中国。

Ancient form ᚠ

夂 is a pictograph. Its original meaning is (*a person*) *coming towards you*. In modern Chinese, 夂 is used only as a radical. As a radical, 夂 often appears on the top, bottom, or lower-left of a compound, such as 冬 (dōng; *winter*), 复 (fù; *again*), and 处 (chù; *place*). The original meaning of 夏 (Xià) is *people of China*. That is, people of the Xia Dynasty, or Xia Nation. According to the legendary story, the name of Emperor for the Xia Dynasty called Xia Yu. 华夏 is also often used to mean *China*.

故事 Story

夏至和冬至 (Xià zhì hé dōng zhì)
夏 summer 至 arrive 和 and 冬 winter 至 arrive

In the Chinese lunar calendar, in addition to twelve months based on the moon, the lunar year is also divided into twenty-four solar periods based on the solar year. Each solar period is approximately 15 days and is named after natural phenomenon that generally occur during that period. 夏至 and 冬至 are two names of the 24 solar periods. The 10th of the 24 solar periods is called *the Summer Solstice* (夏至). It usually occurs around June 21 to 22 in the Gregorian Calendar. *The Winter Solstice* (冬至) is the 22nd of the 24 solar periods. It usually occurs sometime between December 21 to 23. The 24 solar periods are very useful to Chinese farmers because they signal the best time for planting and harvesting.

97. 矢（shǐ）部 Arrow

古字形

“矢”是象形字，古文字像箭矢之形，本义为箭矢。作为部首，“矢”通常位于汉字的左侧，例如“短”。矢部的字多与箭或速度等意义有关。“矫”是形声字，从矢乔声，本是一种器具的名称，该器具的作用是把箭杆揉直，引申为使变直、使合适等意义，例如“矫正”“矫形”。“知”是形声字，从口矢声，本义是知识。

Ancient form

矢 is a pictograph. The ancient form of 矢 looks like an arrow. Therefore, the original meaning of 矢 is *arrow*. As a radical, 矢 often appears on the left side of a compound. Characters with 矢 have meanings related to arrows or speed. 短 is a phonetic-semantic compound, 豆 hints the pronunciation—duǎn. 短 means *short* (*time*). 矫 is another phonetic-semantic compound. 乔 represents its pronunciation—jiǎo. The original meaning of 矫 is *a tool used to make the shaft of arrow straight*. So its extended meaning is *to make an adjustment*. 知 is a phonetic-semantic compound which consists of two components: 口 is the semantic radical and the 矢 signifies the pronunciation of the character. Its original meaning is *knowledge*.

故事 Story

有的放矢 (Yǒu dì fàng shǐ)
有 have 的 target 放 release 矢 arrow

有的放矢 means to shoot the arrow at the target. It is used to describe a person who has a well-defined objective and a feasible plan in mind before taking actions. The following is a Chinese fable that illustrates this idea.

Long ago, there were two monks living in a temple deep in the mountains. They both wanted to travel to the South Sea to see the ocean. Monk Wang planned to walk there on foot. He said: "It may take a very long time to get there by walking, but it is feasible. There are thousands of temples in China. I can find a temple or monastery in almost every village, where I can beg for food and sleep." So Monk Wang set out on his journey the next day. Monk Li, however, thought that he should make a ship and ride down the river to the South Sea, but later, he did not have enough money to pay for the experienced carpenter to finish building a suitable ship, thus, he had changed his mind of pursuing his plan. After a year, Monk Wang had not only made it to the South Sea, he had also returned to the mountains. He told Monk Li of his experiences travelling and the beauty of the South Sea. Monk Li realized that Monk Wang's success was owing to his 有的放矢 . And he himself failed to reach the South Sea because he did not have a feasible plan to reach the goal.

漢字部首教程

98. 斤（jīn）部 Axe

古字形

“斤”是象形字，古文字像斧头之形。“斤”的本义是斧头，假借指重量单位，例如“斤两”“五斤”。作为部首，“斤”通常位于汉字的右侧，例如“断”，有时位于汉字的左侧或下面，例如“欣”“斧”。斤部的字多与砍伐等意义有关。“斩”是会意字，从车从斤，在中国古代有“车裂”之刑，所以“斩”字中有“车”，“斤”则指表示杀人所用的工具。“斩”引申指砍杀，例如“斩草除根”。“断”本来指用斧头将物体分离、截开，引申指不能连续做某事。

Ancient form

斤 is a pictograph. The ancient form of 斤 looks like an axe. Therefore, the original meaning of 斤 is *axe*. In modern Chinese the character 斧 (fǔ) is used for axe, so 斤 now only represents a unit of weight—one jin. 斤 was used to represent this weight because it shared the same pronunciation as the ancient word for axe. One 斤 is about 500 grams, or 1.102 pounds. As a radical, 斤 can appear on the left, right, or bottom of a compound, such as in 欣 (xīn), 断 (duàn), and 斧 (fǔ). Characters with 斤 often have meanings related to cutting or chopping. 斩 (zhǎn; *to slay*) is an ideograph consisting of two radicals 车 and 斤. In ancient China, one of the cruelest forms of capital punishment was to tie a person's hands, legs, and head to a five-horse-drawn chariot, then send the horses running in different directions. The person would be torn into pieces which is similar to the English expression "drawing and quartering." This is why we see 斩 having 车 and 斤 in it. 断 (duàn) means *to cut off*. Its extended meaning is *to discontinue*.

故事 Story

疑邻盗斧 (Yí lín dào fǔ)
疑 suspect 邻 neighbor 盗 steal 斧 axe

Once upon a time, a village man lost his axe. He suspected that his neighbor's son, Dadong, had stolen it. Suspiciously, he began to watch Dadong's every move. The more he watched, the more sure he felt that Dadong was the thief. But a few days later, the villager found his axe in the valley where he had been chopping trees before. On his way home, he bumped into Dadong again. This time, he found that Dadong did not look like a thief.

This story criticizes people who like to accuse others of wrong-doing based on personal feeling rather than facts.

99. 舌（shé）部 Tongue

古字形

“舌”是象形字，古文字像人的舌头之形，本义指舌头。舌头有两大主要功能：一是用于表达，即说话；二是用于别味，即品尝味道。作为部首，“舌”通常位于汉字的左侧，例如“甜”。舌部的字多与舌头的作用有关。“甜”是会意字，从舌从甘，指像糖或蜜的味道，引申用来形容生活舒适愉悦，“甜”也常用来形容话语好听。“舔”指用舌头接触东西。

Ancient form

舌 is a pictograph. The ancient script indicates a person's tongue stretching out from the mouth. The meaning of 舌 is *tongue*. The tongue has two major functions: one is to speak, the other is to taste. As a radical, 舌 is often placed on the left side of a compound, such as in the character 甜 (tián; *sweet taste*). Characters with the 舌 radical often have meanings related to tongue. 甜 is also used to describe a sweet life or sweet words. 舔 (tiǎn) means *to lick*.

故事 Story

舌战群儒 (Shé zhàn qún rú)
舌 tongue 战 fight 群 group 儒 scholars

This story took place in the end of the Eastern Han Period. Cao Cao intended to conquer Liu Bei and Sun Quan. Cao's plan was to make friends with Sun Quan first, so that he could use Sun's army to defeat Liu Bei. Most of Sun Quan's military counselors were in favor of establishing an alliance with Cao Cao. Only Lu Su proposed that Sun Quan unite with Liu Bei and fight with Cao Cao. Lu Su knew it would be difficult for him to convince Sun Quan to adopt his idea because it was not favored by the majority. So he invited the Statesman Zhuge Liang to lobby Sun Quan's military counselors in support of his idea. After a series of heated debates with seven military counselors, Zhuge Liang finally convinced Sun Quan to form an alliance with Liu Bei. Together, they formed a united army and defeated Cao Cao. Zhuge Liang's feat of using his tongue to fight with seven military counselors was widely renowned.

100. 身（shēn）部 Body

古字形

“身”是象形字，像人的身躯，突出腹部，以与“人”（）相别。本义指人的身体。作为部首，“身”通常位于汉字的左侧，例如“躺”。身部的字大都与身体或身体的动作有关系。“躯”是形声字，从身区声，指身体。“躲”是形声字，从身朵声，为避开、隐匿之义，例如“躲避”“躲闪”“躲开”。“躬”也是形声字，从身弓声，为自身、亲自之义。

Ancient form

身 is a pictograph. It looks like a person with abdomen sticking out to differentiate from the character 人 ( ). The original meaning of 身 is *human body*.As a radical, 身 often appears on the left side of a compound. Characters with the 身 radical often have meanings related to the body or actions of body. For example, 躺 (tǎng) means *to lie down*; 躯 (qū) means *human body*; 躲 (duǒ) means *to hide* (*from attack*); and 躬 (gōng) means *personally*.

故事 Story

身在曹营心在汉 (Shēn zài Cáo yíng xīn zài Hàn)

身 body 在 present 曹营 Cao's place
心 heart 在 present 汉 Han

This idiom was derived from a story in the novel *Three Kingdoms*. It is said that during the Eastern Han Period, Liu Bei was defeated by Cao Cao. Liu Bei's important military officer, Guan Yu, was captured by Cao Cao. Cao Cao wanted to use Guan Yu's wisdom to benefit his army, so he did not kill him. Rather, Cao Cao appointed Guan Yu as his military officer. Although Guan Yu appreciated Cao Cao's benevolence and recognition, he was still loyal to Liu Bei. Later, when he learned of Liu Bei's whereabouts, he escaped from Cao Cao's lands and returned to Liu Bei. People knew Guan Yu's body was with Cao Cao but his heart was with Liu Bei —身在曹营心在汉 . Later people used this idiom to describe situations in which a person is not wholeheartedly devoted to his current job, and is longing for something else.

附录 Appendices

拼音检索 *Pinyin* Index

拼音 *Pinyin*	部首 Radical	英文意思 Meaning	编号 Number of Radicals	页码 Page
B				
bā	八（丷）	to divide; to separate	40	92
bái	白	white	73	157
bāo	勹	to wrap up; to packet	87	185
bèi	贝（貝）	seashell	34	80
bīng	仌（冫）	ice	63	137
bǔ	卜（⺊）	divination	79	169
C				
cǎo	艸（艹）	grass	2	17
chē	车（車 ⻋）	cart; vehicle	35	82
chǐ	齿（齒）	tooth	80	171
chì	彳	small steps	49	110
huǐ; chóng	虫	insect	12	37
chuò	辵（辶）	walking; movement	25	63
cùn	寸	Chinese unit of length	95	201
D				
dà	大	man; big	45	102
dāo	刀（刂 ⺈）	knife	29	70
E				
è; dǎi	歹（歺）	remains; skeleton	67	145
ěr	耳	ear	72	155

F

fāng	匚	box; container	91	193
fāng	方	square	81	173
fù	阜（阝在左）	hill	36	84

G

gē	戈	weapon	52	116
gé	革	leather	50	112
gōng	工	ruler	93	197
gōng	弓	bow	66	143
gǔ	骨	bone	74	159

H

hǎn; chǎng	厂	house; shelter	59	129
hé	禾	grain	32	76
hēi	黑	black	82	175
hù	户	single-leaf door	92	195
huǒ	火（灬）	fire	16	45

J

jiàn	见（見）	to see	76	163
jīn	巾	towel; cloth	42	96
jīn	斤	axe	98	207
jīn	金（钅）	gold; metals	7	27

K

kǒu	口	mouth	3	19

L

lì	力	strength	55	121
lì	立	to stand	75	161

M

mǎ	马（馬）	horse	33	78
máo	毛	hair	78	167
mén	门（門）	gate; door	43	98
mǐ	米	rice	46	104

mì	糸（糹纟）	silk	11	35
mián	宀	house	31	74
mǐn	皿	container	62	135
mù	木（朩）	tree	4	21
mù	目	eye	28	68

N

nè	疒	sickness	24	61
niǎo	鸟（鳥）	bird	23	59
niú	牛（牜）	cattle	61	133
nǚ	女	female	14	41

P

pū	攴（攵）	action by using hands	51	114

Q

qì	气	air; gas	86	183
qiàn	欠	breath	69	149
quǎn	犬（犭）	dog; animal	27	66

R

rén	人（亻）	person	6	25
rén; ér	儿	child	84	179
rì	日（曰）	sun	18	49

S

shān	彡	to embellish	85	181
shān	山	mountain	21	55
shé	舌	tongue	99	209
shēn	身	body	100	211
shī	尸	house; corpse	53	118
shí	十	perfect; many	48	108
shí	石	stone; rock	19	51
shí	食（飠饣）	food	38	88
shǐ	矢	arrow	97	205
shì	示（礻）	to show	37	86
shǒu	手（龵扌）	hand	5	23
shū	殳	ancient weapon	83	177
shuǐ	水（氵氺）	water	1	15

sī	厶	privacy	77	165

T

tián	田	land; field	47	106
tǔ	土	soil; earth	9	31

W

wǎ	瓦	tile	89	189
wáng	王（玉）	king; jade	17	47
wéi	囗	to enclose	57	125

X

xiǎo	小（⺌）	small	68	147
xié; yè	页（頁）	head	41	94
xīn	心（忄⺗）	heart	8	29
xué	穴	hole; cave; den	54	119

Y

yán	言（讠）	speech	13	39
yǎn; guǎng	广	big house	44	110
yáng	羊（⺶⺷）	goat; sheep	65	141
yī	衣（衤）	clothes; clothing	26	64
yì	邑（阝在右）	city	30	72
yǒu	酉	alcohol	39	90
yòu	又	hand	60	131
yú	鱼（魚）	fish	20	53
yǔ	雨（⻗）	rain	58	127
yǔ	羽	feather	64	139
yuè	月（⺝）	moon; flesh	10	33

Z

zhǎo	爪（爫）	claw	88	187
zhǐ	夂	arriving	96	203
zhǐ	止	foot	94	199
zhōu	舟	boat	56	123
zhú	竹（⺮）	bamboo	15	43
zhuī	隹	short-tailed bird	71	153
zǐ	子	baby	70	151
zǒu	走	to run; to walk	90	191
zú	足（⻊）	foot	22	57

英文检索 English Index

英文意思 Meaning	部首 Radical	拼音 *Pinyin*	编号 Number of Radicals	页码 page
A				
action by using hands	攴（攵）	pū	51	114
air; gas	气	qì	86	183
alcohol	酉	yǒu	39	90
ancient weapon	殳	shū	83	177
animal; dog	犬（犭）	quǎn	27	66
arriving	夂	zhǐ	96	203
arrow	矢	shǐ	97	205
axe	斤	jīn	98	207
B				
baby	子	zǐ	70	151
bamboo	竹（⺮）	zhú	15	43
big house	广	yǎn; guǎng	44	100
big; man	大	dà	45	102
bird	鸟（鳥）	niǎo	23	59
black	黑	hēi	82	175
boat	舟	zhōu	56	123
body	身	shēn	100	211
bone	骨	gǔ	74	159
bow	弓	gōng	66	143
box; container	匚	fāng	91	193
breath	欠	qiàn	69	149
C				
cart; vehicle	车（車 钅）	chē	35	82
cattle	牛（牜）	niú	61	133

cave; den; hole	穴	xué	54	119
child	儿	rén; ér	84	179
Chinese unit of length	寸	cùn	95	201
city	邑（阝在右）	yì	30	72
claw	爪（爫）	zhǎo	88	187
cloth; towel	巾	jīn	42	96
clothes; clothing	衣（衤）	yī	26	64
container; box	匚	fāng	91	193
container	皿	mǐn	62	135
corpse; house	尸	shī	53	118

D

den; hole; cave	穴	xué	54	119
divination	卜（⺊）	bǔ	79	169
dog; animal	犬（犭）	quǎn	27	66
door; gate	门（門）	mén	43	98

E

ear	耳	ěr	72	155
earth; soil	土	tǔ	9	31
eye	目	mù	28	68

F

feather	羽	yǔ	64	139
female	女	nǚ	14	41
field; land	田	tián	47	106
fire	火（灬）	huǒ	16	45
fish	鱼（魚）	yú	20	53
flesh; moon	月（⺝）	yuè	10	33
food	食（飠饣）	shí	38	88
foot	止	zhǐ	94	199
foot	足（⻊）	zú	22	57

G

gas; air	气	qì	86	183
gate; door	门（門）	mén	43	98
goat; sheep	羊（⺶⺷）	yáng	65	141
gold; metals	金（钅）	jīn	7	27
grain	禾	hé	32	76
grass	艸（艹）	cǎo	2	17

H

hair	毛	máo	78	167
hand	手（龵 扌）	shǒu	5	23
hand	又	yòu	60	131
head	页（頁）	xié; yè	41	94
heart	心（忄⺗）	xīn	8	29
hill	阜（阝在左）	fù	36	84
hole; cave; den	穴	xué	54	119
horse	马（馬）	mǎ	33	78
house	宀	mián	31	74
house; corpse	尸	shī	53	118
house; shelter	厂	hǎn; chǎng	59	129

I

ice	仌（冫）	bīng	63	137
insect	虫	huǐ; chóng	12	37

J

jade;king	王（玉）	wáng	17	47

K

king; jade	王（玉）	wáng	17	47
knife	刀（刂⺈）	dāo	29	70

L

land; field	田	tián	47	106
leather	革	gé	50	112

M

man; big	大	dà	45	102
many; perfect	十	shí	48	108
metals; gold	金（钅）	jīn	7	27
moon; flesh	月（⺼）	yuè	10	33
mountain	山	shān	21	55
mouth	口	kǒu	3	19
movement; walking	辵（辶）	chuò	25	63

P

perfect; many	十	shí	48	108
person	人（亻）	rén	6	25
privacy	厶	sī	77	165

R

rain	雨（⻗）	yǔ	58	127
remains; skeleton	歹（歺）	è; dǎi	67	145
rice	米	mǐ	46	104
rock;stone	石	shí	19	51
ruler	工	gōng	93	197

S

seashell	贝	bèi	34	80
sheep; goat	羊（⺶⺷）	yáng	65	141
shelter; house	厂	hǎn; chǎng	59	129
short-tailed bird	隹	zhuī	71	153
sickness	疒	nè	24	61
silk	糸（糹纟）	mì	11	35
single-leaf door	户	hù	92	195
skeleton;remains	歹（歺）	è; dǎi	67	145
small steps	彳	chì	49	110
small	小（⺌）	xiǎo	68	147
soil; earth	土	tǔ	9	31
speech	言（讠）	yán	13	39
square	方	fāng	81	173
stone; rock	石	shí	19	51
strength	力	lì	55	121
sun	日（曰）	rì	18	49

T

tile	瓦	wǎ	89	189
to divide; to separate	八（丷）	bā	40	92
to embellish	彡	shān	85	181
to enclose	囗	wéi	57	125
to packet; to wrap up	勹	bāo	87	185
to run; to walk	走	zǒu	90	191
to see	见（見）	jiàn	76	163
to separate; to divide	八（丷）	bā	40	92

to show	示（礻）	shì	37	86
to stand	立	lì	75	161
to walk; to run	走	zǒu	90	191
to wrap up; to packet	勹	bāo	87	185
tongue	舌	shé	99	209
tooth	齿（齒）	chǐ	80	171
towel; cloth	巾	jīn	42	96
tree	木（朩）	mù	4	21

V

vehicle;cart	车（車 车）	chē	35	82

W

walking; movement	辵（辶）	chuò	25	63
water	水（氵氺）	shuǐ	1	15
weapon	戈	gē	52	116
white	白	bái	73	157

笔画检索 Strokes Index

部首 Radical	拼音 *Pinyin*	英文意思 Meaning	编号 Number of Radicals	页码 Page
二画				
人（亻）	rén	person	6	25
儿	rén; ér	child	84	179
八（丷）	bā	to divide; to separate	40	92
刀（刂⺈）	dāo	knife	29	70
力	lì	strength	55	121
勹	bāo	to wrap up; to packet	87	185
匚	fāng	box; container	91	193
十	shí	perfect; many	48	108
卜（⺊）	bǔ	divination	79	169
厂	hǎn; chǎng	house; shelter	59	129
厶	sī	privacy	77	165
又	yòu	hand	60	131
三画				
口	kǒu	mouth	3	19
囗	wéi	to enclose	57	125
土	tǔ	soil; earth	9	31
夂	zhǐ	arriving	96	203
大	dà	man; big	45	102
女	nǚ	female	14	41
子	zǐ	baby	70	151
宀	mián	house	31	74
寸	cùn	Chinese unit of length	95	201
小（⺌）	xiǎo	small	68	147
尸	shī	house; corpse	53	118

山	shān	mountain	21	55
工	gōng	ruler	93	197
巾	jīn	towel; cloth	42	96
广	yǎn; guǎng	big house	44	100
弓	gōng	bow	66	143
彡	shān	to embellish	85	181
彳	chì	small steps	49	110
门（門）	mén	gate; door	43	98
马（馬）	mǎ	horse	33	78

四画

仌（冫）	bīng	ice	63	137
心（忄⺗）	xīn	heart	8	29
戈	gē	weapon	52	116
户	hù	single-leaf door	92	195
手（龵扌）	shǒu	hand	5	23
攴（攵）	pū	action by using hands	51	114
斤	jīn	axe	98	207
方	fāng	square	81	173
日（曰）	rì	sun	18	49
月（⺝）	yuè	moon; flesh	10	33
木（朩）	mù	tree	4	21
欠	qiàn	breath	69	149
止	zhǐ	foot	94	199
歹（歺）	è; dǎi	remains; skeleton	67	145
殳	shū	ancient weapon	83	177
毛	máo	hair	78	167
气	qì	air; gas	86	183
水（氵氺）	shuǐ	water	1	15
火（灬）	huǒ	fire	16	45
爪（爫）	zhǎo	claw	88	187
牛（牜）	niú	cattle	61	133
犬（犭）	quǎn	dog; animal	27	66
王（玉）	wáng	king; jade	17	47
瓦	wǎ	tile	89	189
见（見）	jiàn	to see	76	163
贝（貝）	bèi	seashell	34	80
车（車 车）	chē	cart; vehicle	35	82

五画

田	tián	land; field	47	106
疒	nè	sickness	24	61

白	bái	white	73	157
皿	mǐn	container	62	135
目	mù	eye	28	68
矢	shǐ	arrow	97	205
石	shí	stone; rock	19	51
示（礻）	shì	to show	37	86
禾	hé	grain	32	76
穴	xué	hole; cave; den	54	119
立	lì	to stand	75	161
鸟（鳥）	niǎo	bird	23	59

六画

艸（艹）	cǎo	grass	2	17
竹（⺮）	zhú	bamboo	15	43
米	mǐ	rice	46	104
糸（糹纟）	mì	silk	11	35
羊（⺶⺷）	yáng	goat; sheep	65	141
羽	yǔ	feather	64	139
耳	ěr	ear	72	155
舌	shé	tongue	99	209
舟	zhōu	boat	56	123
虫	huǐ; chóng	insect	12	37
衣（衤）	yī	clothes; clothing	26	64
页（頁）	xié; yè	head	41	94

七画

言（讠）	yán	speech	13	39
走	zǒu	to run; to walk	90	191
足（⻊）	zú	foot	22	57
身	shēn	body	100	211
辵（辶）	chuò	walking; movement	25	63
邑（阝在右）	yì	city	30	72
酉	yǒu	alcohol	39	90

八画

金（钅）	jīn	gold; metals	7	27
阜（阝在左）	fù	hill	36	84
隹	zhuī	short-tailed bird	71	153
雨（⻗）	yǔ	rain	58	127
鱼（魚）	yú	fish	20	53
齿（齒）	chǐ	tooth	80	171

九画

革	gé	leather	50	112
食（飠 饣）	shí	food	38	88
骨	gǔ	bone	74	159

十二画

黑	hēi	black	82	175

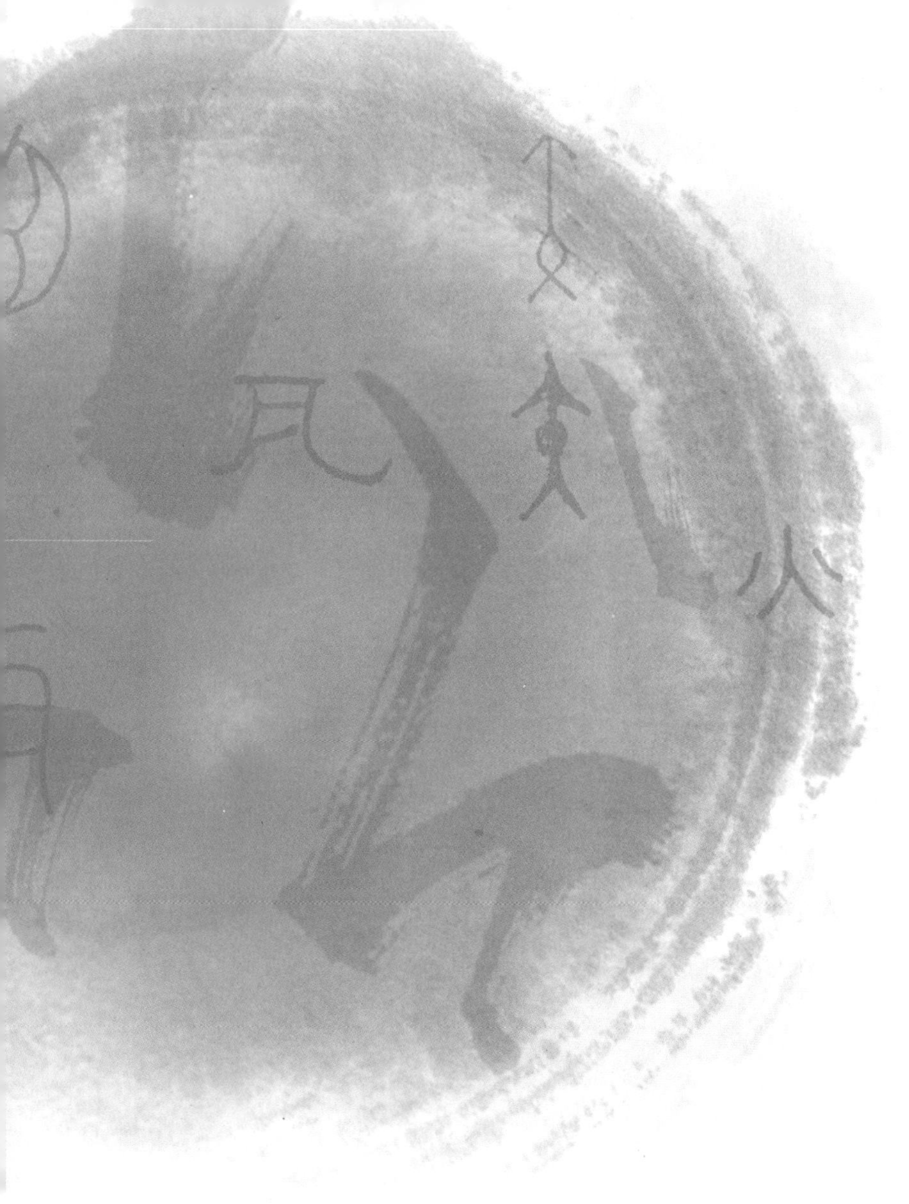

北大版海外汉语教材

汉字部首教程（第二版）

[美]蔡真慧（Chen-hui Tsai）
[美]沈禾玲（Helen H. Shen）　编著
王　平（Ping Wang）

Learning 100 Chinese Radicals (Workbook)
(Second Edition)

北京大学出版社
PEKING UNIVERSITY PRESS

Contents

Introduction

The Structure of the Workbook

The workbook consists of the following three units: basic Chinese strokes, individual radical exercises, and comprehensive radical lesson exercises. The first unit is comprised of eleven basic Chinese strokes. The second unit, individual radical exercises cover 100 targeted radicals. The nine of 100 radicals have two versions in writing, simplified and traditional versions: 鱼(魚), 鸟(鳥), 马(馬), 贝(貝), 车(車), 页(頁), 门(門), 见(見), 齿(齒). However, in this workbook, we require students practice writing the simplified version but not require them write the traditional version. We hope that students focus on learning radical writing in one version to reduce their cognitive load at this very beginning stage. As the traditional version radicals are basic characters, students will learn how to write those characters when they choose to learn Chinese lessons in traditional version characters. The third unit provides comprehensive and integral radical exercises for each lesson, which includes ten radicals. Exercise answer keys are attached at the end of the workbook for self-study.

At the end of this workbook, you will find a set of radical flash cards. On each reverse side of the cards, you will need to fill in the information of sound, shape, and meaning of the radical displayed on the obverse side when the teacher introduces the radical in the class. From the flash cards, you may find that some ancient forms of the radicals provided in the flash cards differ from those in the textbook. Please do not consider them wrong. They are just the variations. By providing these variations, you can get an idea of how the same radical was written in different ways in the ancient time.

Principle for Choosing Targeted Characters

High-frequency characters are the top choices for inclusion in the exercises. When working with semantic radicals, appropriate characters are selected to make the exercises interesting and understandable. However, when the exercises focus on practicing radical decomposition skills, characters containing the target radical and those introduced in previous exercises are given higher priority. Based on the design of spiral learning, learners can accumulate and utilize their accumulated radical knowledge.

Principles for Designing Exercises

Research has shown that Chinese radicals play an important role in word recognition and Chinese vocabulary acquisition. This workbook intends to reinforce stroke/radical information, develop learners' radical perception skills, and prepare learners to develop radical knowledge application skills. In order to achieve these goals, the exercises are designed to help learners to accomplish the following aspects:

- Familiarize themselves with every targeted radical's sound, shape, and meaning. Each radical exercise starts with radical strokes and other basic information. The learners are then directed to focus on the radical within a character. The increase in levels of complexity is intended to help learners achieve the capability of immediate radical recognition.

- Develop the ability to quickly identify the targeted radical in a compound character. Every radical exercise presents specific characters with the targeted radical in common positions in order to acquaint learners with possible structures (an example is shown below), thereby facilitating the speed and accuracy of radical recognition.

Part 4. Find and circle the 木(木) radical in the characters below:

- Develop the ability to approximate the meaning of a character based on its radical component. The exercises draw learners' attention to the relationship between the semantic components and the compound characters, thereby helping them develop the ability to construct a connection between the semantic radical and the meaning of the compound character. This type of exercises enables learners to practice utilizing semantic radicals as processing units for their future improvement of character recognition.

- Develop the ability to deduce the pronunciation of a compound character based on its phonetic radical. The exercises make use of available phonetic cues to aid in the sound representation of a character. Phonetic radicals, if applicable, cue the pronunciation of compound characters, and this offers learners an efficient way to learn the sound of a Chinese character.

- Develop the ability to deconstruct a character into radicals. To fulfill the final task of each radical exercise, learners must identify the radicals to which they have been introduced and decompose characters into smaller components.

The development of the skills that are required to decompose compound characters into radical units will contribute to the skills that are necessary to reproduce compound characters with radical units in the long term. The exercises help learners to perceive radicals effectively. We hope this workbook will help our learners lay a solid foundation for their future Chinese characters studies.

Chinese Basic Strokes Exercise 1

汉字基本笔画练习一

Part I: Please fill in the missing information and circle the basic stroke in each character:

Basic stroke	Direction	*Pinyin*	English	Circle the basic stroke in each character.
丶		diǎn		小 small　六 six　你 you　字 character

Part II: Practice the basic stroke “丶”:

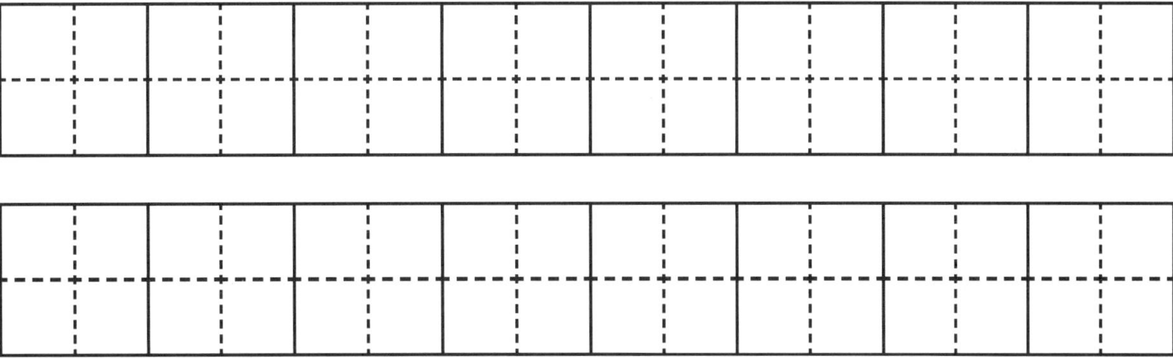

Part III: Practice the basic stroke “丶” in characters:

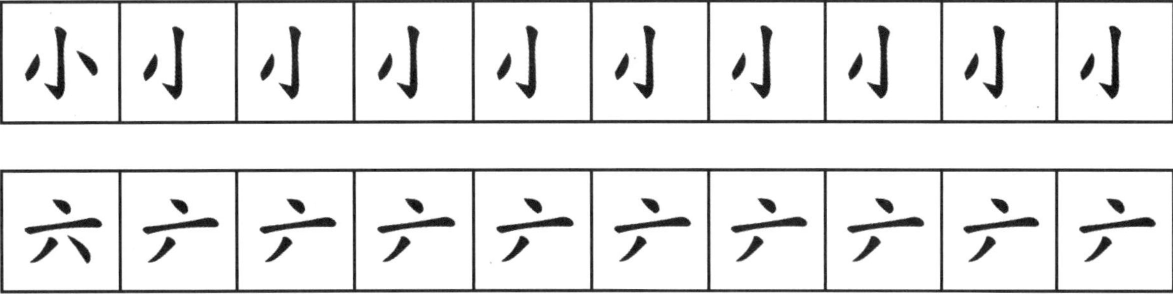

Homework

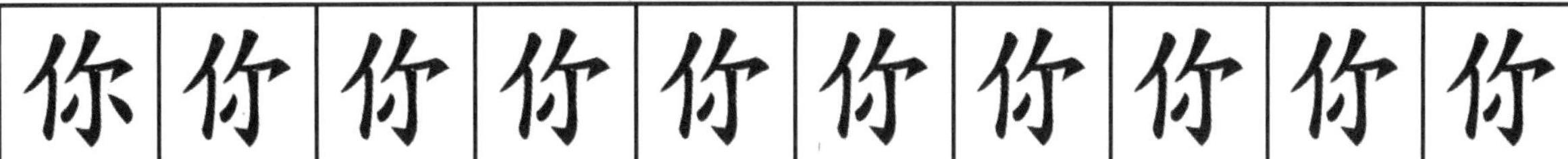

Homework

字	字	字	字	字	字	字	字	字	字

Section: ____________________ Chinese Name: ____________________

Chinese Basic Strokes Exercise 2
汉字基本笔画练习二

Part I: Please fill in the missing information and circle the basic stroke(s) in each character:

Basic stroke	Direction	*Pinyin*	English	Circle the basic stroke(s) in each character.
一		héng		大 big　三 three　女 female　师 master

Part II: Practice the basic stroke "一":

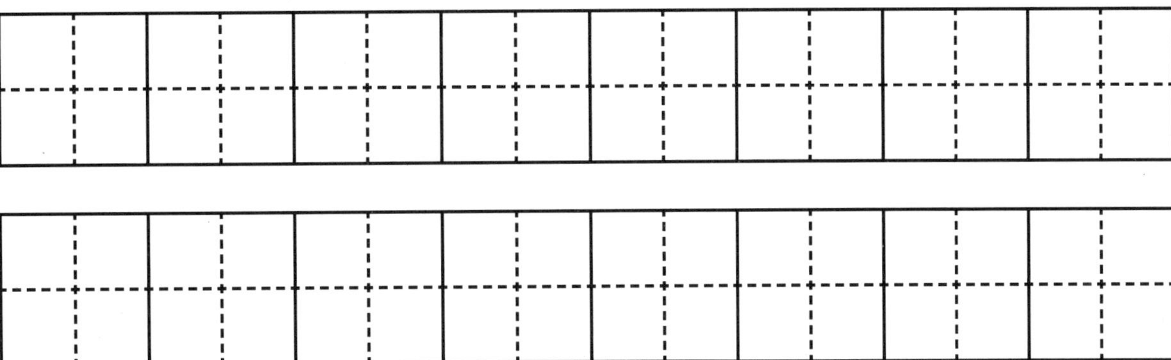

Part III: Practice the basic stroke "一" in characters:

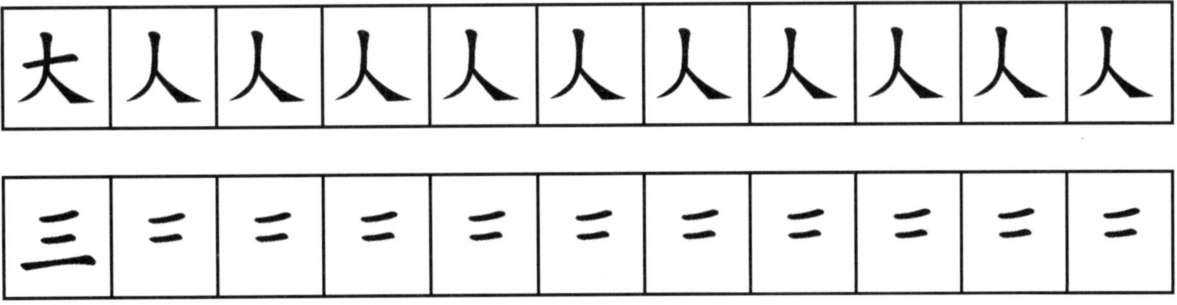

Homework

女	女	女	女	女	女	女	女	女	女	女

Homework

师	帅	帅	帅	帅	帅	帅	帅	帅	帅	帅

Section: ____________________ Chinese Name: ____________________

Chinese Basic Strokes Exercise 3

汉字基本笔画练习三

Part I: Please fill in the missing information and circle the basic stroke in each character:

Basic stroke	Direction	*Pinyin*	English	Circle the basic stroke in each character.
丨		shù		上 up　中 middle　十 ten　牛 cattle

Part II: Practice the basic stroke "丨":

Part III: Practice the basic stroke "丨" in characters:

上	二	二	二	二	二	二	二	二	二	二
中	口	口	口	口	口	口	口	口	口	口

Homework

十	一	一	一	一	一	一	一	一	一	一

Homework

牛	𠂉	𠂉	𠂉	𠂉	𠂉	𠂉	𠂉	𠂉	𠂉	𠂉

Section: ____________________ **Chinese Name:** ____________________

Chinese Basic Strokes Exercise 4

汉字基本笔画练习四

Part I: Please fill in the missing information and circle the basic stroke in each character:

Basic stroke	Direction	*Pinyin*	English	Circle the basic stroke in each character.
丿		piě		四 千 才 他 four thousand just he

Part II: Practice the basic stroke "丿":

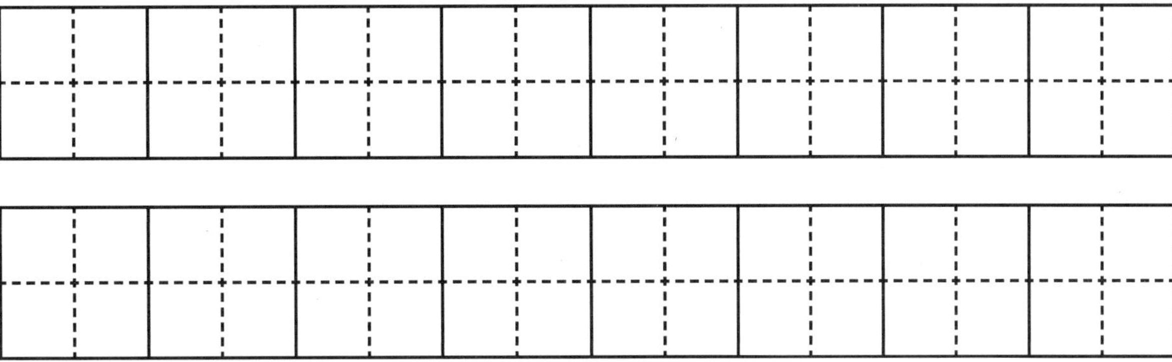

Part III: Practice the basic stroke "丿" in characters:

四	四	四	四	四	四	四	四	四	四	四

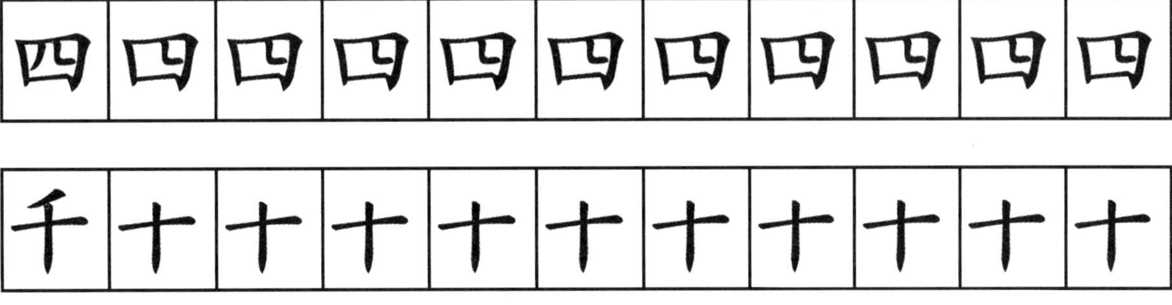

Homework

才	才	才	才	才	才	才	才	才	才	才

Homework

他	他	他	他	他	他	他	他	他	他	他

Section: ______________ Chinese Name: ______________

Chinese Basic Strokes Exercise 5
汉字基本笔画练习五

Part I: Please fill in the missing information and circle the basic stroke in each character:

Basic stroke	Direction	*Pinyin*	English	Circle the basic stroke in each character.
㇏		nà		大 big　人 person　木 wood　八 eight

Part II: Practice the basic stroke "㇏":

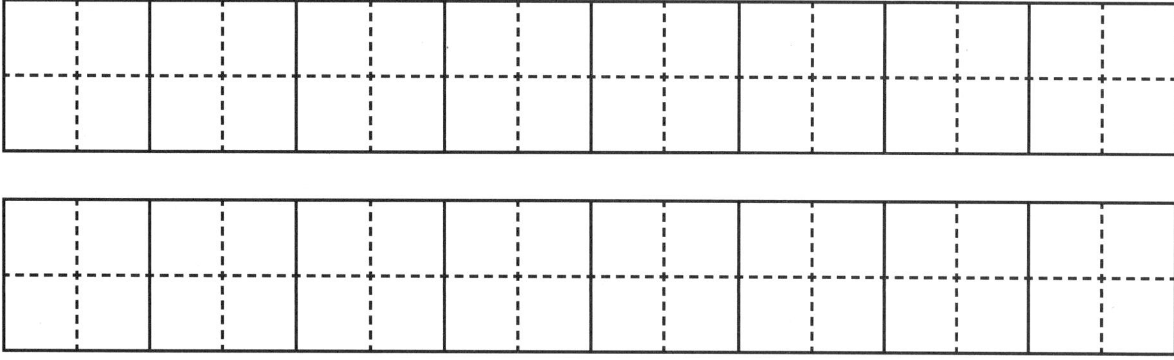

Part III: Practice the basic stroke "㇏" in characters:

Homework

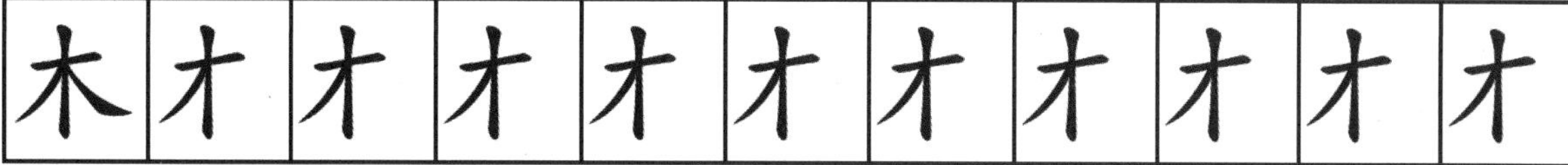

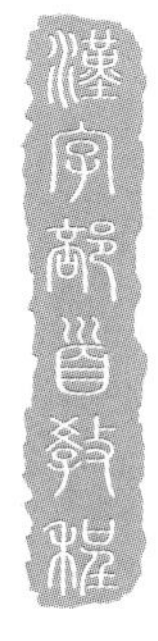

Homework

八	丿	丿	丿	丿	丿	丿	丿	丿	丿	丿

Section: ____________ **Chinese Name:** ____________

Chinese Basic Strokes Exercise 6

汉字基本笔画练习六

Part I: Please fill in the missing information and circle the basic stroke in each character:

Basic stroke	Direction	*Pinyin*	English	Circle the basic stroke in each character.
㇀		tí		海 sea　我 I　打 to hit　冰 ice

Part II: Practice the basic stroke "㇀":

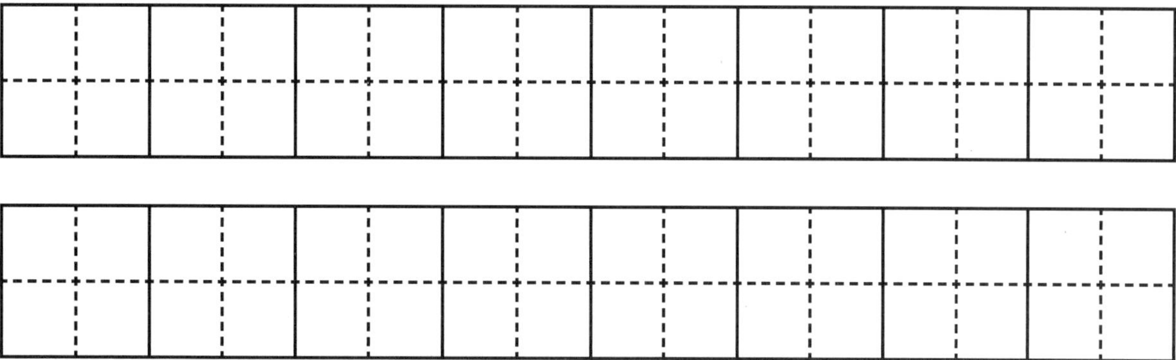

Part III: Practice the basic stroke "㇀" in characters:

海	海	海	海	海	海	海	海	海	海	海

我	我	我	我	我	我	我	我	我	我	我

Homework

打	打	打	打	打	打	打	打	打	打	打

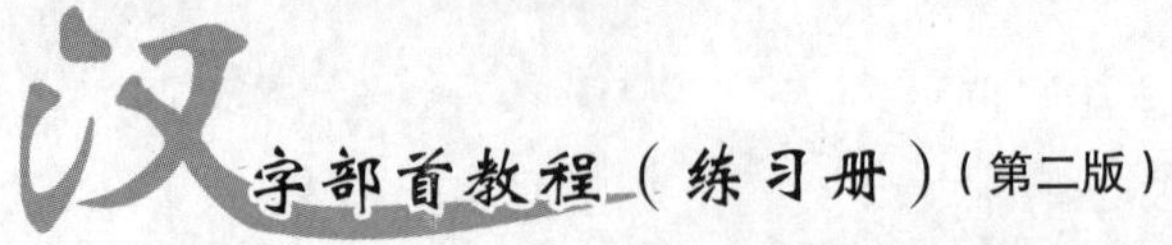

Homework

冰	冰	冰	冰	冰	冰	冰	冰	冰	冰	冰

Section: ____________ Chinese Name: ____________

Chinese Basic Strokes Exercise 7
汉字基本笔画练习七

Part I: Please fill in the missing information and circle the basic stroke(s) in each character:

Basic stroke	Direction	*Pinyin*	English	Circle the basic stroke(s) in each character.
㇖		hénggōu		字 character 爱 love 家 home 序 sequence

Part II: Practice the basic stroke "㇖":

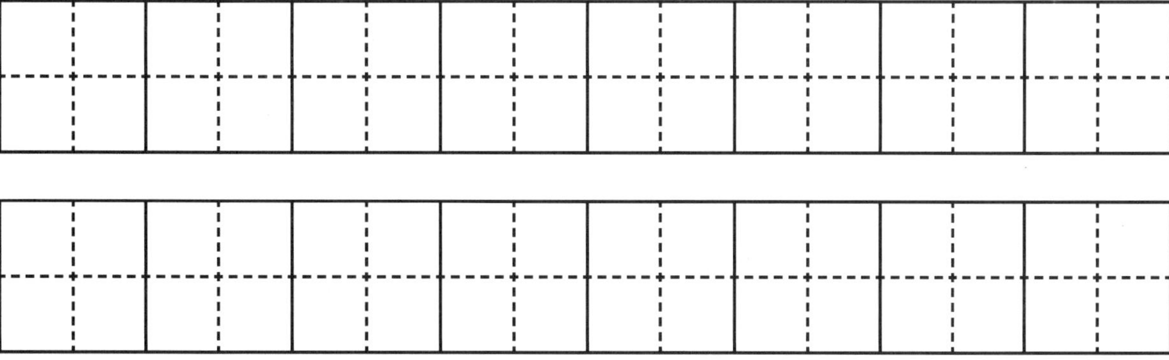

Part III: Practice the basic stroke "㇖" in characters:

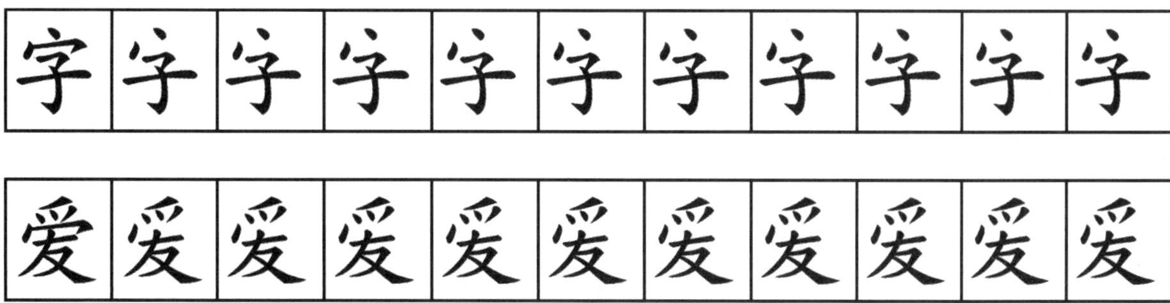

Homework

Homework

序	序	序	序	序	序	序	序	序	序	序

Section: ____________________ Chinese Name: ____________________

Chinese Basic Strokes Exercise 8
汉字基本笔画练习八

Part I: Please fill in the missing information and circle the basic stroke in each character:

Basic stroke	Direction	*Pinyin*	English	Circle the basic stroke in each character.
亅		shùgōu		哥 brother　你 you　小 small　预 in advance

Part II: Practice the basic stroke "亅":

Part III: Practice the basic stroke "亅" in characters:

哥

你

Homework

小

Homework

预	预	预	预	预	预	预	预	预	预	预

Section: ____________________ Chinese Name: ____________________

Chinese Basic Strokes Exercise 9

汉字基本笔画练习九

Part I: Please fill in the missing information and circle the basic stroke in each character:

Basic stroke	Direction	*Pinyin*	English	Circle the basic stroke in each character.
㇂		xiégōu		戏 drama　我 I　浇 to water　代 to substitute

Part II: Practice the basic stroke "㇂":

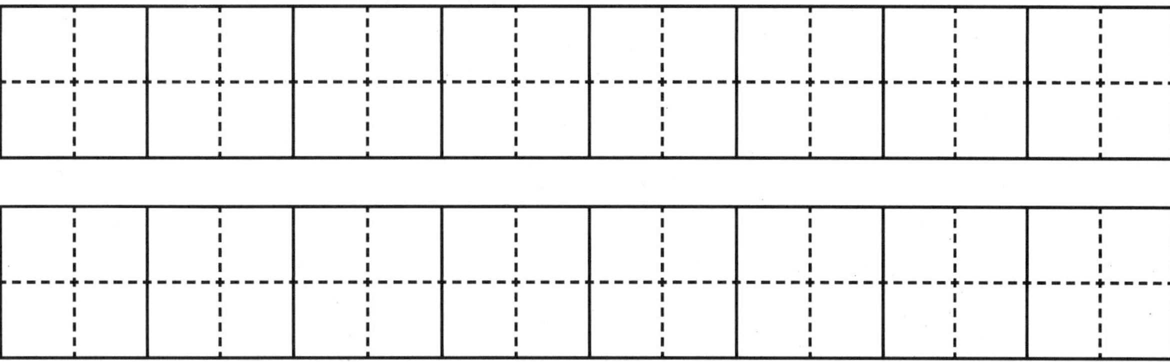

Part III: Practice the basic stroke "㇂" in characters:

戏

我

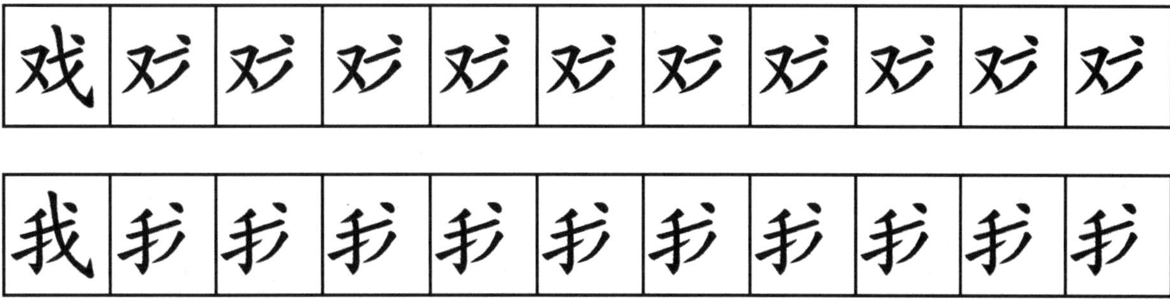

Homework

浇

Homework

代	亻一	亻一	亻一	亻一	亻一	亻一	亻一	亻一	亻一	亻一

Section: ____________________ Chinese Name: ____________________

Chinese Basic Strokes Exercise 10

汉字基本笔画练习十

Part I: Please fill in the missing information and circle the basic stroke in each character:

Basic stroke	Direction	*Pinyin*	English	Circle the basic stroke in each character.
𠃍		héngzhé		见 口 姐 票 to see mouth sister ticket

Part II: Practice the basic stroke "𠃍":

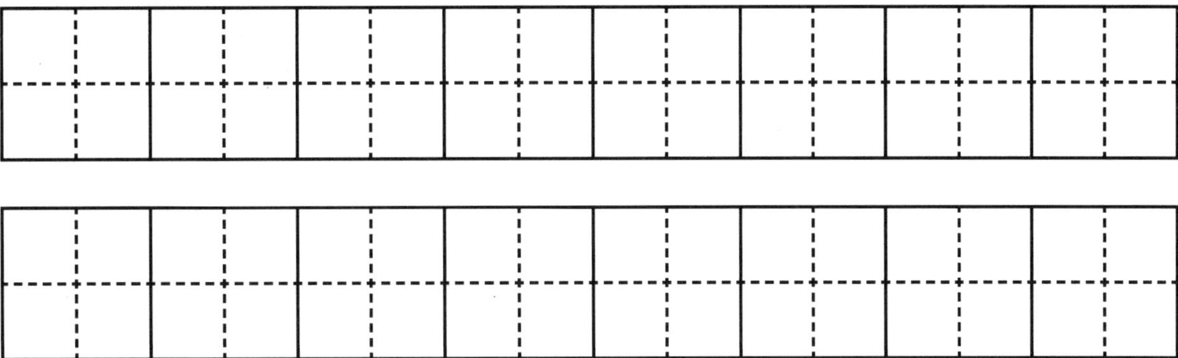

Part III: Practice the basic stroke "𠃍" in characters:

见	儿	儿	儿	儿	儿	儿	儿	儿	儿	儿
口	ㄴ	ㄴ	ㄴ	ㄴ	ㄴ	ㄴ	ㄴ	ㄴ	ㄴ	ㄴ

Homework

姐	姐	姐	姐	姐	姐	姐	姐	姐	姐	姐

Homework

票	票	票	票	票	票	票	票	票	票	票

Section: ________________ **Chinese Name:** ________________

Chinese Basic Strokes Exercise 11

汉字基本笔画练习十一

Part I: Please fill in the missing information and circle the basic stroke in each character:

Basic stroke	Direction	*Pinyin*	English	Circle the basic stroke in each character.
ㄴ		shùzhé		忙 busy　忘 to forget　医 to cure　每 every

Part II: Practice the basic stroke "ㄴ":

Part III: Practice the basic stroke "ㄴ" in characters:

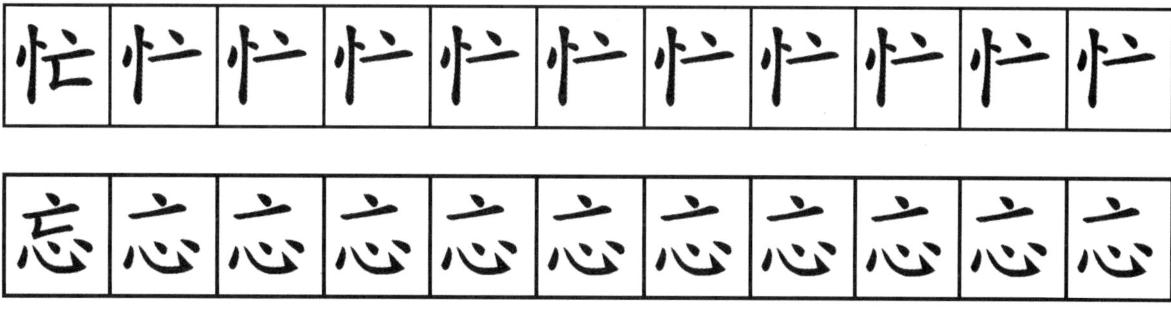

Homework

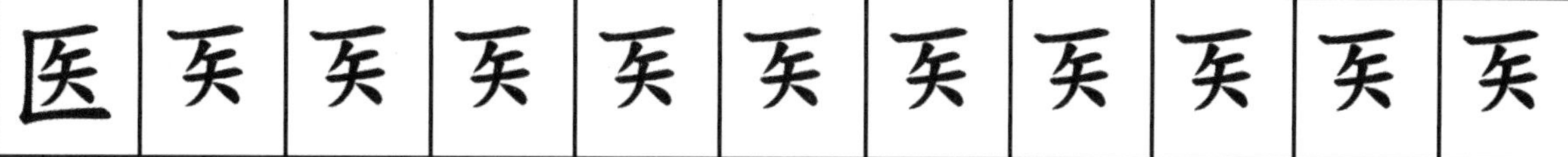

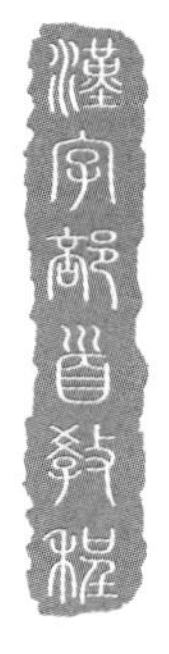

Homework

每	每	每	每	每	每	每	每	每	每	每

Section: ______________ Chinese Name: ______________

Chinese Basic Strokes Exercise

丶

一

丨

丿

㇏

㇀

乛

亅

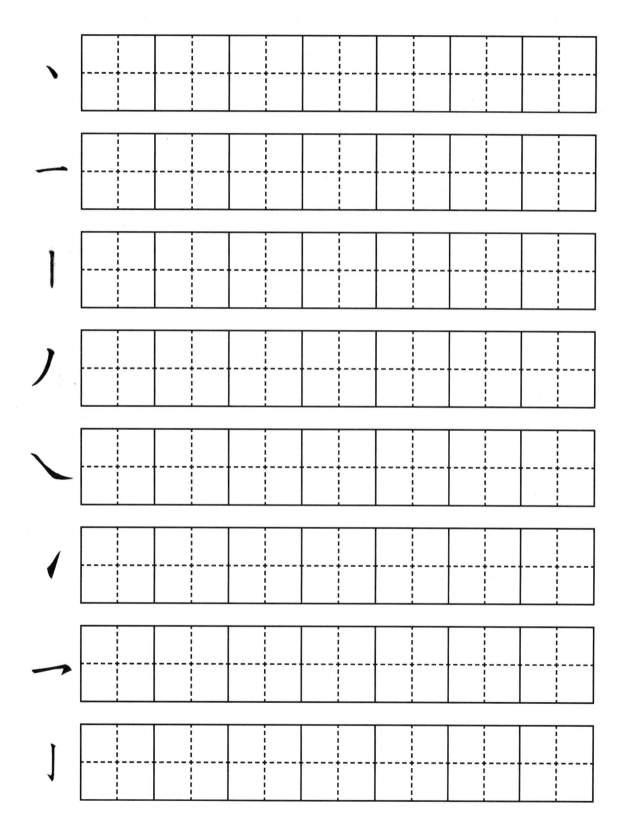

㇏

㇆

㇗

Individual Radical Exercises

Chinese Radical Exercise 1

Part 1. Write out the meaning for the radical below:

Radical and its variants	*Pinyin*	Meaning
水(氵 氺)	shuǐ	

Part 2. Copy the radical 水 (氵 氺):

Part 3. Add the radical for each character according to the sample given:

汉	又	又	又	又	又	又	又

Han nation

Part 4. Find and circle the 水 (氵 氺) radical in the characters below:

永　酒　沓　泰　黎　慕

漢字部首教程

Part 5. Based on the meaning of the 水 radical, please choose an appropriate meaning for the following characters from the three possible choices:

1. (　　) 江　a. mountain　b. river　c. sun
2. (　　) 汽　a. steam　b. smoke　c. plastic
3. (　　) 漂　a. to leap　b. to fly　c. to float
4. (　　) 湿　a. wet　b. dry　c. stinky

Part 6. Please find the 水 radical in the characters below and copy into the brackets:

1. 瀑 waterfall　[　　]
2. 浆 thick liquid　[　　]

Chinese Radical Exercise 2

Part 1. Write out the meaning for the radical below:

Radical and its variant	*Pinyin*	Meaning
艸 (艹)	cǎo	

Part 2. Copy the radical 艹:

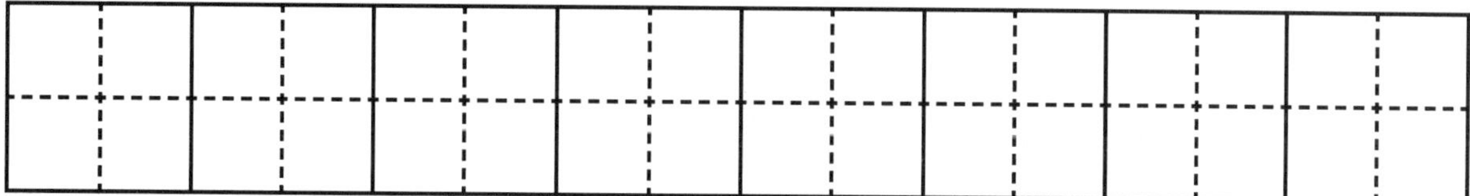

Part 3. Add the radical for each character according to the sample given:

茶	余	余	余	余	余	余	余

tea

Part 4. Find and circle the 艹 radical in the characters below:

英　讲　节　岳　草　带

Part 5. Based on the meanings of the radicals you have learned, please choose the appropriate Chinese characters for the following English equivalents:

1. (　　) vegetable　　a. 菜　　b. 鱼　　c. 肉
2. (　　) celery　　a. 米　　b. 蛋　　c. 芹
3. (　　) swim　　a. 泳　　b. 草　　c. 大

Part 6. Please find the components shared by the Chinese characters below and copy into the brackets:

萍　　莎　[　　　][　　　]

Chinese Radical Exercise 3

Part 1. Write out the meaning for the radical below:

Radical	*Pinyin*	Meaning
口	kǒu	

Part 2. Copy the radical 口:

Part 3. Add the radical for each character according to the sample given:

叫	丩	丩	丩	丩	丩	丩	丩

to call

Part 4. Find and circle the 口 radical in the characters below:

眼 吓 员 导 虽 央

Part 5. Based on the sounds of the radicals you have learned, please choose the correct *pinyin* for the following characters from the lists below:

1. ( ) 叩 a. suǒ b. shuì c. kòu
2. ( ) 草 a. sǐ b. cǎo c. piě

Part 6. Please identify the components you have learned so far for each of the characters below and copy into the brackets:

1. 哎 hey [ ][ ]
2. 治 to manage [ ][ ]

汉字部首教程

Chinese Radical Exercise 4

Part 1. Write out the meaning for the radical below:

Radical and its variant	*Pinyin*	Meaning
木(朩)	mù	

Part 2. Copy the radical 木(朩):

Part 3. Add the radical for each character according to the sample given:

茶	艾	艾	艾	艾	艾	艾	艾

tea

Part 4. Find and circle the 木(朩) radical in the characters below:

大　校　李　臬　才　弄

Part 5. Based on the meanings of the radicals you have learned, please choose the appropriate Chinese characters for the following English equivalents:

1. (　　) pine　　a. 瀑　　b. 松　　c. 歌
2. (　　) woods　　a. 业　　b. 林　　c. 如
3. (　　) to sign　　a. 叹　　b. 术　　c. 氽

Part 6. Please find the components shared by the Chinese characters in the lists below and copy into the brackets:

1. 渠　染　[　　][　　]
2. 棠　啉　[　　][　　]

Chinese Radical Exercise 5

Part 1. Write out the meaning for the radical below:

Radical and its variants	*Pinyin*	Meaning
手(龵 扌)	shǒu	

Part 2. Copy the radical 手 (龵 扌):

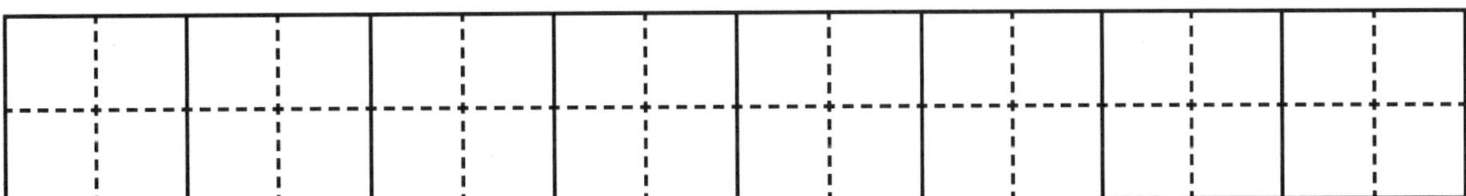

Part 3. Add the radical for each character according to the sample given:

打	丁	丁	丁	丁	丁	丁	丁

to hit

Part 4. Find and circle the 手 (龵 扌) radical in the characters below:

挲　看　在　艳　拜　钱

Part 5. Based on the meaning of the 手 radical, please choose an appropriate meaning for the following characters from the three possible choices:

1. (　　) 拳　a. fist　b. knees　c. legs
2. (　　) 拾　a. to jump　b. to sink　c. to pick up
3. (　　) 推　a. to kick　b. to push　c. to smell

Part 6. Please find the 手 radical in the characters below and copy into the brackets:

1. 找 to look for [ ]
2. 掌 palm [ ]
3. 掰 to separate with hands [ ] [ ]

Chinese Radical Exercise 6

Part 1. Write out the meaning for the radical below:

Radical and its variant	*Pinyin*	Meaning
人（亻）	rén	

Part 2. Copy the radical 人（亻）:

Part 3. Add the radical for each character according to the sample given:

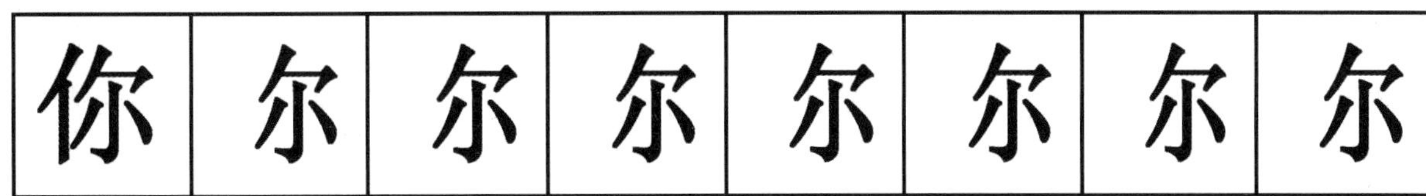

you

Part 4. Find and circle the 人（亻）radical in the characters below:

价　低　后　以　化　见

Part 5. Based on the meanings of the radicals you have learned, please choose the appropriate Chinese characters for the following English equivalents:

1. (　　) uncle　　a. 梦　　b. 滑　　c. 伯
2. (　　) to live　　a. 住　　b. 黄　　c. 洗
3. (　　) to swallow　　a. 但　　b. 吞　　c. 棒

Part 6. Please identify the components you have learned so far for each of the characters below and copy into the brackets:

1. 保 to protect [ ] [ ] [ ]
2. 休 to rest [ ] [ ]
3. 侣 companion [ ] [ ]

Chinese Radical Exercise 7

Part 1. Write out the meaning for the radical below:

Radical and its variant	*Pinyin*	Meaning
金 (钅)	jīn	

Part 2. Copy the radical 金 (钅):

Part 3. Add the radical for each character according to the sample given:

money

Part 4. Find and circle the 金 (钅) radical in the characters below:

鉴　针　馆　铅　级　记

Part 5. Based on your understanding of each radical's meaning, please choose an appropriate meaning for the following characters from the three possible choices:

1. (　　) 钩　a. hook　b. bait　c. tippet
2. (　　) 伴　a. partner　b. penmanship　c. skill
3. (　　) 锤　a. blackboard　b. table　c. hammer

Part 6. Among the characters below, there are some words which are related to metallic elements and share the same radical 金. Please find and circle them:

钴　吵　铝　镍　银　伯　铁　波　铜

Chinese Radical Exercise 8

Part 1. Write out the meaning for the radical below:

Radical and its variants	*Pinyin*	Meaning
心(忄 ⺗)	xīn	

Part 2. Copy the radical 心 (忄 ⺗):

Part 3. Add the radical for each character according to the sample given:

想	相	相	相	相	相	相	相

to think

Part 4. Find and circle the 心 (忄 ⺗) radical in the characters below:

忽 忙 热 录 暴 恭

Part 5. Please find the 心 radical in the characters below and copy into the brackets:

1. 怡 joyous [ ]
2. 懲 to punish [ ]
3. 慕 to admire [ ]

漢字部首教程

Part 6. Please identify the components you have learned so far for each of the characters below and copy into the brackets:

1. 恕 to forgive [ ][ ]
2. 懂 to understand [ ][ ]

Chinese Radical Exercise 9

Part 1. Write out the meaning for the radical below:

Radical	*Pinyin*	Meaning
土	tǔ	

Part 2. Copy the radical 土:

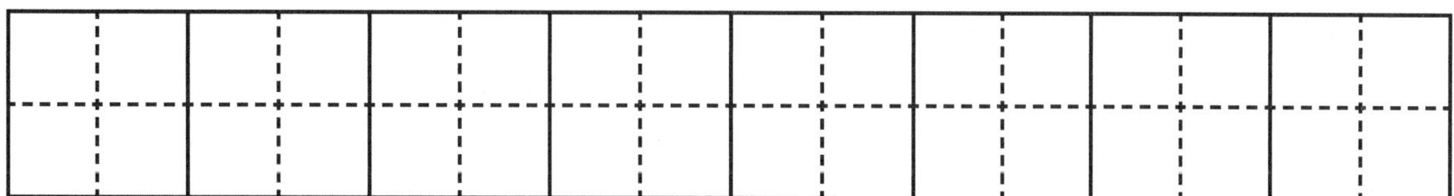

Part 3. Add the radical for each character according to the sample given:

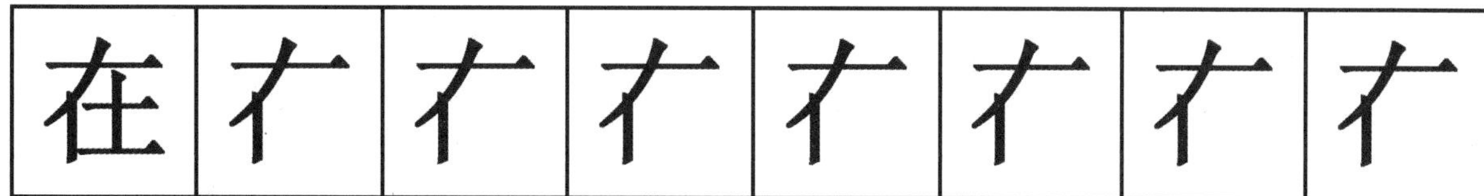

at (preposition)

Part 4. Find and circle the 土 radical in the characters below:

寺　功　基　去　块　劳

Part 5. Based on the meanings of the radicals you have learned, please choose the appropriate Chinese characters for the following English equivalents:

1. (　　) slope　a. 海　b. 台　c. 坡
2. (　　) to pitch　a. 从　b. 投　c. 慢
3. (　　) mound　a. 今　b. 集　c. 堆

Part 6. Please identify the components you have learned so far for each of the characters below and copy into the brackets:

1. 墓 tomb [ ][ ]
2. 坐 to sit [ ][ ]

Chinese Radical Exercise 10

Part 1. Write out the meaning for the radical below:

Radical and its variant	*Pinyin*	Meaning
月(⺼)	yuè	

Part 2. Copy the radical 月(⺼):

Part 3. Add the radical for each character according to the sample given:

有	𠂇	𠂇	𠂇	𠂇	𠂇	𠂇	𠂇

to have

Part 4. Find and circle the 月(⺼) radical in the characters below:

育　赢　期　朋　刘　背

Part 5. Please find and circle the 月 radical in the characters below and copy into the brackets:

1. 肥 fat [ ]
2. 胃 stomach [ ]
3. 朗 bright [ ]

漢字部首教程

Part 6. Please identify the components you have learned so far for each of the characters below and copy into the brackets:

1. 肚 belly　　[　　][　　]
2. 胎 fetus　　[　　][　　]

Chinese Radical Exercise 11

Part 1. Write out the meaning for the radical below:

Radical and its variants	*Pinyin*	Meaning
糸(糹纟)	mì	

Part 2. Copy the radical 糸 (纟):

Part 3. Add the radical for each character according to the sample given:

给	合	合	合	合	合	合	合

to give

Part 4. Find and circle the 糸 (纟) radical in the characters below:

紧 纪 汤 红 紫 素

Part 5. Based on the meaning of the 糸 radical, please choose an appropriate meaning for the following characters form the three possible choices:

1. ( ) 绢 a. big rocks b. thin silk c. deep sea
2. ( ) 缝 a. to sew b. to vomit c. to kick
3. ( ) 线 a. thread b. chair c. knife

Part 6. Please find the components shared by the Chinese characters in the lists below and copy into the brackets:

1. 绘　纵　[　　][　　]
2. 结　络　[　　][　　]

Chinese Radical Exercise 12

Part 1. Write out the meaning for the radical below:

Radical	*Pinyin*	Meaning
虫	huǐ chóng	

Part 2. Copy the radical 虫:

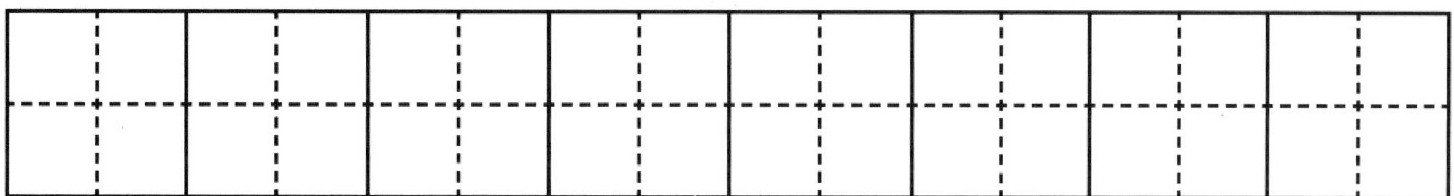

Part 3. Add the radical for each character according to the sample given:

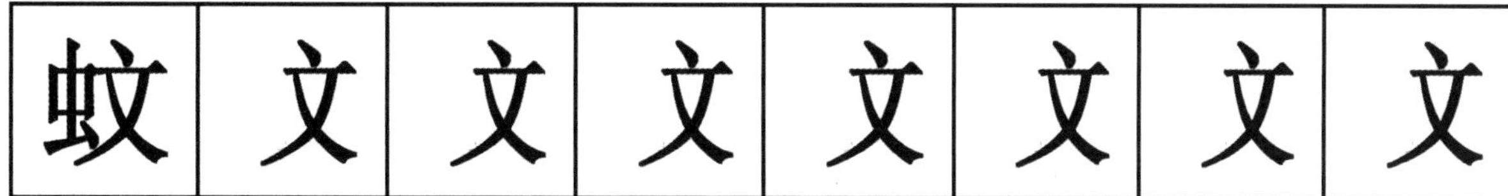

mosquito

Part 4. Find and circle the 虫 radical in the characters below:

蜇　使　蚕　整　蠢　贵

Part 5. Based on the meanings of the radicals you have learned, please choose the appropriate Chinese characters for the following English equivalents:

1. (　　) cockroach　a. 例　b. 紧　c. 蟑
2. (　　) embroidery　a. 蚤　b. 绣　c. 名
3. (　　) shrimp　a. 墙　b. 纸　c. 虾

Part 6. Please identify the components you have learned so far for each of the characters below and copy into the brackets:

1. 螺 snail [ ][ ]
2. 虽 although [ ][ ]

Chinese Radical Exercise 13

Part 1. Write out the meaning for the radical below:

Radical and its variant	*Pinyin*	Meaning
言（讠）	yán	

Part 2. Copy the radical 言 (讠):

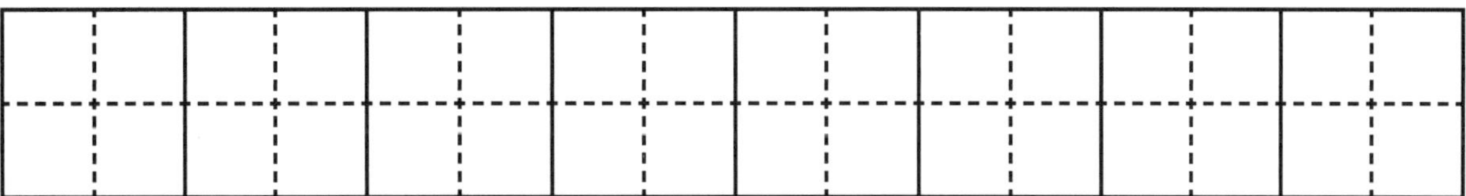

Part 3. Add the radical for each character according to the sample given:

说	兑	兑	兑	兑	兑	兑	兑

to say

Part 4. Find and circle the 言 (讠) radical in the characters below:

计 们 譬 记 饭 誉

Part 5. Based on your understanding of each radical's meaning, please choose an appropriate meaning for the following characters from the three possible choices:

1. (   ) 诵 a. to laugh b. to recite c. to cry
2. (   ) 语 a. hint b. gesture c. language
3. (   ) 蝶 a. butterfly b. handkerchief c. bush

Part 6. Please identify the components you have learned so far for each of the characters below and copy into the brackets:

1. 信 letter [ ][ ]
2. 认 to recognize [ ][ ]

Chinese Radical Exercise 14

Part 1. Write out the meaning for the radical below:

Radical	*Pinyin*	Meaning
女	nǚ	

Part 2. Copy the radical 女:

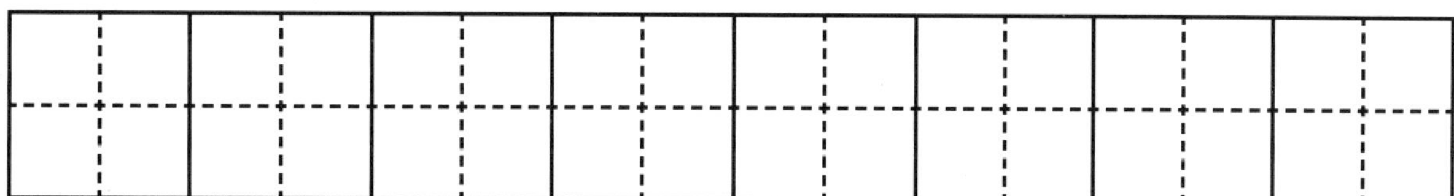

Part 3. Add the radical for each character according to the sample given:

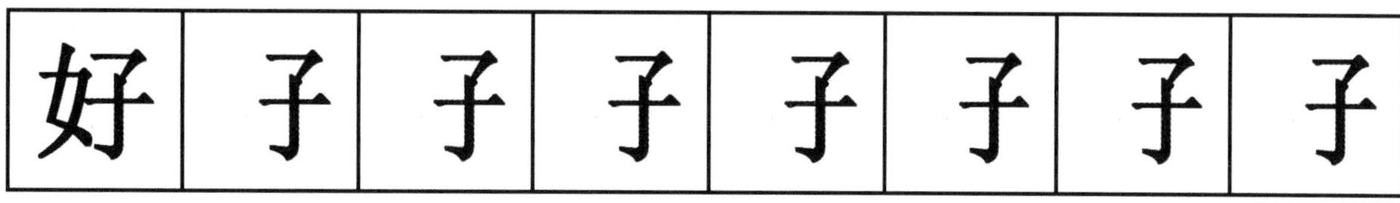

good

Part 4. Find and circle the 女 radical in the characters below:

姓　娃　动　娶　姿　冬

Part 5. Based on the meanings of the radicals you have learned, please choose the appropriate Chinese characters for the following English equivalents:

1. (　　) she　　a. 她　　b. 谁　　c. 级
2. (　　) mother　　a. 给　　b. 妈　　c. 蕊
3. (　　) speech　　a. 姐　　b. 话　　c. 好

Part 6. Please identify the components you have learned so far for each of the characters below and copy into the brackets:

1. 婆 old woman [ ][ ]
2. 妹 younger sister [ ][ ]

Chinese Radical Exercise 15

Part 1. Write out the meaning for the radical below:

Radical and its variant	*Pinyin*	Meaning
竹(⺮)	zhú	

Part 2. Copy the radical 竹(⺮):

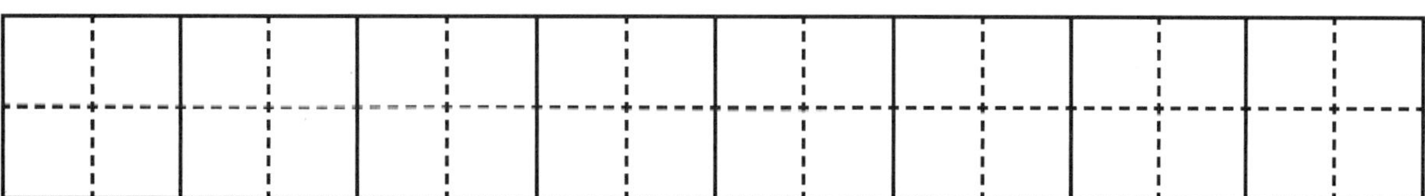

Part 3. Add the radical for each character according to the sample given:

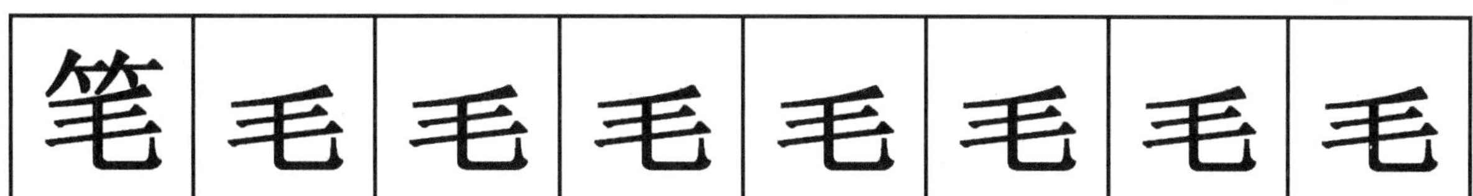

pen

Part 4. Find and circle the 竹(⺮) radical in the characters below:

笑　第　花　算　篇　赛

Part 5. Based on your understanding of each radical's meaning, please choose an appropriate meaning for the following characters from the three possible choices:

1. (　　) 篮　a. basket　b. sculpture　c. water fall
2. (　　) 妹　a. younger sister　b. younger brother　c. grandchildren
3. (　　) 筷　a. guardian　b. fly　c. chopsticks

Part 6. Please identify the components you have learned so far for each of the characters below and copy into the brackets:

1. 笨 stupid [ ][ ]
2. 等 to wait [ ][ ]
3. 答 to answer [ ][ ][ ]

Chinese Radical Exercise 16

Part 1. Write out the meaning for the radical below:

Radical and its variant	*Pinyin*	Meaning
火(灬)	huǒ	

Part 2. Copy the radical 火(灬):

Part 3. Add the radical for each character according to the sample given:

热	执	执	执	执	执	执	执

hot

Part 4. Find and circle the火(灬) radical in the characters below:

点　烦　试　照　灵　然

Part 5. Based on the meanings of the radicals you have learned, please choose the appropriate Chinese characters for the following English equivalents:

1. (　　) coal　　a. 泪　　b. 煤　　c. 信
2. (　　) vocabulary　　a. 姑　　b. 词　　c. 燕
3. (　　) to burn　　a. 烧　　b. 骨　　c. 经

Part 6. Please identify the components you have learned so far for each of the characters below and copy into the brackets:

1. 谈 to talk [ ][ ]
2. 燃 to burn [ ][ ]
3. 煲 to cook slowly [ ][ ][ ][ ]

Chinese Radical Exercise 17

Part 1. Write out the meaning for the radical below:

Radical and its variant	*Pinyin*	Meaning
王（玉）	wáng	

Part 2. Copy the radical 王 (玉):

Part 3. Add the radical for each character according to the sample given:

玩	元	元	元	元	元	元	元
to play							

Part 4. Find and circle the 王 (玉) radicals in the characters below:

枝　珏　球　璧　琴　珊

Part 5. Among the characters below, there are some words which are related to different kinds of jades or stones like pearls. They all share the same radical 王. Please find and circle them:

琳　琅　玛　竽　瑙　社　琥　珀　纽　珠　珥

Part 6. Please identify the components you have learned so far for each of the characters below and copy into the brackets:

1. 噩 unlucky [ ][ ]
2. 钰 treasure [ ][ ]
3. 望 to look [ ][ ]

Chinese Radical Exercise 18

Part 1. Write out the meaning for the radical below:

Radical and its variant	*Pinyin*	Meaning
日（⺜）	rì	

Part 2. Copy the radical 日（⺜）:

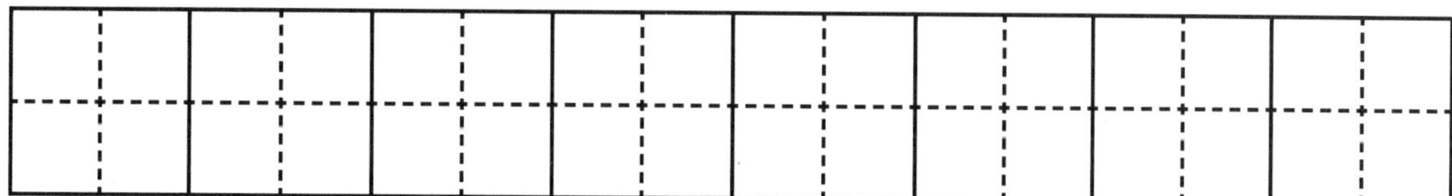

Part 3. Add the radical for each character according to the sample given:

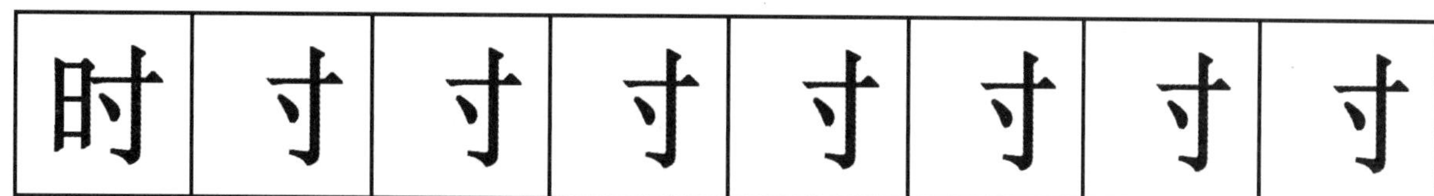

time

Part 4. Find and circle the 日（⺜） radical in the characters below:

旺　是　春　昨　售　曲

Part 5. Based on the meaning of the 日 radical, please choose an appropriate meaning for the following characters from the three possible choices:

1. (　　) 暑　a. hot weather　b. cold weather　c. flood
2. (　　) 早　a. food　b. morning　c. debate

Part 6. Please identify the components you have learned so far for each of the characters below and copy into the brackets:

1. 暮 dust [ ][ ]
2. 照 to shine [ ][ ][ ]
3. 明 clear; bright [ ][ ]

Chinese Radical Exercise 19

Part 1. Write out the meaning for the radical below:

Radical	*Pinyin*	Meaning
石	shí	

Part 2. Copy the radical 石:

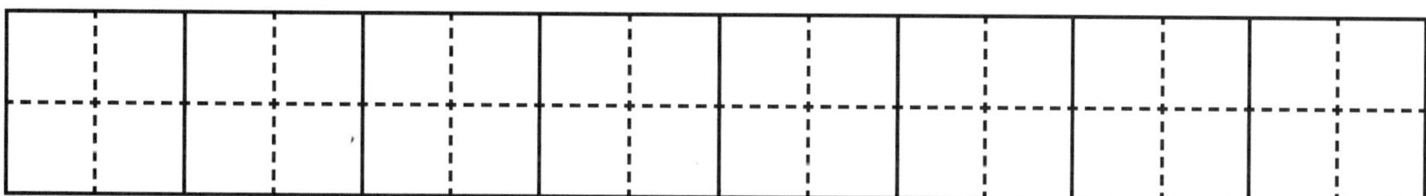

Part 3. Add the radical for each character according to the sample given:

sand

Part 4. Find and circle the 石 radical in the characters below:

破　碧　右　研　磊　福

Part 5. Based on the meanings of the radicals you have learned, please choose the appropriate Chinese characters for the following English equivalents:

1. (　　) hard　a. 潮　b. 签　c. 硬
2. (　　) mine　a. 要　b. 矿　c. 证
3. (　　) to cook　a. 理　b. 煮　c. 纽

Part 6. Please identify the components you have learned so far for each of the characters below and copy into the brackets:

1. 硼 boron [ ][ ]
2. 泵 pump [ ][ ]

Chinese Radical Exercise 20

Part 1. Write out the meaning for the radical below:

Radical and its vaiant	*Pinyin*	Meaning
鱼(魚)	yú	

Part 2. Copy the radical 鱼:

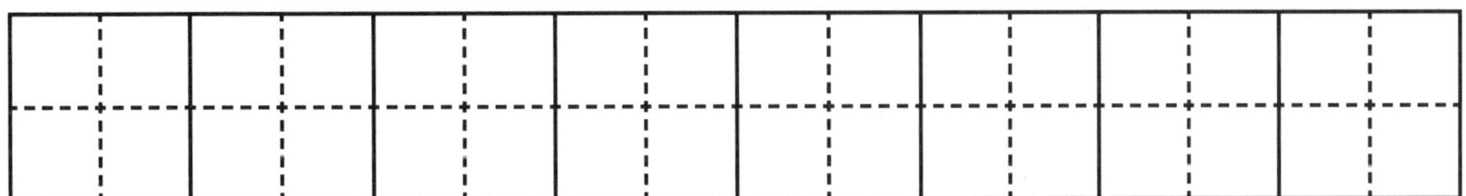

Part 3. Add the radical for each character according to the sample given:

鲜	羊	羊	羊	羊	羊	羊	羊

fresh

Part 4. Find and circle the 鱼 radical in the characters below:

鳕　得　鲁　艳　谢　鳖

Part 5. Based on your understanding of each radical's meaning, please choose an appropriate meaning for the following characters from the three possible choices:

1. (　　) 鲨　a. shark　b. heat　c. knot
2. (　　) 碧　a. green jade　b. fine silk　c. thin bamboo
3. (　　) 鱿　a. burnt　b. squid　c. hairy

Part 6. Please identify the components you have learned so far for each of the characters below and copy into the brackets:

1. 鲳 butterfish [ ][ ]
2. 鲑 salmon [ ][ ]
3. 鲔 tuna [ ][ ]

Chinese Radical Exercise 21

Part 1. Write out the meaning for the radical below:

Radical	*Pinyin*	Meaning
山	shān	

Part 2. Copy the radical 山:

Part 3. Add the radical for each character according to the sample given:

years old

Part 4. Find and circle the 山 radical in the characters below:

岸　峡　业　岛　幽　岳

Part 5. Based on your understanding of each radical's meaning, please choose an appropriate meaning for the following characters from the three possible choices:

1. (　　) 峰　a. apex　b. bee　c. gold
2. (　　) 岘　a. rotten meat　b. broken heart　c. steep hill
3. (　　) 晴　a. sunny　b. windy　c. cloudy

Part 6. Please identify the components you have learned so far for each of the characters below and copy into the brackets:

1. 岩 crag [ ][ ]
2. 炭 charcoal [ ][ ]
3. 峙 to stand erectly [ ][ ]

Chinese Radical Exercise 22

Part 1. Write out the meaning for the radical below:

Radical and its variant	*Pinyin*	Meaning
足(⻊)	zú	

Part 2. Copy the radical 足(⻊):

Part 3. Add the radical for each character according to the sample given:

跳	兆	兆	兆	兆	兆	兆	兆

to jump

Part 4. Find and circle the 足(⻊) radical in the characters below:

距　蹩　识　跑　址　路

Part 5. Based on the meanings of the radicals you have learned, please choose the appropriate Chinese characters for the following English equivalents:

1. (　　) to kick　　a. 怕　　b. 踢　　c. 请
2. (　　) to stomp　　a. 机　　b. 灰　　c. 跺
3. (　　) high mountains　　a. 姨　　b. 岳　　c. 鲤

Part 6. Please identify the components you have learned so far for each of the characters below and copy into the brackets:

1. 跖 tread [ ][ ]
2. 踏 to step [ ][ ][ ]
3. 蹦 to leap [ ][ ][ ]

Chinese Radical Exercise 23

Part 1. Write out the meaning for the radical below:

Radical and its variant	*Pinyin*	Meaning
鸟(鳥)	niǎo	

Part 2. Copy the radical 鸟:

Part 3. Add the radical for each character according to the sample given:

鸭	甲	甲	甲	甲	甲	甲	甲

duck

Part 4. Find and circle the 鸟 radical in the characters below:

鸠　鹃　吗　鸳　鸽　乌

Part 5. Based on your understanding of each radical's meaning, please choose an appropriate meaning for the following characters from the three possible choices:

1. (　　) 鹰　a. hawk　b. frog　c. snake
2. (　　) 跳　a. to lick　b. to jump　c. to tap
3. (　　) 鸵　a. panda　b. dolphin　c. ostrich

Part 6. Please identify the components you have learned so far for each of the characters below and copy into the brackets:

1. 鸣 to chirp [ ][ ]
2. 鹏 roc [ ][ ]
3. 鹭 aigrette [ ][ ][ ]

Chinese Radical Exercise 24

Part 1. Write out the meaning for the radical below:

Radical	*Pinyin*	Meaning
疒	nè	

Part 2. Copy the radical 疒:

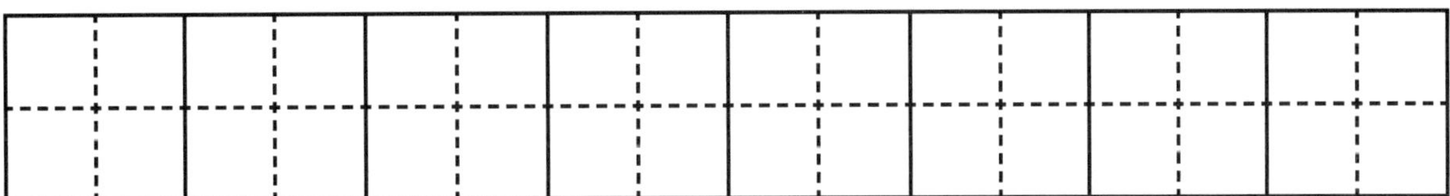

Part 3. Add the radical for each character according to the sample given:

病	丙	丙	丙	丙	丙	丙	丙

sick

Part 4. Find and circle the 疒 radical in the characters below:

症　疼　疗　厅　应　瘦

Part 5. Based on the meanings of the radicals you have learned, please choose the appropriate Chinese characters for the following English equivalents:

1. (　　) malaria　a. 疟　b. 跑　c. 凉
2. (　　) crazy　a. 球　b. 疯　c. 路
3. (　　) she　a. 她　b. 有　c. 考

Part 6. Please identify the components you have learned so far for each of the characters below and copy into the brackets:

1. 癌 cancer [ ][ ][ ]
2. 痰 sputum [ ][ ]

Chinese Radical Exercise 25

Part 1. Write out the meaning for the radical below:

Radical and its variant	*Pinyin*	Meaning
辵(辶)	chuò	

Part 2. Copy the radical 辶:

Part 3. Add the radical for each character according to the sample given:

进	井	井	井	井	井	井	井

to enter

Part 4. Find and circle the 辶 radical in the characters below:

近　连　迎　之　建　边

Part 5. Based on your understanding of each radical's meaning, please choose an appropriate meaning for the following characters from the three possible choices:

1. (　　) 迟　a. to fly away　b. to float　c. to be late
2. (　　) 痛　a. change　b. pain　c. happiness
3. (　　) 追　a. to chase　b. to hover　c. to dive

Part 6. Please find the components shared by the Chinese characters below and copy into the brackets:

逛　逞　[　　][　　]

Chinese Radical Exercise 26

Part 1. Write out the meaning for the radical below:

Radical and its variant	*Pinyin*	Meaning
衣（衤）	yī	

Part 2. Copy the radical 衣（衤）:

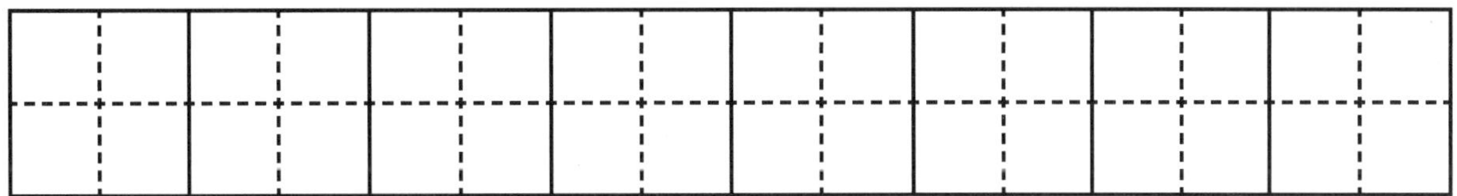

Part 3. Add the radical for each character according to the sample given:

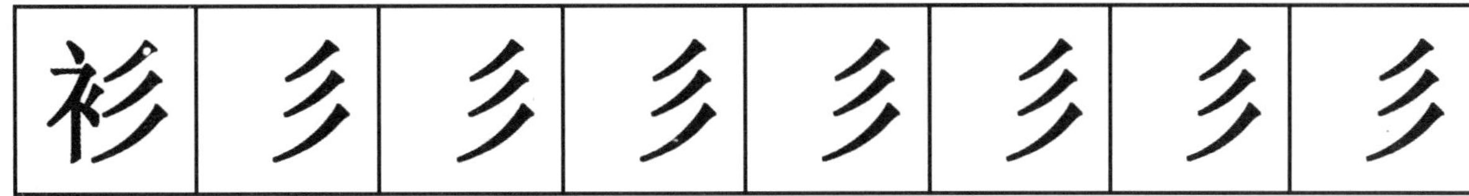

shirt

Part 4. Find and circle the 衣（衤）radical in the characters below:

袜　裙　畏　袋　被　神

Part 5. Based on the meanings of the radicals you have learned, please choose the appropriate Chinese characters for the following English equivalents:

1. (　　) pants　　a. 送　　b. 裤　　c. 疼
2. (　　) to go back　　a. 返　　b. 病　　c. 鲜
3. (　　) shirts　　a. 出去　　b. 衬衫　　c. 茶水

Part 6. Please identify the components you have learned so far for each of the characters below and copy into the brackets:

1. 褓 cloth for carrying baby [ ][ ][ ][ ]
2. 哀 sorrow [ ][ ]

Chinese Radical Exercise 27

Part 1. Write out the meaning for the radical below:

Radical and its variant	*Pinyin*	Meaning
犬 (犭)	quǎn	

Part 2. Copy the radical 犬 (犭):

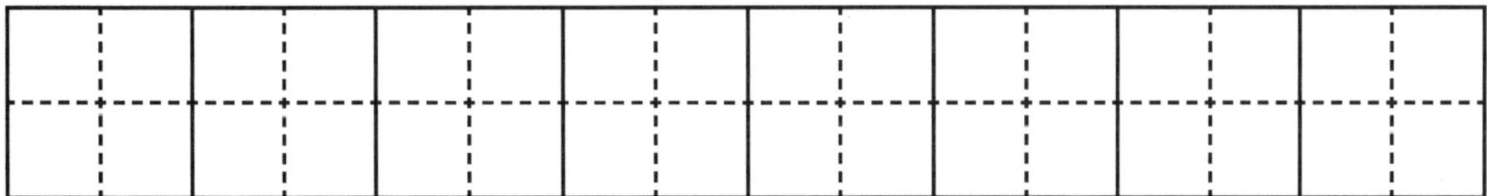

Part 3. Add the radical for each character according to the sample given:

狗	句	句	句	句	句	句	句

dog

Part 4. Find and circle the 犬 (犭) radical in the characters below:

哭　美　猛　作　须　猜

Part 5. Please find the 犬 radical in the characters below and copy into the brackets:

1. 狼 wolf　[　　]
2. 臭 stink　[　　]

Part 6. Among the characters below, there are some words which are related to different kinds of animals. They all share the same radical 犭. Please find the characters and circle them:

猫　杀　狗　狮　遛　狐　猴　吼　猿

Chinese Radical Exercise 28

Part 1. Write out the meaning for the radical below:

Radical	*Pinyin*	Meaning
目 (stroke order 1–5)	mù	

Part 2. Copy the radical 目:

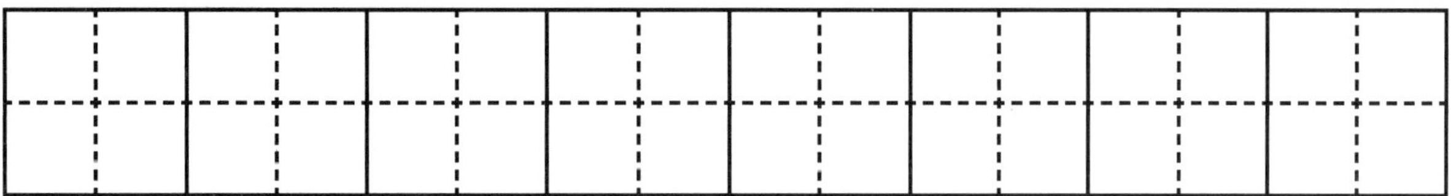

Part 3. Add the radical for each character according to the sample given:

盲	亡	亡	亡	亡	亡	亡	亡

blind

Part 4. Find and circle the 目 radical in the characters below:

睡　晴　眼　盼　省　真

Part 5. Based on your understanding of each radical's meaning, please choose an appropriate meaning for the following characters from the three possible choices:

1. (　　) 眉　a. eyebrow　b. nose　c. mouth
2. (　　) 盯　a. to stare　b. to smell　c. to feel
3. (　　) 逛　a. to scare　b. to throw　c. to stroll

漢字部首教程

Part 6. Please identify the components you have learned so far for the character below and copy into the brackets:

想 to think [ ][ ][ ]

Chinese Radical Exercise 29

Part 1. Write out the meaning for the radical below:

Radical and its variants	*Pinyin*	Meaning
刀(刂⺈)	dāo	

Part 2. Copy the radical 刀(刂⺈):

Part 3. Add the radical for each character according to the sample given:

别	另	另	另	另	另	另	另

to differentiate

Part 4. Find and circle the 刀(刂⺈) radical in the characters below:

召　动　刚　免　师　条

Part 5. Please find the 刀 radical in the characters below and copy into the brackets:

1. 切 to cut [ ]
2. 刻 to engrave [ ]
3. 争 to dispute [ ]

汉字部首教程

Part 6. Based on the sounds of the radicals you have learned, please choose the correct *pinyin* for the following characters from the lists below:

1. (　　) 到　a. shàn　b. niǎo　c. dào
2. (　　) 苜　a. diāo　b. mù　c. chuáng

Chinese Radical Exercise 30

Part 1. Write out the meaning for the radical below:

Radical and its variant	*Pinyin*	Meaning
邑（阝）	yì	

Part 2. Copy the radical 邑（阝）:

Part 3. Add the radical for each character according to the sample given:

那	冄	冄	冄	冄	冄	冄	冄

that

Part 4. Find and circle the 邑（阝）radical in the characters below:

郡　际　邮　跑　都　陈

Part 5. Based on the meanings of the radicals you have learned, please choose the appropriate Chinese characters for the following English equivalents:

1. (　　) nation　a. 到　b. 相　c. 邦
2. (　　) capital　a. 都　b. 跳　c. 鲜
3. (　　) shaving　a. 被　b. 过　c. 刮

Part 6. Please identify the components you have learned so far for each of the characters below and copy into the brackets:

1. 邵 a Chinese surname [ ][ ][ ]
2. 都 capital [ ][ ][ ]

Chinese Radical Exercise 31

Part 1. Write out the meaning for the radical below:

Radical	*Pinyin*	Meaning
宀	mián	

Part 2. Copy the radical 宀:

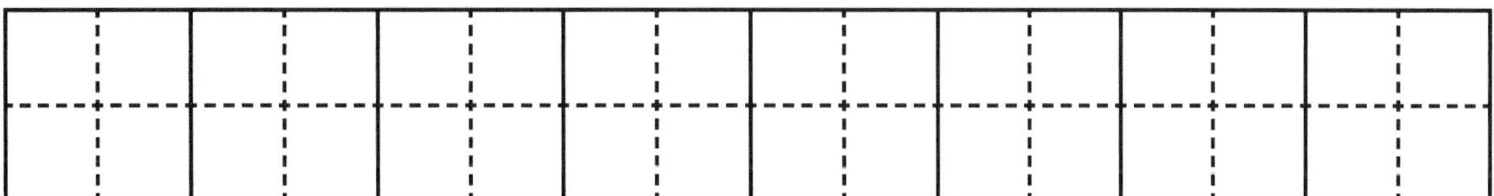

Part 3. Add the radical for each character according to the sample given:

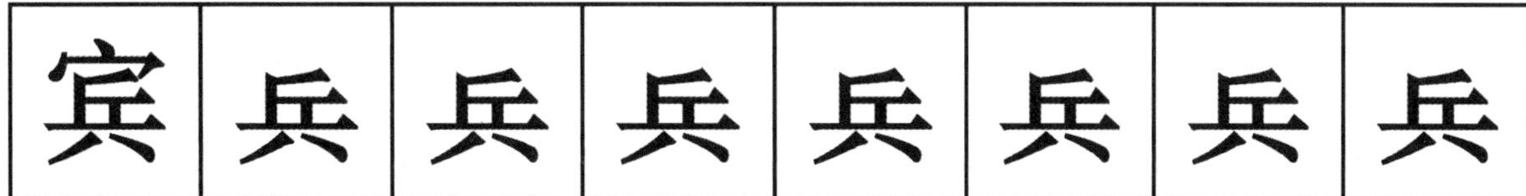

guest

Part 4. Find and circle the 宀 radical in the characters below:

寄　写　客　字　要　完

Part 5. Based on your understanding of each radical's meaning, please choose an appropriate meaning for the following characters from the three possible choices:

1. (　　) 家　a. garden　b. home　c. pool
2. (　　) 室　a. fox　b. room　c. vine
3. (　　) 袜　a. socks　b. feet　c. table

Part 6. Please identify the components you have learned so far for each of the characters below and copy into the brackets:

1. 灾 disaster [ ][ ]
2. 宝 treasure [ ][ ]
3. 安 safe; calm [ ][ ]

Chinese Radical Exercise 32

Part 1. Write out the meaning for the radical below:

Radical	*Pinyin*	Meaning
禾	hé	

Part 2. Copy the radical 禾:

Part 3. Add the radical for each character according to the sample given:

秋	火	火	火	火	火	火	火

autumn

Part 4. Find and circle the 禾 radical in the characters below:

和　乘　秦　枝　私　季

Part 5. Based on the meanings of the radicals you have learned, please choose the appropriate Chinese characters for the following English equivalents:

1. (　　) rice　　a. 字　　b. 郊　　c. 稻
2. (　　) broomcorn　　a. 渴　　b. 黍　　c. 定
3. (　　) house　　a. 宅　　b. 狗　　c. 这

汉字部首教程

Part 6. Please identify the components you have learned so far for each of the characters below and copy into the brackets:

1. 利 sharp [ ][ ]
2. 香 good-smelling [ ][ ]
3. 秋 autumn [ ][ ]

Chinese Radical Exercise 33

Part 1. Write out the meaning for the radical below:

Radical and its variant	*Pinyin*	Meaning
马(馬)	mǎ	

Part 2. Copy the radical 马:

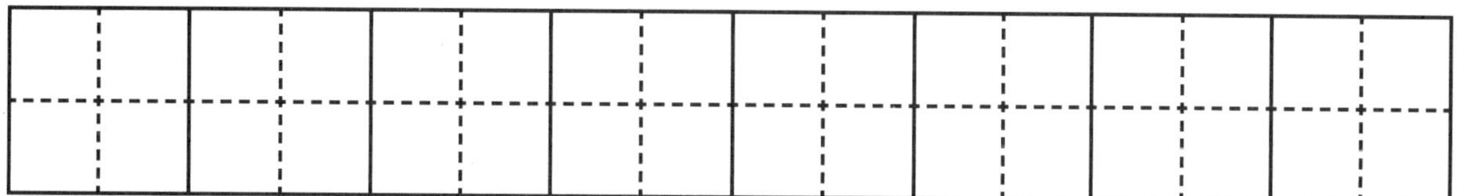

Part 3. Add the radical for each character according to the sample given:

骗	扁	扁	扁	扁	扁	扁	扁

to cheat

Part 4. Find and circle the 马 radical in the characters below:

骑　驭　鳞　鸦　驽　写

Part 5. Based on your understanding of each radical's meaning, please choose an appropriate meaning for the following characters from the three possible choices:

1. (　　) 骑　a. to ride on　b. to doze off　c. to wriggle
2. (　　) 宫　a. grassland　b. desert　c. palace
3. (　　) 驰　a. to sleep　b. to sing　c. to gallop

Part 6. Please identify the components you have learned so far for each of the characters below and copy into the brackets:

1. 妈 mother [ ][ ]
2. 骂 to scold [ ][ ]
3. 骡 mule [ ][ ]

Chinese Radical Exercise 34

Part 1. Write out the meaning for the radical below:

Radical and its variant	*Pinyin*	Meaning
贝(貝)	bèi	

Part 2. Copy the radical 贝:

Part 3. Add the radical for each character according to the sample given:

贵	虫	虫	虫	虫	虫	虫	虫

expensive

Part 4. Find and circle the 贝 radical in the characters below:

责　费　朋　财　真　贯

Part 5. Based on the sounds of the radicals you have learned, please choose the correct *pinyin* for the following characters from the lists below:

1. (　　) 狈　a. yán　b. bèi　c. huǒ
2. (　　) 吗　a. ma　b. lù　c. yī

Part 6. Please identify the components you have learned so far for each of the characters below and copy into the brackets:

1. 赛 competition　[　　][　　]
2. 赢 to win　[　　][　　][　　]

Chinese Radical Exercise 35

Part 1. Write out the meaning for the radical below:

Radical and its variants	*Pinyin*	Meaning
车(車 ⻋)	chē	

Part 2. Copy the radical 车(⻋):

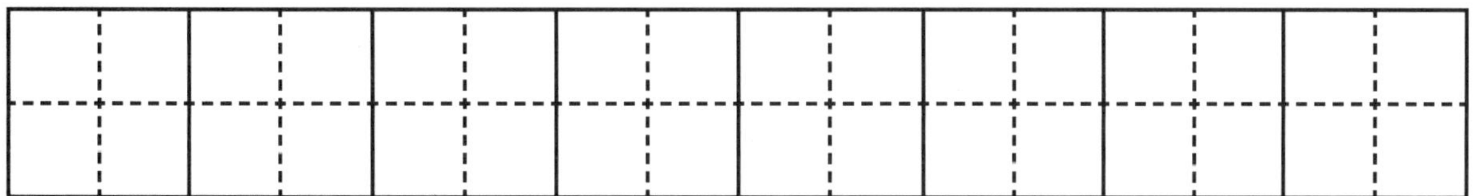

Part 3. Add the radical for each character according to the sample given:

轻	𢀖	𢀖	𢀖	𢀖	𢀖	𢀖	𢀖

light

Part 4. Find and circle the 车(⻋) radical in the characters below:

转　辆　轰　陈　载　软

Part 5. Based on the meanings of the radicals you have learned, please choose the appropriate Chinese characters for the following English equivalents:

1. (　　) railway　a. 字　b. 费　c. 轨
2. (　　) expensive　a. 宜　b. 贵　c. 香
3. (　　) wheel　a. 财　b. 轮　c. 宋

Part 6. Please identify the components you have learned so far for each of the characters below and copy into the brackets:

1. 辔 bridle [ ][ ][ ]
2. 轵 axletree terminal [ ][ ]

Chinese Radical Exercise 36

Part 1. Write out the meaning for the radical below:

Radical and its variant	*Pinyin*	Meaning
阜 (阝)	fù	

Part 2. Copy the radical 阜 (阝):

Part 3. Add the radical for each character according to the sample given:

院	完	完	完	完	完	完	完

yard

Part 4. Find and circle the 阜 (阝) radical in the characters below:

陆　险　都　除　阿　附

Part 5. Based on your understanding of each radical's meaning, please choose an appropriate meaning for the following characters from the three possible choices:

1. (　　) 陵　a. high mound　b. high building　c. great canal
2. (　　) 秧　a. bedroom　b. bike　c. seedling

Part 6. Please identify the components you have learned so far for each of the characters below and copy into the brackets:

1. 阵 battle array　[　　][　　]
2. 队 team　[　　][　　]
3. 阳 sun　[　　][　　]

Chinese Radical Exercise37

Part 1. Write out the meaning for the radical below:

Radical and its variant	*Pinyin*	Meaning
示(礻)	shì	

Part 2. Copy the radical 示 (礻):

Part 3. Add the radical for each character according to the sample given:

视	见	见	见	见	见	见	见

to see; to consider as

Part 4. Find and circle the 示 (礻) radical in the characters below:

祖　衬　祟　神　京　社

Part 5. Please find the 示 radical in the characters below and copy into the brackets:

1. 祭 obit　[　　]
2. 神 divinity　[　　]
3. 祝 to wish　[　　]

汉字部首教程

Part 6. Please identify the components you have learned so far for each of the characters below and copy into the brackets:

1. 际 border [ ][ ]
2. 禁 ban [ ][ ]
3. 祁 a place name [ ][ ]

Chinese Radical Exercise 38

Part 1. Write out the meaning for the radical below:

Radical and its variants	*Pinyin*	Meaning
食（飠饣）	shí	

Part 2. Copy the radical 食（饣）:

Part 3. Add the radical for each character according to the sample given:

饱	包	包	包	包	包	包	包

full

Part 4. Find and circle the 食（饣）radical in the characters below:

饮　钱　餐　饼　饲　课

Part 5. Based on your understanding of each radical's meaning, please choose an appropriate English equivalent for each of the following characters from the three possible choices:

1. (　　) 饭　a. ceiling　b. meal　c. lamp
2. (　　) 饺　a. dumpling　b. vase　c. mop
3. (　　) 饿　a. sleepy　b. hungry　c. tired

汉字部首教程

Part 6. Please identify the components you have learned so far for each of the characters below and copy into the brackets:

1. 蚀 to erode [ ][ ]
2. 馆 restaurant [ ][ ]
3. 馅 filling (in a pie) [ ][ ]

Chinese Radical Exercise 39

Part 1. Write out the meaning for the radical below:

Radical	*Pinyin*	Meaning
酉	yǒu	

Part 2. Copy the radical 酉:

Part 3. Add the radical for each character according to the sample given:

配	己	己	己	己	己	己	己

to match

Part 4. Find and circle the 酉 radical in the characters below:

酿　醉　酸　洒　醋　酱

Part 5. Based on your understanding of each radical's meaning, please choose an appropriate meaning for the following characters from the three possible choices:

1. (　　) 醉　a. fast　b. drunk　c. full
2. (　　) 馆　a. tunnel　b. bridge　c. restaurant
3. (　　) 酌　a. to pour out liquor　b. to chop wood　c. to stroll the beach

汉字部首教程

Part 6. Please identify the components you have learned so far for each of the characters below and copy into the brackets:

1. 酥 crisp [ ][ ]
2. 醒 to wake [ ][ ]

Chinese Radical Exercise 40

Part 1. Write out the meaning for the radical below:

Radical and its variant	*Pinyin*	Meaning
八 (丷)	bā	

Part 2. Copy the radical 八 (丷):

Part 3. Add the radical for each character according to the sample given:

共	共	共	共	共	共	共	共

altogether

Part 4. Find and circle the 八 (丷) radical in the characters below:

弟　兴　关　兰　爱　养

Part 5. Please find the 八 radical in the characters below and copy into the brackets:

1. 单　[　　]
2. 公　[　　]

Part 6. Please identify the components you have learned so far for each of the characters below and copy into the brackets:

1. 贫 poor [ ][ ][ ]
2. 酋 chief of a tribe [ ][ ]
3. 曾 ever [ ][ ]

Chinese Radical Exercise 41

Part 1. Write out the meaning for the radical below:

Radical and its variant	*Pinyin*	Meaning
页(頁)	xié yè	

Part 2. Copy the radical 页:

Part 3. Add the radical for each character according to the sample given:

预	予	予	予	予	予	予	予

in advance

Part 4. Find and circle the 页 radical in the characters below:

颜　颖　赏　颈　题　顾

Part 5. Based on the meaning of the 页 radical, please choose an appropriate meaning for the following characters from the three possible choices:

1. (　　) 额　a. foot　b. forehead　c. elbow
2. (　　) 颌　a. fingers　b. knee　c. jaw

Part 6. Please identify the components you have learned so far for each of the characters below and copy into the brackets:

1. 烦 annoyed　[　　][　　]
2. 硕 large　[　　][　　]

Chinese Radical Exercise 42

Part 1. Write out the meaning for the radical below:

Radical	*Pinyin*	Meaning
巾 (stroke order 1, 2, 3)	jīn	

Part 2. Copy the radical 巾:

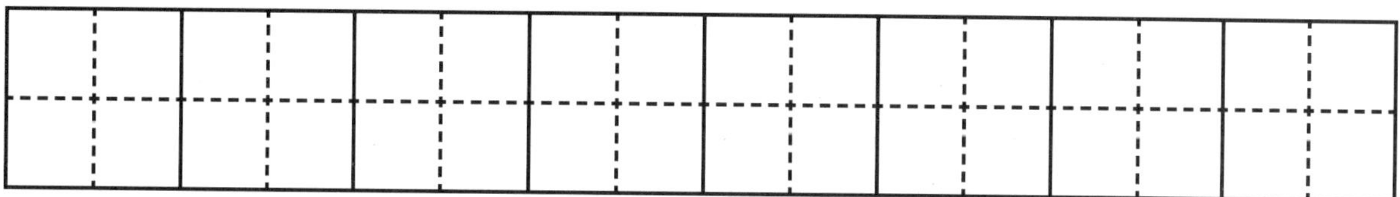

Part 3. Add the radical for each character according to the sample given:

帮	邦	邦	邦	邦	邦	邦	邦

to help

Part 4. Find and circle the 巾 radical in the characters below:

常　帅　帽　布　帆　篇

Part 5. Based on the meaning of the 巾 radical, please choose an appropriate meaning for the following characters from the three possible choices:

1. (　　) 帜　a. drum　b. flag　c. carriage
2. (　　) 帐　a. door　b. window　c. curtain
3. (　　) 帕　a. plow　b. bracelet　c. handkerchief

Part 6. Please identify the components you have learned so far for each of the characters below and copy into the brackets:

1. 帮 to help [ ][ ]
2. 幕 screen [ ][ ]

Chinese Radical Exercise 43

Part 1. Write out the meaning for the radical below:

Radical and its variant	*Pinyin*	Meaning
门 (門)	mén	

Part 2. Copy the radical 门:

Part 3. Add the radical for each character according to the sample given:

问	口	口	口	口	口	口	口

to ask

Part 4. Find and circle the 门 radical in the characters below:

闪　间　同　闰　冒　国

Part 5. Based on the sound of the 门 radical, please choose the correct *pinyin* for the following characters from the lists below:

1. (　　) 闷　a. bīn　b. yà　c. mēn
2. (　　) 问　a. jiào　b. wèn　c. yǒu

Part 6. Please identify the components you have learned so far for each of the characters below and copy into the brackets:

1. 闯 to barge in　[　　][　　]
2. 闲 not busy　[　　][　　]

Chinese Radical Exercise 44

Part 1. Write out the meaning for the radical below:

Radical	*Pinyin*	Meaning
广	yǎn guǎng	

Part 2. Copy the radical 广:

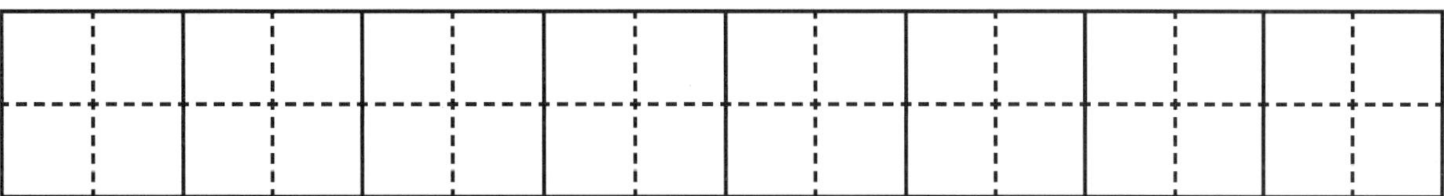

Part 3. Add the radical for each character according to the sample given:

庆	大	大	大	大	大	大	大

to celebrate

Part 4. Find and circle the 广 radical in the characters below:

床　应　新　店　厅　庭

Part 5. Based on the meaning of the 广 radical, please choose an appropriate meaning for the following characters from the three possible choices:

1. (　　) 库　a. warehouse　b. tea pot　c. disease
2. (　　) 庄　a. fee　b. door stop　c. village
3. (　　) 府　a. jacket　b. mansion　c. drink

Part 6. Please identify the components you have learned so far for each of the characters below and copy into the brackets:

1. 席 mat [ ][ ]
2. 麻 hemp [ ][ ]

Chinese Radical Exercise 45

Part 1. Write out the meaning for the radical below:

Radical	*Pinyin*	Meaning
大	dà	

Part 2. Copy the radical 大:

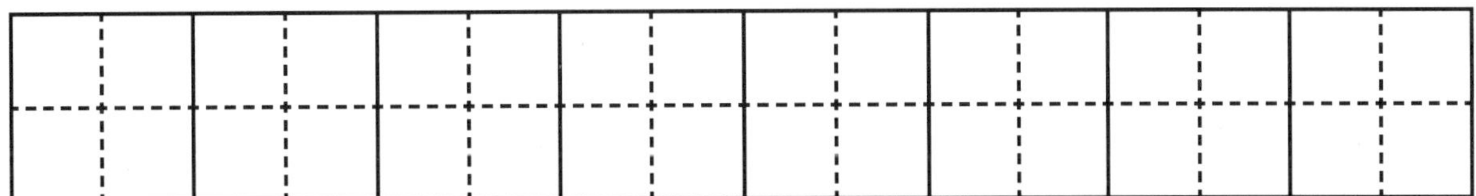

Part 3. Add the radical for each character according to the sample given:

奇	可	可	可	可	可	可	可

strange

Part 4. Find and circle the 大 radical in the characters below:

头　夺　太　集　套　奖

Part 5. Based on the meanings of the radicals you have learned, please choose the appropriate Chinese characters for the following English equivalents:

1. (　　) too　a. 太　b. 常　c. 闷
2. (　　) extravagant　a. 奢　b. 市　c. 间
3. (　　) profound　a. 带　b. 奥　c. 烦

Part 6. Please identify the components you have learned so far for each of the characters below and copy into the brackets:

1. 奈 how [ ][ ]
2. 奠 to establish [ ][ ][ ]

Chinese Radical Exercise 46

Part 1. Write out the meaning for the radical below:

Radical	*Pinyin*	Meaning
米	mǐ	

Part 2. Copy the radical 米:

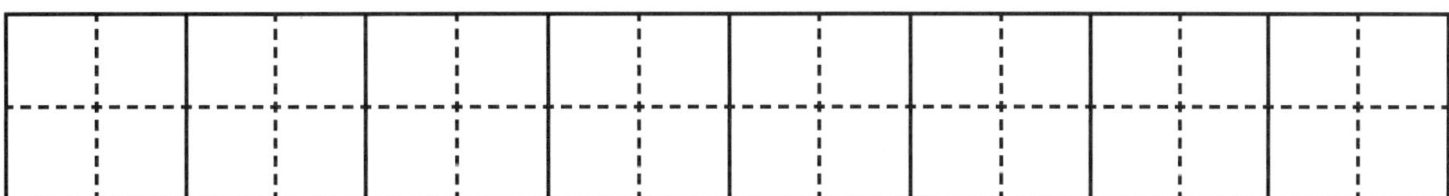

Part 3. Add the radical for each character according to the sample given:

messed up

Part 4. Find and circle the 米 radical in the characters below:

老 粒 娄 奖 粪 学

Part 5. Based on the meanings of the radicals you have learned, please choose the appropriate Chinese characters for the following English equivalents:

1. ( ) porridge a. 妈 b. 岩 c. 粥
2. ( ) millet a. 头 b. 粟 c. 门
3. ( ) cake a. 颜 b. 糕 c. 帮

Part 6. Please identify the components you have learned so far for each of the characters below and copy into the brackets:

1. 粽 rice dumpling [ ][ ][ ]
2. 类 kind [ ][ ]

Chinese Radical Exercise 47

Part 1. Write out the meaning for the radical below:

Radical	*Pinyin*	Meaning
田	tián	

Part 2. Copy the radical 田:

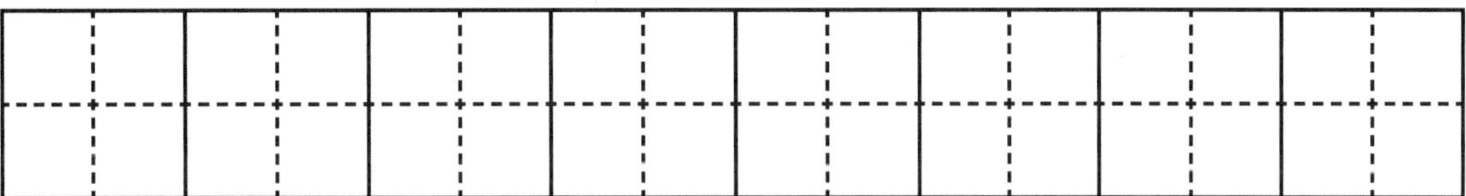

Part 3. Add the radical for each character according to the sample given:

男	力	力	力	力	力	力	力

man

Part 4. Find and circle the 田 radical in the characters below:

累　略　电　音　留　畏

Part 5. Based on the meaning of the 田 radical, please choose an appropriate meaning for the following characters from the three possible choices:

1. (　　) 界　a. boundary　b. sign　c. banner
2. (　　) 畦　a. forest　b. tower　c. farmland

Part 6. Please identify the components you have learned so far for each of the characters below and copy into the brackets:

1. 累 tired [ ][ ]
2. 胃 stomach [ ][ ]

Chinese Radical Exercise 48

Part 1. Write out the meaning for the radical below:

Radical	*Pinyin*	Meaning
十	shí	

Part 2. Copy the radical 十:

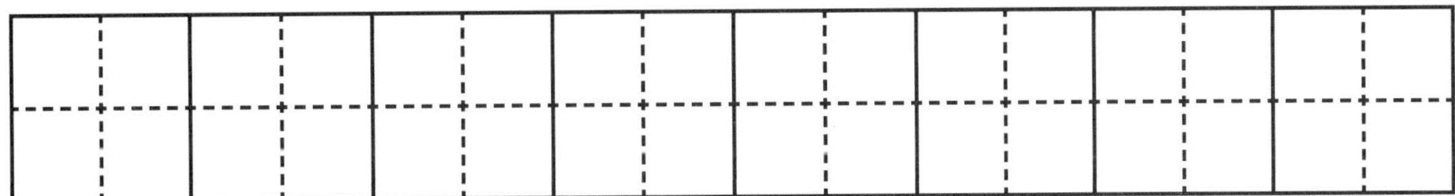

Part 3. Add the radical for each character according to the sample given:

协	办	办	办	办	办	办	办

to assist

Part 4. Find and circle the 十 radical in the characters below:

华　南　卉　丧　博　直

Part 5. Please find the components shared by the Chinese characters below and copy into the brackets:

1. 卓　朝　[　　][　　]
2. 克　古　[　　][　　]

Part 6. Please identify the components you have learned so far for each of the characters below and copy into the brackets:

1. 卖 to sell　[　　][　　]
2. 华 splendid　[　　][　　]

Chinese Radical Exercise 49

Part 1. Write out the meaning for the radical below:

Radical	*Pinyin*	Meaning
彳	chì	

Part 2. Copy the radical 彳:

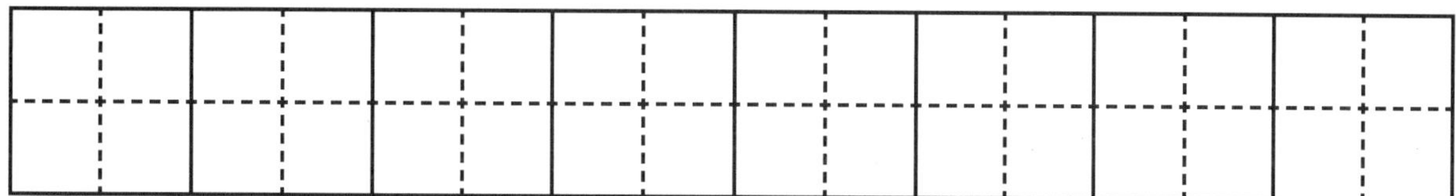

Part 3. Add the radical for each character according to the sample given:

很	艮	艮	艮	艮	艮	艮	艮

very

Part 4. Find and circle the 彳 radical in the characters below:

行　很　做　徊　街　衍

Part 5. Based on the meaning of the 彳 radical, please choose an appropriate meaning for the following characters from the three possible choices:

1. (　　) 往　a. to head for　b. to lay down　c. to dig in
2. (　　) 征　a. to dive into a pool　b. to plant on a farm　c. to go on a journey

Part 6. Please identify the components you have learned so far for each of the characters below and copy into the brackets:

1. 德 virtue; morals [ ][ ][ ]
2. 得 to get [ ][ ]

Chinese Radical Exercise 50

Part 1. Write out the meaning for the radical below:

Radical	*Pinyin*	Meaning
革	gé	

Part 2. Copy the radical 革:

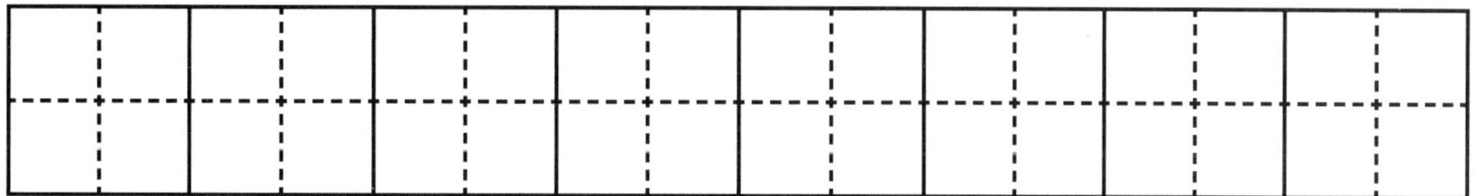

Part 3. Add the radical for each character according to the sample given:

鞋	圭	圭	圭	圭	圭	圭	圭

shoe(s)

Part 4. Find and circle the 革 radical in the characters below:

蛙　靴　甜　鞍　勒　带

Part 5. Based on the meaning of the 革 radical, please choose an appropriate meaning for the following characters from the three possible choices:

1. (　　) 靴　a. handkerchief　b. sweater　c. boots
2. (　　) 鞘　a. sheath　b. umbrella　c. table

Part 6. Please identify the components you have learned so far for each of the characters below and copy into the brackets:

1. 鞍 saddle　[　　][　　][　　]
2. 鞭 whip　[　　][　　]

Chinese Radical Exercise 51

Part 1. Write out the meaning for the radical below:

Radical and its variant	*Pinyin*	Meaning
攴(攵)	pū	

Part 2. Copy the radical 攴 (攵):

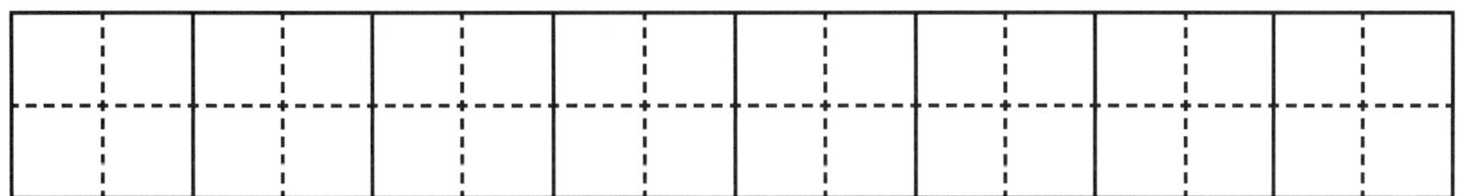

Part 3. Add the radical for each character according to the sample given:

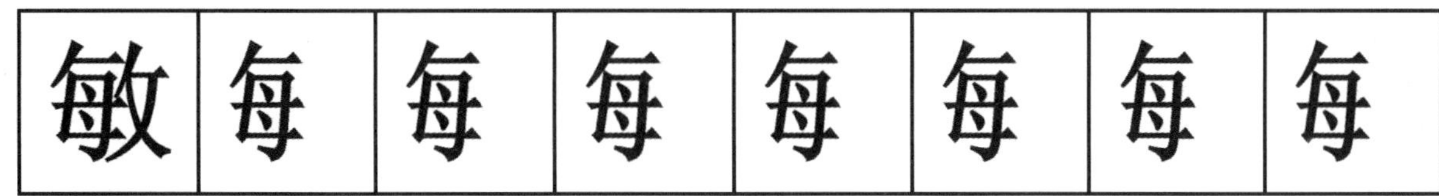

quick

Part 4. Find and circle the 攴 (攵) radical in the characters below:

政　敢　收　枝　敬　次

Part 5. Based on the meaning of the 攴 radical, please choose an appropriate meaning for the following characters from the three possible choices:

1. (　　) 教　a. to teach　b. to watch　c. to brag
2. (　　) 敷　a. to laugh at　b. to talk about　c. to lay out

Part 6. Please identify the components you have learned so far for each of the characters below and copy into the brackets:

1. 故 on purpose [ ] [ ] [ ]
2. 败 to fail [ ] [ ]
3. 数 to count [ ] [ ] [ ]

Chinese Radical Exercise 52

Part 1. Write out the meaning for the radical below:

Radical	*Pinyin*	Meaning
戈	gē	

Part 2. Copy the radical 戈 :

Part 3. Add the radical for each character according to the sample given:

划	刂	刂	刂	刂	刂	刂	刂

to paddle

Part 4. Find and circle the 戈 radical in the characters below:

戎　或　代　戒　必　戳

Part 5. Based on the meaning of the 戈 radical, please choose an appropriate meaning for the following characters from the three possible choices:

1. (　　) 战　a. war　b. party　c. tutor
2. (　　) 成　a. to jump　b. to succeed　c. to laugh
3. (　　) 戎　a. material affairs　b. love affairs　c. military affairs

漢字部首教程

Part 6. Please find the components shared by the Chinese characters below and copy into the brackets:

幾　戴　　[　　][　　]

Chinese Radical Exercise 53

Part 1. Write out the meaning for the radical below:

Radical	*Pinyin*	Meaning
尸	shī	

Part 2. Copy the radical 尸 :

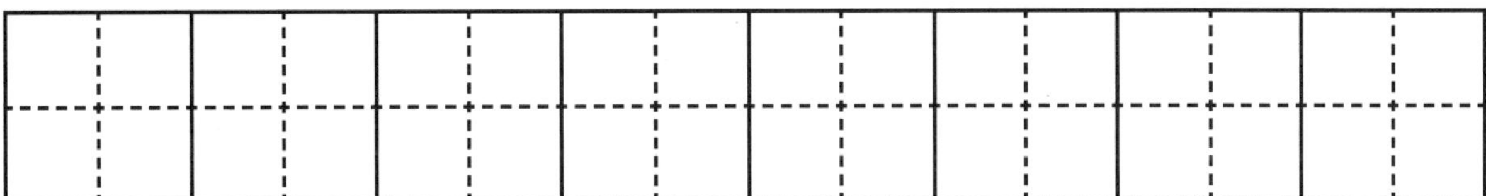

Part 3. Add the radical for each character according to the sample given:

尼	匕	匕	匕	匕	匕	匕	匕

nun

Part 4. Find and circle the 尸 radical in the characters below:

层　尾　眉　属　屏　肩

Part 5. Based on your understanding of each radical's meaning, please choose an appropriate meaning for the following characters from the three possible choices:

1. (　　) 屠　a. holiday　b. reunion　c. slaughter
2. (　　) 威　a. by force　b. on sale　c. off duty

Part 6. Please identify the components you have learned so far for each of the characters below and copy into the brackets:

1. 屎 excrement [ ][ ]
2. 居 to live [ ][ ][ ]

Chinese Radical Exercise 54

Part 1. Write out the meaning for the radical below:

Radical	*Pinyin*	Meaning
穴 (stroke order 1–5)	xué	

Part 2. Copy the radical 穴 :

Part 3. Add the radical for each character according to the sample given:

空	工	工	工	工	工	工	工

empty

Part 4. Find and circle the 穴 radical in the characters below:

穷 穿 写 家 窗 高

Part 5. Based on the meanings of the radicals you have learned, please choose the appropriate Chinese characters for the following English equivalents:

1. ( ) window a. 放 b. 窗 c. 我
2. ( ) narrow a. 呢 b. 或 c. 窄

汉字部首教程

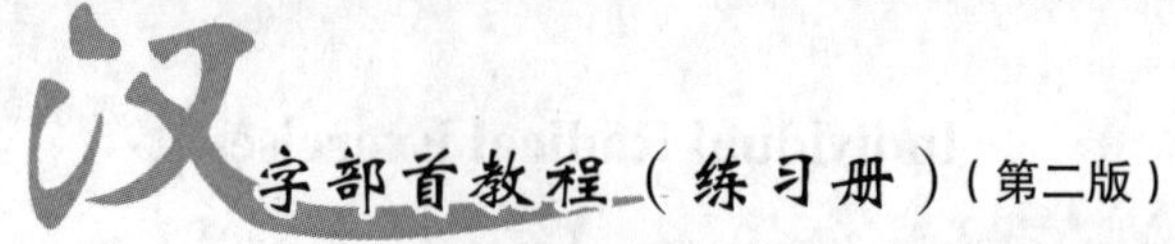

Part 6. Please identify the components you have learned so far for each of the characters below and copy into the brackets:

1. 突 sticking out; sudden [ ][ ]
2. 帘 curtain [ ][ ]

Chinese Radical Exercise 55

Part 1. Write out the meaning for the radical below:

Radical	*Pinyin*	Meaning
力	lì	

Part 2. Copy the radical 力 :

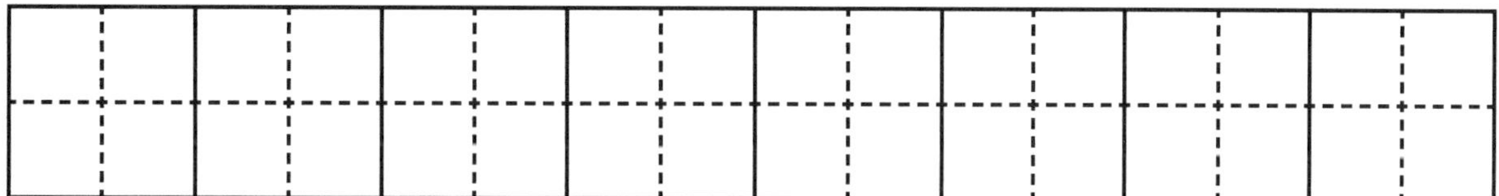

Part 3. Add the radical for each character according to the sample given:

加	口	口	口	口	口	口	口

to add

Part 4. Find and circle the 力 radical in the characters below:

劣　助　分　劲　易　动

Part 5. Based on the sounds of the radicals you have learned, please choose the correct *pinyin* for the following characters from the lists below:

1. (　　) 历　a. lì　b. fàn　c. shuō
2. (　　) 屎　a. shǐ　b. pǎo　c. lù
3. (　　) 荔　a. tāng　b. chǔn　c. lì

Part 6. Please identify the components you have learned so far for each of the characters below and copy into the brackets:

1. 男 man [ ][ ]
2. 架 fight; frame [ ][ ][ ]

Chinese Radical Exercise 56

Part 1. Write out the meaning for the radical below:

Radical	*Pinyin*	Meaning
舟	zhōu	

Part 2. Copy the radical 舟 :

Part 3. Add the radical for each character according to the sample given:

船	㕣	㕣	㕣	㕣	㕣	㕣	㕣

boat

Part 4. Find and circle the 舟 radical in the characters below:

盘　丹　舰　每　般　服

Part 5. Based on your understanding of each radical's meaning, please choose an appropriate meaning for the following characters from the three possible choices:

1. (　　) 航　a. holiday　b. to navigate　c. slaughter
2. (　　) 舵　a. basement　b. wheel　c. rudder
3. (　　) 劳　a. to work hard　b. to think fast　c. to run slowly

漢字部首教程

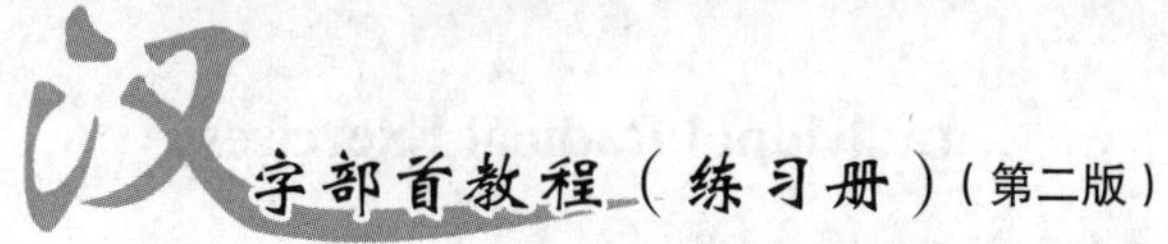

Part 6. Please identify the components you have learned so far for each of the characters below and copy into the brackets:

1. 舱 a cabin of a ship [ ][ ]
2. 船 ship; boat [ ][ ]
3. 舵 a rudder or helm [ ][ ]

Chinese Radical Exercise 57

Part 1. Write out the meaning for the radical below:

Radical	*Pinyin*	Meaning
囗	wéi	

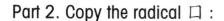

Part 2. Copy the radical 囗 :

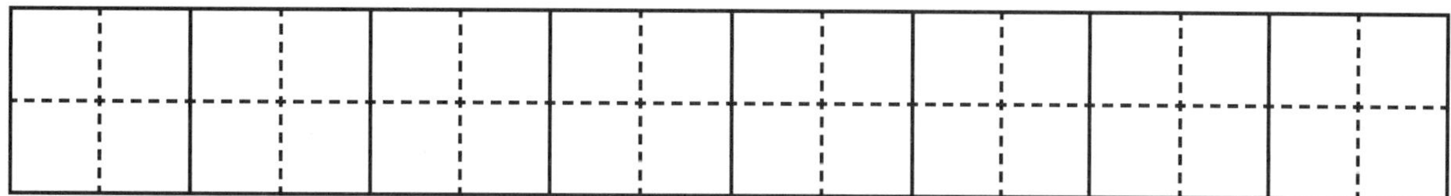

Part 3. Add the radical for each character according to the sample given:

回	口	口	口	口	口	口	口

to return

Part 4. Find and circle the 囗 radical in the characters below:

团　回　吃　齿　图　明

Part 5. Based on your understanding of each radical's meaning, please choose an appropriate meaning for the following characters from the three possible choices:

1. (　　) 囚　a. to imprison　b. to set free　c. sold out
2. (　　) 墙　a. ocean　b. moonlight　c. wall
3. (　　) 困　a. to surround　b. to quarrel　c. to exercise

Part 6. Please identify the components you have learned so far for each of the characters below and copy into the brackets:

1. 回 to return [ ][ ]
2. 国 country [ ][ ]
3. 因 because; due to [ ][ ]

Chinese Radical Exercise 58

Part 1. Write out the meaning for the radical below:

Radical and its variant	*Pinyin*	Meaning
雨 (⻗)	yǔ	

Part 2. Copy the radical 雨 (⻗):

Part 3. Add the radical for each character according to the sample given:

雪	彐	彐	彐	彐	彐	彐	彐

snow

Part 4. Find and circle the 雨 (⻗) radical in the characters below:

需 要 霉 罚 雷 霞

Part 5. Based on the meanings of the radicals you have learned, please choose the appropriate Chinese characters for the following English equivalents:

1. ( ) thunder a. 雷 b. 空 c. 成
2. ( ) dew a. 船 b. 露 c. 图

Part 6. Please identify the components you have learned so far for each of the characters below and copy into the brackets:

1. 霸 to dominate [ ][ ][ ]
2. 雷 thunder [ ][ ]

漢字部首教程

Chinese Radical Exercise 59

Part 1. Write out the meaning for the radical below:

Radical	*Pinyin*	Meaning
厂 (stroke order: 1→, 2↓)	hǎn chǎng	

Part 2. Copy the radical 厂 :

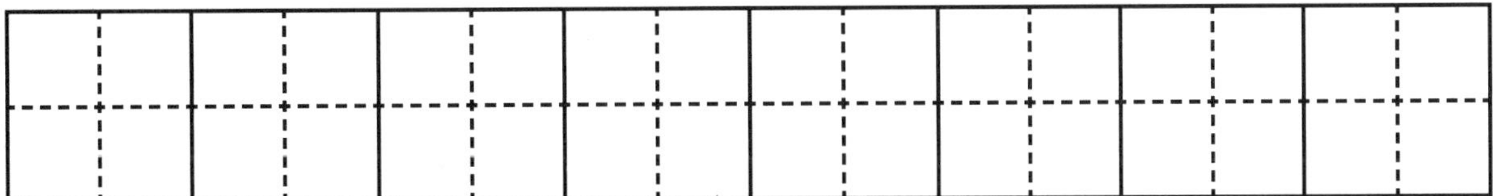

Part 3. Add the radical for each character according to the sample given:

厅	丁	丁	丁	丁	丁	丁	丁
hall							

Part 4. Find and circle the 厂 radical in the characters below:

床　厨　后　病　历　厕

Part 5. Based on the meanings of the radicals you have learned, please choose the appropriate Chinese characters for the following English equivalents:

1. (　　) mansion　a. 盘　b. 厦　c. 四
2. (　　) compartment　a. 雪　b. 厢　c. 层
3. (　　) collapse　a. 压　b. 收　c. 生

Part 6. Please identify the components you have learned so far for each of the characters below and copy into the brackets:

1. 厕 restroom [ ][ ][ ]
2. 历 to go through [ ][ ]

Chinese Radical Exercise 60

Part 1. Write out the meaning for the radical below:

Radical	*Pinyin*	Meaning
又	yòu	

Part 2. Copy the radical 又 :

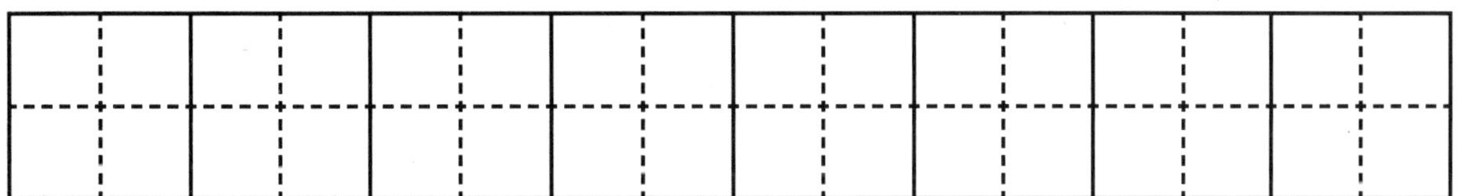

Part 3. Add the radical for each character according to the sample given:

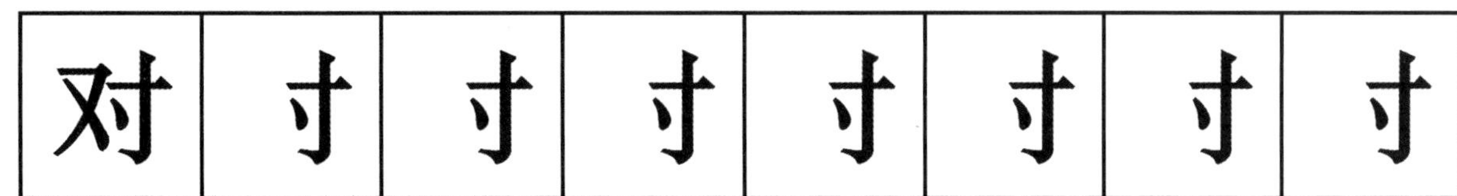

right

Part 4. Find and circle the 又 radical in the characters below:

邓　双　爸　欢　难　受

Part 5. Based on your understanding of each radical's meaning, please choose the appropriate Chinese characters for the following English equivalents:

1. (　　) double　a. 双　b. 律　c. 妹
2. (　　) snow　a. 在　b. 雪　c. 般
3. (　　) overlap　a. 钢　b. 叠　c. 醋

Part 6. Please identify the components you have learned so far for each of the characters below and copy into the brackets:

1. 戏 a play [ ][ ]
2. 慢 slow [ ][ ][ ]

漢字部首教程

Chinese Radical Exercise 61

Part 1. Write out the meaning for the radical below:

Radical and its variant	*Pinyin*	Meaning
牛(牜)	niú	

Part 2. Copy the radical 牛 (牜):

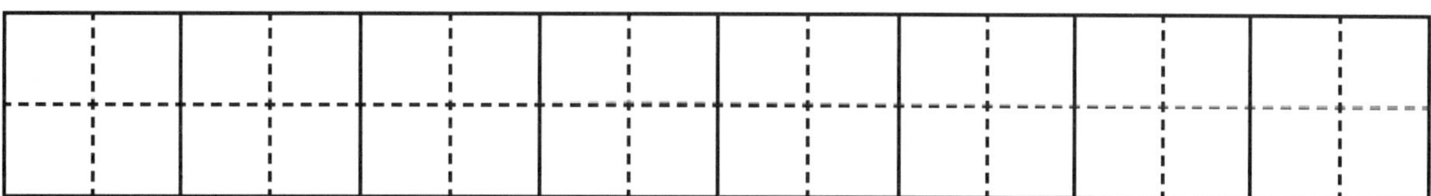

Part 3. Add the radical for each character according to the sample given:

特	寺	寺	寺	寺	寺	寺	寺

special

Part 4. Find and circle the 牛 (牜) radical in the characters below:

物　程　犟　坏　牡　报

Part 5. Based on the meanings of the radicals you have learned, please choose the appropriate Chinese characters for the following English equivalents:

1. (　　) calf　　a. 厅　　b. 犊　　c. 难
2. (　　) livestock　　a. 牲　　b. 很　　c. 和
3. (　　) right　　a. 对　　b. 床　　c. 酒

Part 6. Please identify the components you have learned so far for each of the characters below and copy into the brackets:

1. 犁 to work with a plough [ ][ ][ ]
2. 牧 to herd [ ][ ]

Chinese Radical Exercise 62

Part 1. Write out the meaning for the radical below:

Radical	*Pinyin*	Meaning
皿 (stroke order 1–5)	mǐn	

Part 2. Copy the radical 皿 :

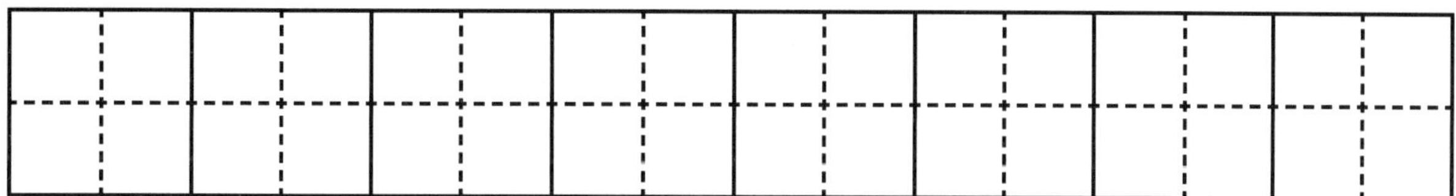

Part 3. Add the radical for each character according to the sample given:

盐	圤	圤	圤	圤	圤	圤	圤

salt

Part 4. Find and circle the 皿 radical in the characters below:

监　具　益　耶　盛　留

Part 5. Based on the meanings of the radicals you have learned, please choose the appropriate Chinese characters for the following English equivalents:

1. (　　) pot　　a. 友　　b. 靠　　c. 盆
2. (　　) helmet　　a. 办　　b. 盔　　c. 空
3. (　　) to spill over　　a. 视　　b. 间　　c. 盈

Part 6. Please identify the components you have learned so far for each of the characters below and copy into the brackets:

1. 盛 to fill [ ][ ]
2. 盟 alliance [ ][ ][ ]

Chinese Radical Exercise 63

Part 1. Write out the meaning for the radical below:

Radical and its variant	*Pinyin*	Meaning
仌(冫)	bīng	

Part 2. Copy the radical 冫 :

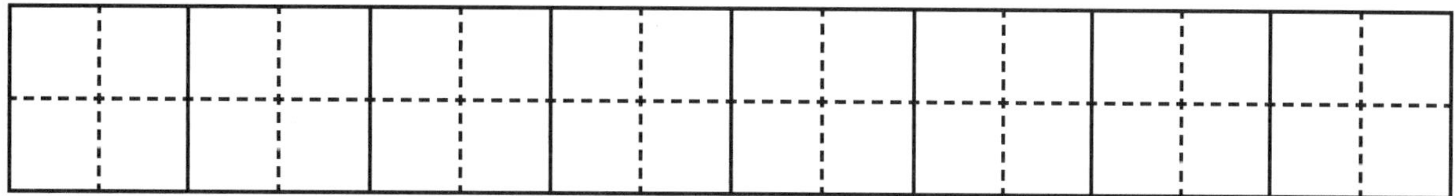

Part 3. Add the radical for each character according to the sample given:

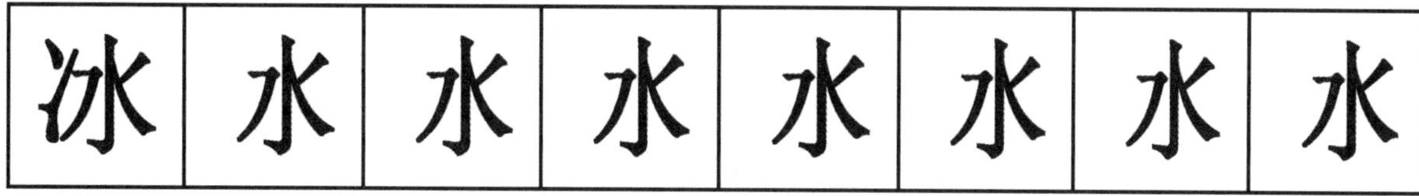

ice

Part 4. Find and circle the 冫 radical in the characters below:

习　次　冲　法　净　壮

Part 5. Based on the meaning of the 冫 radical, please choose an appropriate meaning for the following characters from the three possible choices:

1. (　　) 冷　a. warm　b. cold　c. hot
2. (　　) 凉　a. able　b. amiable　c. cool

Part 6. Please identify the components you have learned so far for each of the characters below and copy into the brackets:

1. 冯 a surname [ ][ ]
2. 凛 piercingly cold [ ][ ][ ][ ]

Chinese Radical Exercise 64

Part 1. Write out the meaning for the radical below:

Radical	*Pinyin*	Meaning
羽	yǔ	

Part 2. Copy the radical 羽 :

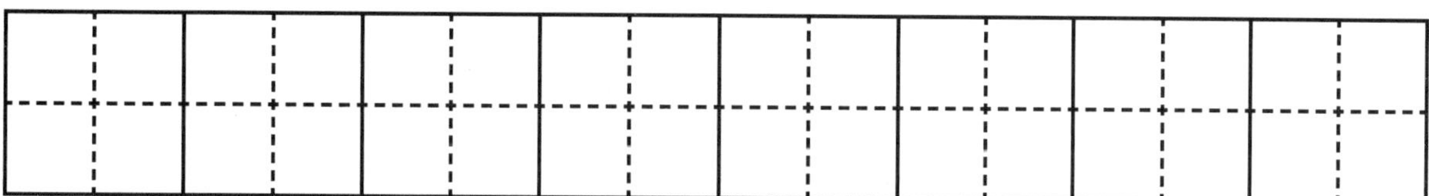

Part 3. Add the radical for each character according to the sample given:

翘	尧	尧	尧	尧	尧	尧	尧

to raise

Part 4. Find and circle the 羽 radical in the characters below:

翠　翟　翩　那　翻　非

Part 5. Based on your understanding of each radical's meaning, please choose the appropriate Chinese characters for the following English equivalents:

1. ( ) wing　a. 翅　b. 习　c. 告
2. ( ) frozen　a. 特　b. 对　c. 冻
3. ( ) to fly　a. 姐　b. 翔　c. 好

Part 6. Please identify the components you have learned so far for each of the characters below and copy into the brackets:

1. 翼 wing [ ][ ][ ]
2. 翱 to hover [ ][ ][ ]

Chinese Radical Exercise 65

Part 1. Write out the meaning for the radical below:

Radical and its variants	*Pinyin*	Meaning
羊(⺶⺷)	yáng	

Part 2. Copy the radical 羊 (⺶⺷):

Part 3. Add the radical for each character according to the sample given:

群	君	君	君	君	君	君	君

a crowd or group

Part 4. Find and circle the 羊 (⺶⺷) radical in the characters below:

姜　着　当　羔　差　前

Part 5. Based on the sounds of the radicals you have learned, please choose the correct *pinyin* for the following characters from the lists below:

1. (　　) 养　a. rè　b.yǎng　c. sù
2. (　　) 冰　a. lù　b. bào　c. bīng
3. (　　) 样　a. yàng　b. hòu　c. kū

Part 6. Please identify the components you have learned so far for each of the characters below and copy into the brackets:

1. 着 auxiliary word [ ][ ]
2. 美 pretty [ ][ ]

Chinese Radical Exercise 66

Part 1. Write out the meaning for the radical below:

Radical	*Pinyin*	Meaning
弓	gōng	

Part 2. Copy the radical 弓 :

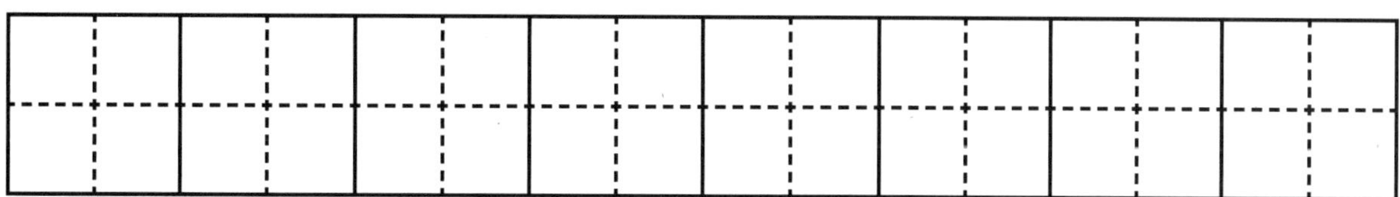

Part 3. Add the radical for each character according to the sample given:

张	长	长	长	长	长	长	长

a sheet of

Part 4. Find and circle the 弓 radical in the characters below:

弛　改　弱　弯　弹　强

Part 5. Based on the meanings of the radicals you have learned, please choose the appropriate Chinese characters for the following English equivalents:

1. (　　) arc　　a. 弧　　b. 姜　　c. 冷
2. (　　) bowstring　　a. 图　　b. 弦　　c. 难
3. (　　) to bend　　a. 弯　　b. 穿　　c. 脚

Part 6. Please identify the components you have learned so far for each of the characters below and copy into the brackets:

1. 疆 boundary [ ][ ][ ]
2. 粥 porridge [ ][ ]
3. 弩 crossbow [ ][ ][ ]

Chinese Radical Exercise 67

Part 1. Write out the meaning for the radical below:

Radical and its variant	*Pinyin*	Meaning
歹(歺)	è dǎi	

Part 2. Copy the radical 歹 (歺):

Part 3. Add the radical for each character according to the sample given:

残	戋	戋	戋	戋	戋	戋	戋

deficient

Part 4. Find and circle the 歹 (歺) radical in the characters below:

死　多　殁　殖　花　殊

Part 5. Based on the meaning of the radical, please choose an appropriate meaning for the following characters from the three possible choices:

1. (　　) 死　a. to blow　b. to live　c. to die
2. (　　) 殆　a. special　b. dangerous　c. beautiful

Part 6. Please identify the components you have learned so far for each of the characters below and copy into the brackets:

1. 餐 meal　[　　][　　][　　]
2. 列 list　[　　][　　]

汉字部首教程

Chinese Radical Exercise 68

Part 1. Write out the meaning for the radical below:

Radical and its variant	*Pinyin*	Meaning
小 (⺌)	xiǎo	

Part 2. Copy the radical 小 (⺌):

Part 3. Add the radical for each character according to the sample given:

当	⺌	⺌	⺌	⺌	⺌	⺌	⺌

to regard as

Part 4. Find and circle the 小 (⺌) radical in the characters below:

尘　京　肖　半　光　尝　关

Part 5. Based on the meaning of the 小 radical, please choose an appropriate meaning for the following characters from the three possible choices:

1. (　　) 少　a. long　b. many　c. few
2. (　　) 雀　a. cloud　b. eagle　c. sparrow

Part 6. Please identify the components you have learned so far for each of the characters below and copy into the brackets:

1. 尖 pointed　[　　][　　]
2. 裳 skirt; clothing　[　　][　　][　　]

汉字部首教程

Chinese Radical Exercise 69

Part 1. Write out the meaning for the radical below:

Radical	*Pinyin*	Meaning
欠 (stroke order 1–4)	qiàn	

Part 2. Copy the radical 欠 :

Part 3. Add the radical for each character according to the sample given:

歇	曷	曷	曷	曷	曷	曷	曷

to rest

Part 4. Find and circle the 欠 radical in the characters below:

欧　收　歌　款　条　饿

Part 5. Based on your understanding of each radical's meaning, please choose an appropriate meaning for the following characters from the three possible choices:

1. (　　) 歌　a. song　b. footprint　c. thought
2. (　　) 尘　a. dust　b. picture　c. breath
3. (　　) 歉　a. to dig　b. to apologize　c. to plant

Part 6. Please identify the components you have learned so far for each of the characters below and copy into the brackets:

1. 软 soft [ ][ ]
2. 欢 cheerful [ ][ ]

Chinese Radical Exercise 70

Part 1. Write out the meaning for the radical below:

Radical	*Pinyin*	Meaning
子 (stroke order 1→ 2↓ 3→)	zǐ	

Part 2. Copy the radical 子 :

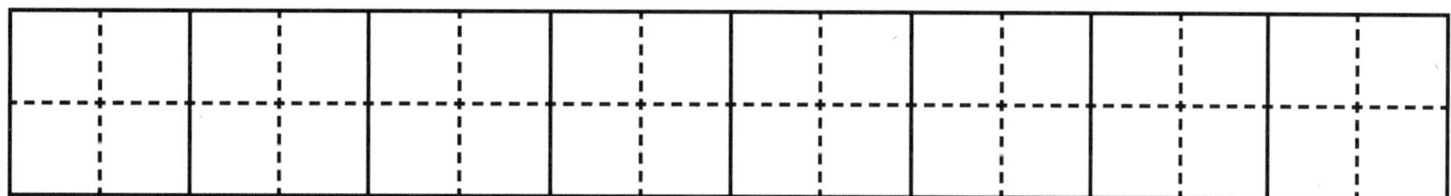

Part 3. Add the radical for each character according to the sample given:

学	𭕄	𭕄	𭕄	𭕄	𭕄	𭕄	𭕄

to learn

Part 4. Find and circle the 子 radical in the characters below:

孔　孩　孕　存　推　熟

Part 5. Based on the meaning of the 子 radical, please choose an appropriate meaning for the following characters from the three possible choices:

1. (　　) 孙　a. father-in-law　b. grandmother　c. grandson
2. (　　) 孤　a. orphan　b. elderly　c. soldier

Part 6. Please identify the components you have learned so far for each of the characters below and copy into the brackets:

1. 李 plum [ ][ ]
2. 盂 a surname [ ][ ]

Chinese Radical Exercise 71

Part 1. Write out the meaning for the radical below:

Radical	*Pinyin*	Meaning
隹	zhuī	

Part 2. Copy the radical 隹:

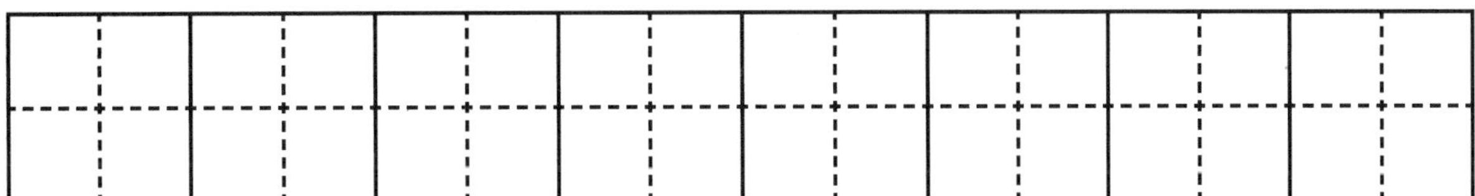

Part 3. Add the radical for each character according to the sample given:

售	口	口	口	口	口	口	口

to sell

Part 4. Find and circle the 隹 radical in the characters below:

焦　作　遍　截　便　雕

Part 5. Based on the meanings of the radicals you have learned, please choose the appropriate Chinese characters for the following English equivalents:

1. (　　) burnt　　a. 共　　b. 焦　　c. 习
2. (　　) sparrow　　a. 迎　　b. 路　　c. 雀
3. (　　) gather　　a. 集　　b. 字　　c. 饺

Part 6. Please identify the components you have learned so far for each of the characters below and copy into the brackets:

1. 售 to sell [ ][ ]
2. 耀 to shine [ ][ ][ ]

Chinese Radical Exercise 72

Part 1. Write out the meaning for the radical below:

Radical	*Pinyin*	Meaning
耳 (stroke order: 1→ 2↓ 3↓ 4→ 5→ 6→)	ěr	

Part 2. Copy the radical 耳 :

Part 3. Add the radical for each character according to the sample given:

聊	卯	卯	卯	卯	卯	卯	卯

to chat

Part 4. Find and circle the 耳 radical in the characters below:

闻　取　联　聚　眼　职

Part 5. Based on your understanding of each radical's meaning, please choose an appropriate meaning for the following characters from the three possible choices:

1. (　　) 闻　a. close　b. lack　c. to hear
2. (　　) 聋　a. busy　b. deaf　c. bored
3. (　　) 雉　a. snail　b. pheasant　c. beaver

Part 6. Please identify the components you have learned so far for each of the characters below and copy into the brackets:

1. 取 to take [ ][ ]
2. 耿 upright [ ][ ]

Chinese Radical Exercise 73

Part 1. Write out the meaning for the radical below:

Radical	*Pinyin*	Meaning
白	bái	

Part 2. Copy the radical 白 :

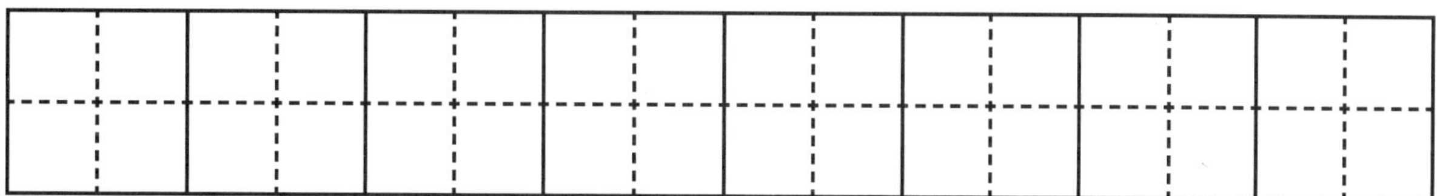

Part 3. Add the radical for each character according to the sample given:

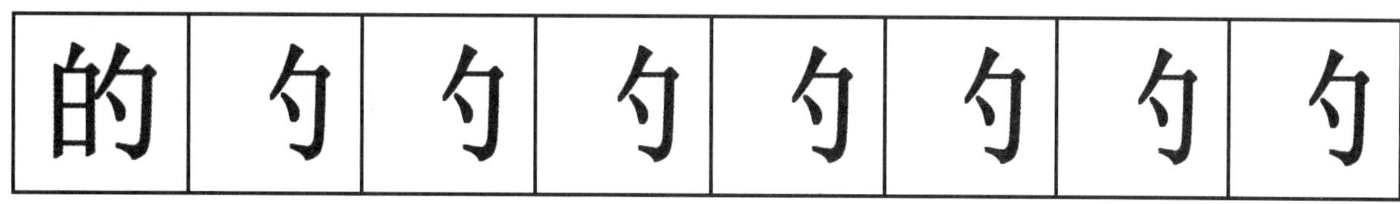

of

Part 4. Find and circle the 白 radical in the characters below:

晳　皆　早　皓　皂　时

Part 5. Based on the sounds of the radicals you have learned, please choose the correct *pinyin* for the following characters from the lists below:

1. (　　) 百　a. bǎi　b. qún　c. wēng
2. (　　) 饵　a. ěr　b. liú　c. jù
3. (　　) 帛　a. chéng　b. wù　c. bó

Part 6. Please identify the components you have learned so far for each of the characters below and copy into the brackets:

1. 皇 emperor [ ][ ]
2. 泉 spring water [ ][ ]

Chinese Radical Exercise 74

Part 1. Write out the meaning for the radical below:

Radical	*Pinyin*	Meaning
骨	gǔ	

Part 2. Copy the radical 骨 :

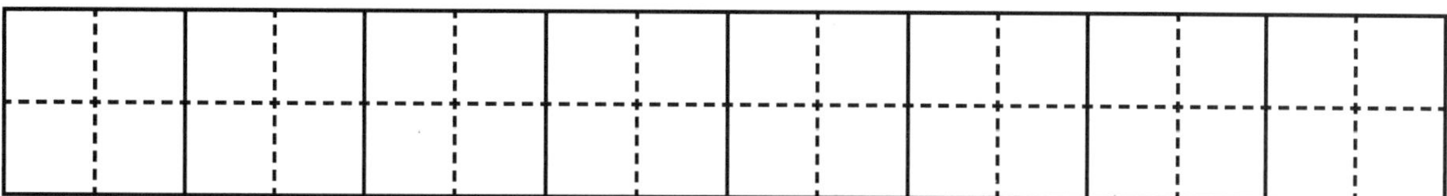

Part 3. Add the radical for each character according to the sample given:

骼	各	各	各	各	各	各	各

bone

Part 4. Find and circle the 骨 radical in the characters below:

骰　局　骸　蜗　骼　橘

Part 5. Based on your understanding of each radical's meaning, please choose an appropriate meaning for the following characters from the three possible choices:

1. (　　) 骸　a. warm　b. skeleton　c. hot
2. (　　) 皙　a. fair-complexioned　b. dark-complexioned　c. political complexion
3. (　　) 骷　a. skin　b. skull　c. vein

Part 6. Please identify the components you have learned so far for each of the characters below and copy into the brackets:

1. 髅 skeleton [ ][ ][ ]
2. 骰 dice [ ][ ]

Chinese Radical Exercise 75

Part 1. Write out the meaning for the radical below:

Radical	*Pinyin*	Meaning
立	lì	

Part 2. Copy the radical 立 :

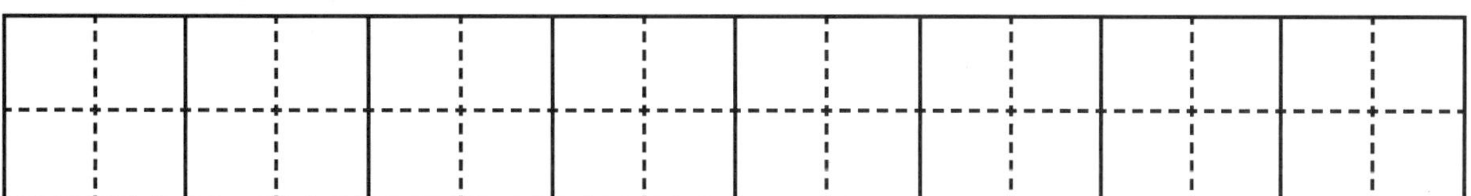

Part 3. Add the radical for each character according to the sample given:

站	占	占	占	占	占	占	占

a station or stop

Part 4. Find and circle the 立 radical in the characters below:

竞　亲　竖　究　教　产

Part 5. Based on your understanding of each radical's meaning, please choose an appropriate meaning for the following characters from the three possible choices:

1. (　　) 端　a. to feed　b. to fill　c. to carry
2. (　　) 竖　a. downward　b. erect　c. horizontal
3. (　　) 聊　a. to choke　b. to swallow　c. to gossip

Part 6. Please identify the components you have learned so far for each of the characters below and copy into the brackets:

1. 章 a seal or stamp [ ][ ][ ]
2. 意 meaning [ ][ ][ ]

Chinese Radical Exercise 76

Part 1. Write out the meaning for the radical below:

Radical and its variant	*Pinyin*	Meaning
见(見)	jiàn	

Part 2. Copy the radical 见 :

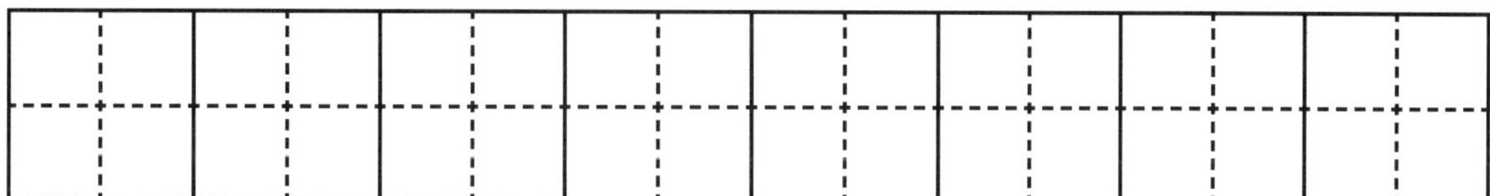

Part 3. Add the radical for each character according to the sample given:

觉	𭕄	𭕄	𭕄	𭕄	𭕄	𭕄	𭕄
asleep							

Part 4. Find and circle the 见 radical in the characters below:

视　览　费　规　厕　觅

Part 5. Based on the meanings of the radicals you have learned, please choose the appropriate Chinese characters for the following English equivalents:

1. (　　) to look at　a. 视　b. 童　c. 聪
2. (　　) chick　a. 雏　b. 翔　c. 好
3. (　　) to view　a. 踢　b. 览　c. 饮

Part 6. Please identify the components you have learned so far for each of the characters below and copy into the brackets:

1. 视 to look at [ ][ ]
2. 现 to show [ ][ ]

Chinese Radical Exercise 77

Part 1. Write out the meaning for the radical below:

Radical	*Pinyin*	Meaning
厶	sī	

Part 2. Copy the radical 厶 :

Part 3. Add the radical for each character according to the sample given:

能	能	能	能	能	能	能	能

to be able to

Part 4. Find and circle the 厶 radical in the characters below:

矣　允　能　范　参　台

Part 5. Please find the components shared by the Chinese characters below and copy into the brackets:

1. 脚　能　[　　][　　]
2. 怡　惨　[　　][　　]

漢字部首教程

Part 6. Please identify the components you have learned so far for the characters below and copy into the brackets:

1. 篡 to seize position illegally [ ][ ][ ][ ]
2. 牟 a surname [ ][ ]

Chinese Radical Exercise 78

Part 1. Write out the meaning for the radical below:

Radical	*Pinyin*	Meaning
毛 (stroke order 1, 2, 3, 4)	máo	

Part 2. Copy the radical 毛 :

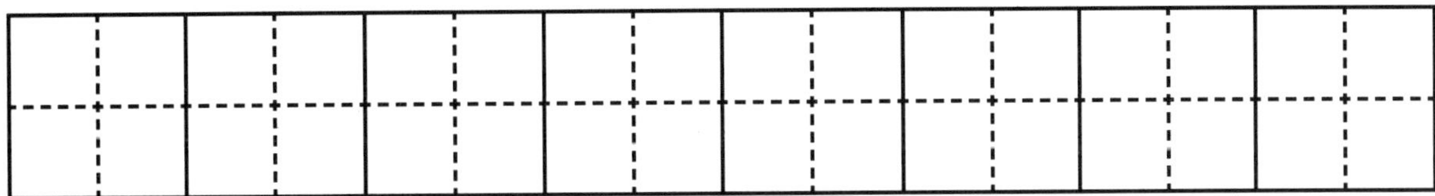

Part 3. Add the radical for each character according to the sample given:

尾	尸	尸	尸	尸	尸	尸	尸

tail

Part 4. Find and circle the 毛 radical in the characters below:

麾　毯　提　毡　街

Part 5. Based on the meaning of the 毛 radical, please choose an appropriate meaning for the following characters from the three possible choices:

1. (　　) 毯　a. notebook　b. plastic　c. rug
2. (　　) 毫　a. thick soup　b. fine hair　c. dark coffee

Part 6. Please identify the components you have learned so far for each of the characters below and copy into the brackets:

1. 笔 pen [ ][ ]
2. 尾 tail; end [ ][ ]

Chinese Radical Exercise 79

Part 1. Write out the meaning for the radical below:

Radical and its variant	*Pinyin*	Meaning
卜 (⺊)	bǔ	

Part 2. Copy the radical 卜 (⺊):

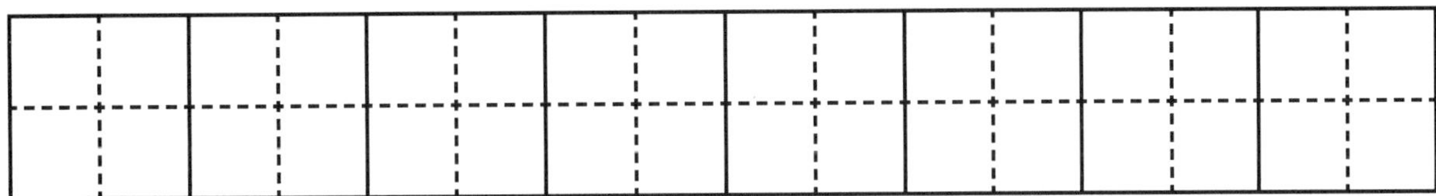

Part 3. Add the radical for each character according to the sample given:

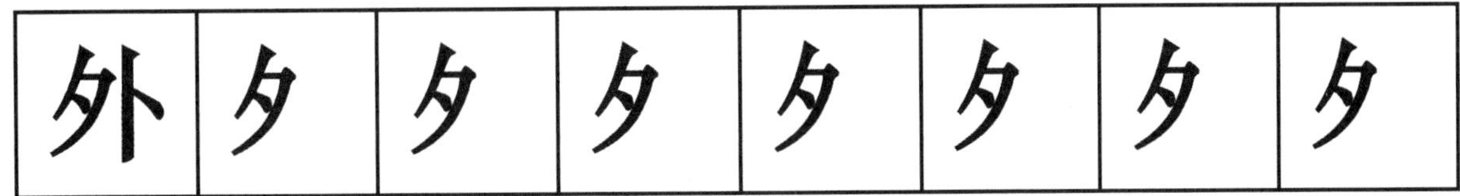

outside

Part 4. Find and circle the 卜 (⺊) radical in the characters below:

占　古　卧　贞　真

Part 5. Based on the sounds of the radicals you have learned, please choose the correct *pinyin* for the following characters from the lists below:

1. (　　) 补　a. wēi　b. bǔ　c. fēn
2. (　　) 赴　a. gāo　b. yǒng　c. fù
3. (　　) 私　a. sī　b. tiáo　c. běn

Part 6. Please identify the components you have learned so far for each of the characters below and copy into the brackets:

1. 卦 divinatory symbols [ ][ ]
2. 桌 table [ ][ ][ ]

Chinese Radical Exercise 80

Part 1. Write out the meaning for the radical below:

Radical and its variant	*Pinyin*	Meaning
齿(齒)	chǐ	

Part 2. Copy the radical 齿 :

Part 3. Add the radical for each character according to the sample given:

龄	令	令	令	令	令	令	令

age

Part 4. Find and circle the 齿 radical in the characters below:

龄　龈　龃　脑　龉

Part 5. Based on the meaning of the 齿 radical, please choose an appropriate meaning for the following characters from the three possible choices:

1. (　　) 龋　a. dental caries　b. toes　c. hands
2. (　　) 龈　a. hip　b. gum　c. chest
3. (　　) 龅　a. fish-bellied　b. bull-headed　c. buck-toothed

汉字部首教程

Part 6. Please identify the components you have learned so far for the character below and copy into the brackets:

齷 filthy　[　　][　　]

Chinese Radical Exercise 81

Part 1. Write out the meaning for the radical below:

Radical	*Pinyin*	Meaning
方	fāng	

Part 2. Copy the radical 方 :

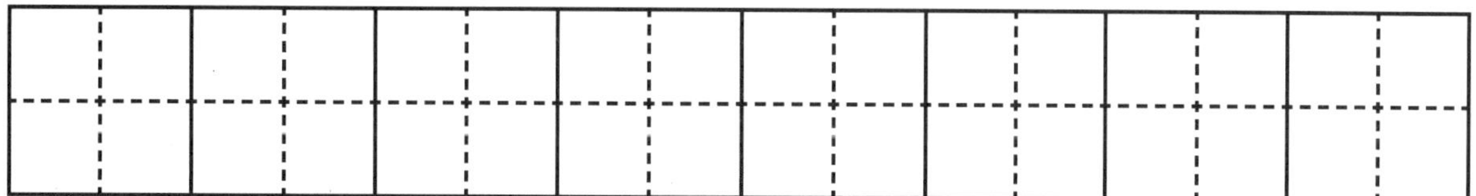

Part 3. Add the radical for each character according to the sample given:

旁	亠	亠	亠	亠	亠	亠	亠

side

Part 4. Find and circle the 方 radical in the characters below:

放　旗　物　族　旅　家

Part 5. Based on the sound of the 方 radical, please choose the correct *pinyin* for the following characters from the lists below:

1. (　　) 房　a. fáng　b. zì　c. hǔ
2. (　　) 芳　a. shè　b. zhū　c. fāng
3. (　　) 访　a. niǔ　b. ěr　c. fǎng

Part 6. Please identify the components you have learned so far for each of the characters below and copy into the brackets:

1. 放 to put [ ][ ]
2. 旎 ancient flag ornament [ ][ ]

Chinese Radical Exercise 82

Part 1. Write out the meaning for the radical below:

Radical	*Pinyin*	Meaning
黑	hēi	

Part 2. Copy the radical 黑 :

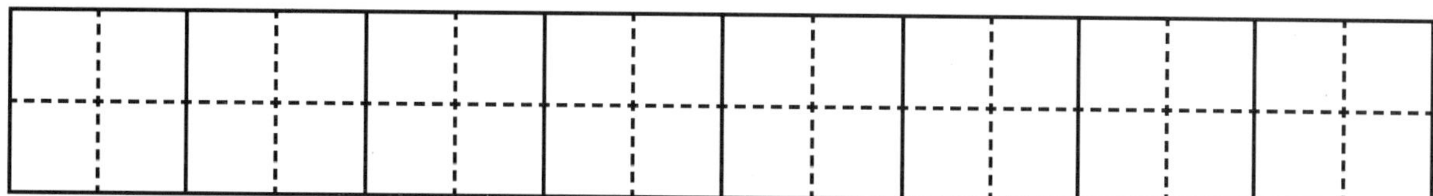

Part 3. Add the radical for each character according to the sample given:

默	犬	犬	犬	犬	犬	犬	犬

silent

Part 4. Find and circle the 黑 radical in the characters below:

墨　黜　然　黛　焦　摩

Part 5. Based on the meaning of the 黑 radical, please choose an appropriate meaning for the following characters from the three possible choices:

1. (　　) 墨　a. pastry　b. ink　c. yolk
2. (　　) 黔　a. to flirt　b. to blacken　c. to pump
3. (　　) 黝　a. dark　b. light　c. medium

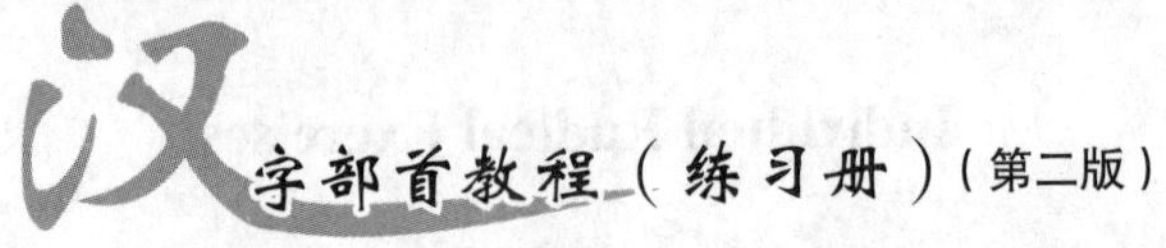

Part 6. Please identify the components you have learned so far for each of the characters below and copy into the brackets:

1. 黯 dim; gloomy [ ][ ][ ]
2. 嘿 hey [ ][ ]

Chinese Radical Exercise 83

Part 1. Write out the meaning for the radical below:

Radical	*Pinyin*	Meaning
殳	shū	

Part 2. Copy the radical 殳 :

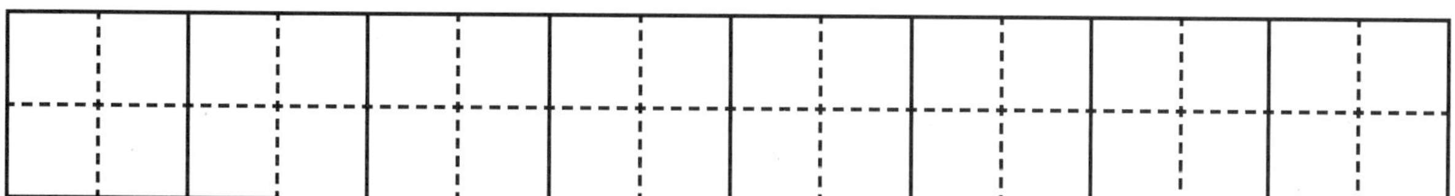

Part 3. Add the radical for each character according to the sample given:

殿	㞋	㞋	㞋	㞋	㞋	㞋	㞋

palace

Part 4. Find and circle the 殳 radical in the characters below:

段　般　友　毅　炼　放

Part 5. Based on the meaning of the 殳 radical, please choose an appropriate meaning for the following characters from the three possible choices:

1. (　　) 殴　a. to drive away　b. to slow down　c. to beat up
2. (　　) 毁　a. to damage　b. gum　c. chest
3. (　　) 殁　a. to talk　b. to die　c. to stand

Part 6. Please identify the components you have learned so far for each of the characters below and copy into the brackets:

1. 股 thigh [ ][ ]
2. 投 to throw [ ][ ]

Chinese Radical Exercise 84

Part 1. Write out the meaning for the radical below:

Radical	*Pinyin*	Meaning
儿	rén ér	

Part 2. Copy the radical 儿 :

Part 3. Add the radical for each character according to the sample given:

先	生	生	生	生	生	生	生

first

Part 4. Find and circle the 儿 radical in the characters below:

党　先　亮　光　风　兆

Part 5. Please find the components shared by the Chinese characters below and copy into the brackets:

1. 说　党　[　　][　　]
2. 竟　竞　[　　][　　]

汉字部首教程

Part 6. Please identify the radicals you have learned so far for each of the characters below and copy the components into the brackets:

1. 允 to permit [ ][ ]
2. 兄 elder brother [ ][ ]

Chinese Radical Exercise 85

Part 1. Write out the meaning for the radical below:

Radical	*Pinyin*	Meaning
彡	shān	

Part 2. Copy the radical 彡 :

Part 3. Add the radical for each character according to the sample given:

影	景	景	景	景	景	景	景
shadow							

Part 4. Find and circle the 彡 radical in the characters below:

形　往　处　彦　彩　钱

Part 5. Based on the sound of the 彡 radical, please choose the correct *pinyin* for the following characters from the lists below:

1. (　　) 衫　a. tuī　b. shān　c. jié
2. (　　) 参　a. cān　b. yíng　c. gòng
3. (　　) 钐　a. què　b. mù　c. shān

Part 6. Please identify the components you have learned so far for each of the characters below and copy into the brackets:

1. 杉 cedar [ ][ ]
2. 须 beard [ ][ ]

Chinese Radical Exercise 86

Part 1. Write out the meaning for the radical below:

Radical	*Pinyin*	Meaning
气	qì	

Part 2. Copy the radical 气 :

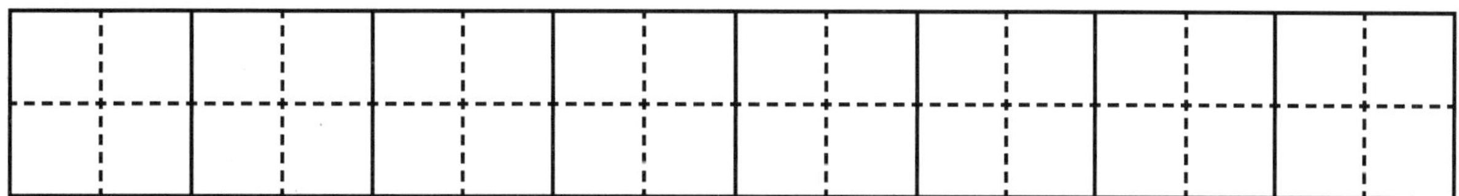

Part 3. Add the radical for each character according to the sample given:

氛	分	分	分	分	分	分	分

atmosphere

Part 4. Find and circle the 气 radical in the characters below:

氧　年　氮　飞　氯　朗

Part 5. Based on the meaning of the 气 radical, please choose an appropriate meaning for the following characters from the three possible choices:

1. (　　) hydrogen　a. 氢　b. 钟　c. 雄
2. (　　) atmosphere　a. 拐　b. 氛　c. 视
3. (　　) nitrogen　a. 聪　b. 氮　c. 鱼

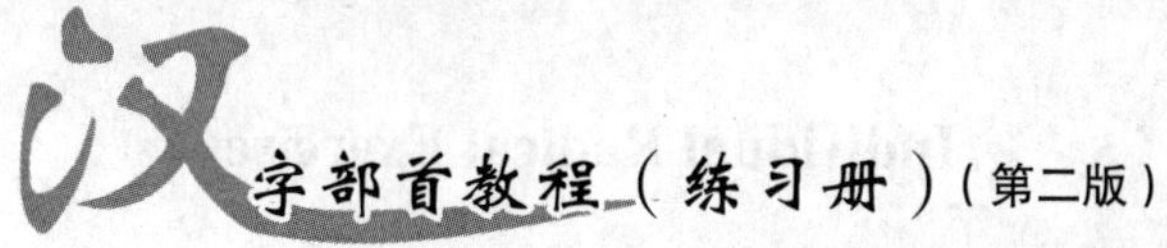

Part 6. Please identify the components you have learned so far for each of the characters below and copy into the brackets:

1. 汽 vapor　　[　　][　　]
2. 氨 ammonia　　[　　][　　][　　]

Chinese Radical Exercise 87

Part 1. Write out the meaning for the radical below:

Radical	*Pinyin*	Meaning
勹 (stroke order 1, 2)	bāo	

Part 2. Copy the radical 勹 :

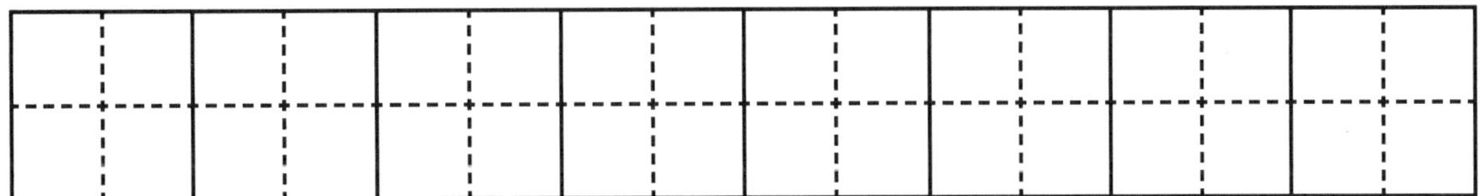

Part 3. Add the radical for each character according to the sample given:

句	口	口	口	口	口	口	口
sentence							

Part 4. Find and circle the 勹 radical in the characters below:

包　同　充　匆　篇　勾

Part 5. Based on the sound of the 勹 radical, please choose the correct *pinyin* for the following characters from the lists below:

1. (　　) 饱　a. qǔ　b. chuò　c. bǎo
2. (　　) 豹　a. gǔ　b. yín　c. bào
3. (　　) 跑　a. jiē　b. pǎo　c. tí

Part 6. Please identify the components you have learned so far for each of the characters below and copy into the brackets:

1. 匀 even up; smooth [ ][ ]
2. 钩 hook [ ][ ][ ]
3. 旬 a period of ten days [ ][ ]

Chinese Radical Exercise 88

Part 1. Write out the meaning for the radical below:

Radical and its variant	*Pinyin*	Meaning
爪（爫）	zhǎo	

Part 2. Copy the radical 爪（爫）:

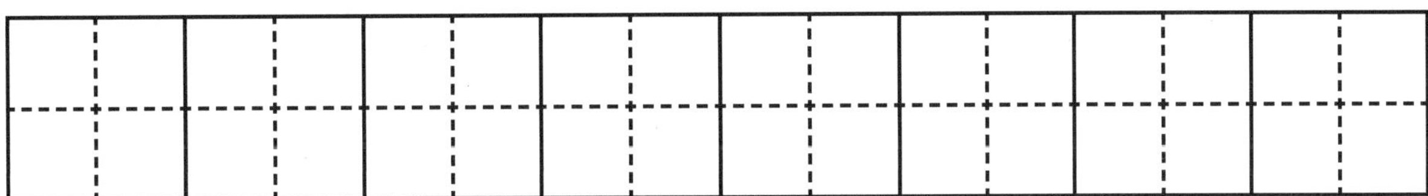

Part 3. Add the radical for each character according to the sample given:

爱	冖友	冖友	冖友	冖友	冖友	冖友	冖友
love							

Part 4. Find and circle the 爪（爫）radical in the characters below:

爬　爱　悉　孚　觅　尾

Part 5. Based on your understanding of each radical's meaning, please choose an appropriate meaning for the following characters from the three possible choices:

1. (　　) 爬　a. to assume　b. to cry　c. to climb
2. (　　) 采　a. to pluck　b. to dance　c. to smile
3. (　　) 舀　a. to yell　b. to scoop　c. to stare

Part 6. Please identify the components you have learned so far for each of the characters below and copy into the brackets:

1. 彩 color [ ][ ][ ]

2. 妥 ready [ ][ ]

Chinese Radical Exercise 89

Part 1. Write out the meaning for the radical below:

Radical	*Pinyin*	Meaning
瓦	wǎ	

Part 2. Copy the radical 瓦 :

Part 3. Add the radical for each character according to the sample given:

瓶	并	并	并	并	并	并	并

bottle

Part 4. Find and circle the 瓦 radical in the characters below:

瓷　每　瓯　瓶　处　散

Part 5. Based on the meanings of the radicals you have learned, please choose the appropriate Chinese characters for the following English equivalents:

1. (　　) vase　a. 爱　b. 元　c. 瓶
2. (　　) porcelain　a. 旅　b. 瓷　c. 影

Part 6. Please identify the components you have learned so far for each of the characters below and copy into the brackets:

1. 瓮 an earthen jar or urn　[　　][　　][　　]
2. 瓷 porcelain　[　　][　　][　　]

Chinese Radical Exercise 90

Part 1. Write out the meaning for the radical below:

Radical	*Pinyin*	Meaning
走	zǒu	

Part 2. Copy the radical 走:

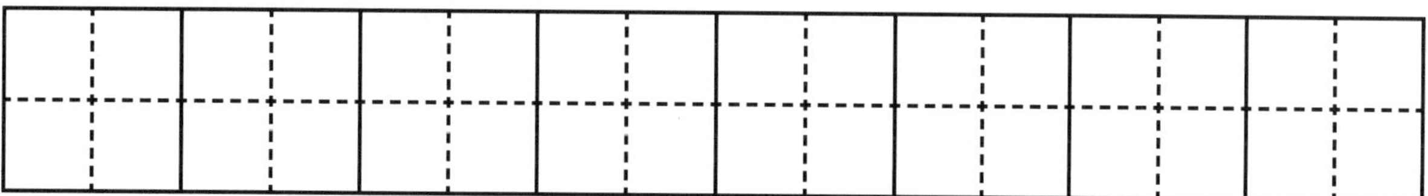

Part 3. Add the radical for each character according to the sample given:

起	己	己	己	己	己	己	己

to get up or rise

Part 4. Find and circle the 走 radical in the characters below:

赵　越　步　超　定　邵

Part 5. Based on the meaning of the 走 radical, please choose an appropriate meaning for the following characters from the three possible choices:

1. (　　) to go beyond　a. 超　b. 受　c. 瓶
2. (　　) to catch up with　a. 影　b. 墨　c. 赶
3. (　　) to hurry off to　a. 旁　b. 趋　c. 汽

Part 6. Please identify the components you have learned so far for each of the characters below and copy into the brackets:

1. 趣 interesting [ ][ ][ ]
2. 赴 to go to [ ][ ]

Chinese Radical Exercise 91

Part 1. Write out the meaning for the radical below:

Radical	*Pinyin*	Meaning
匚	fāng	

Part 2. Copy the radical 匚 :

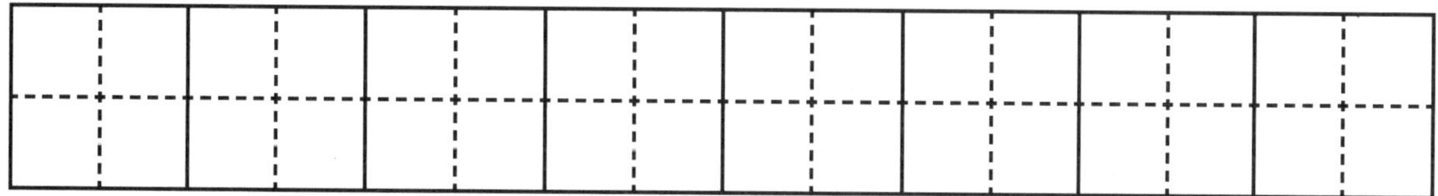

Part 3. Add the radical for each character according to the sample given:

医	矢	矢	矢	矢	矢	矢	矢

doctor

Part 4. Find and circle the 匚 radical in the characters below:

匠　再　区　巨　出　匹

Part 5. Based on the meaning of the 匚 radical, please choose an appropriate meaning for the following characters from the three possible choices:

1. (　　) 匣　a. rolling rock　b. small box　c. spring water
2. (　　) 匿　a. to fight　b. to turn　c. to conceal

Part 6. Please identify the components you have learned so far for each of the characters below and copy into the brackets:

1. 砸 to smash　[　　][　　][　　]
2. 筐 basket　[　　][　　][　　]

Chinese Radical Exercise 92

Part 1. Write out the meaning for the radical below:

Radical	*Pinyin*	Meaning
户	hù	

Part 2. Copy the radical 户 :

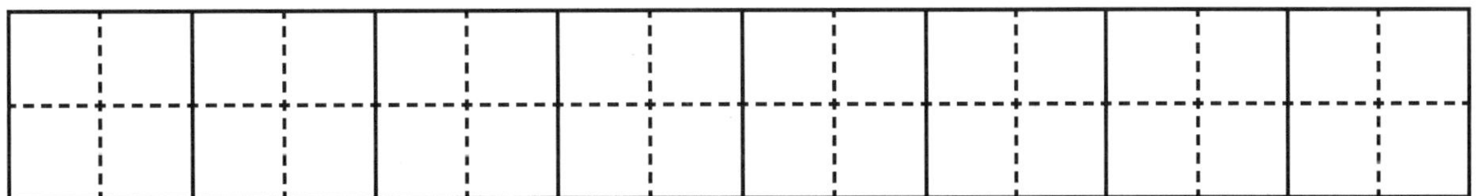

Part 3. Add the radical for each character according to the sample given:

肩	月	月	月	月	月	月	月

shoulder

Part 4. Find and circle the 户 radical in the characters below:

扉　启　局　戾　呃　扈

Part 5. Based on the meaning of the 户 radical, please choose an appropriate meaning for the following characters from the three possible choices:

1. (　　) house　　a. 房　　b. 龄　　c. 站
2. (　　) to open　　a. 么　　b. 启　　c. 船

Part 6. Please identify the components you have learned so far for each of the characters below and copy into the brackets:

1. 扇 a leaf (of doors); a fan　　[　　][　　]
2. 雇 to employ　　[　　][　　]

Chinese Radical Exercise 93

Part 1. Write out the meaning for the radical below:

Radical	*Pinyin*	Meaning
工 (1→ 2↓ 3→)	gōng	

Part 2. Copy the radical 工 :

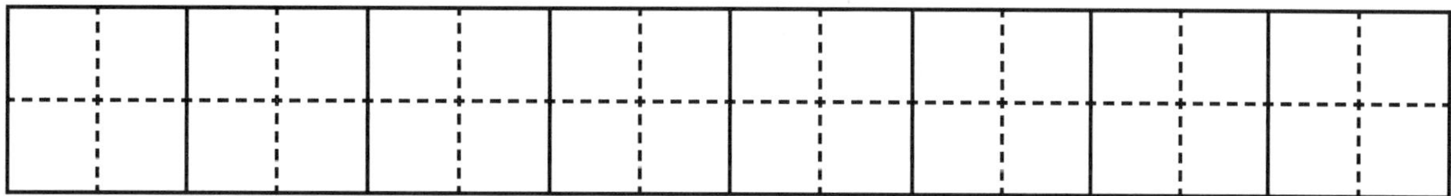

Part 3. Add the radical for each character according to the sample given:

功	力	力	力	力	力	力	力

achievement

Part 4. Find and circle the 工 radical in the characters below:

分　左　巫　贡　地　努

Part 5. Based on the sounds of the radicals you have learned, please choose the correct *pinyin* for the following characters from the lists below:

1. (　　) 功　a. qù　b. tǎn　c. gōng
2. (　　) 护　a. hù　b. yún　c. shì
3. (　　) 红　a. kū　b. de　c. hóng

Part 6. Please identify the components you have learned so far for each of the characters below and copy into the brackets:

1. 攻 to attack [ ][ ]
2. 项 nape of the neck [ ][ ]

Chinese Radical Exercise 94

Part 1. Write out the meaning for the radical below:

Radical	*Pinyin*	Meaning
止 (stroke order 1–4)	zhǐ	

Part 2. Copy the radical 止 :

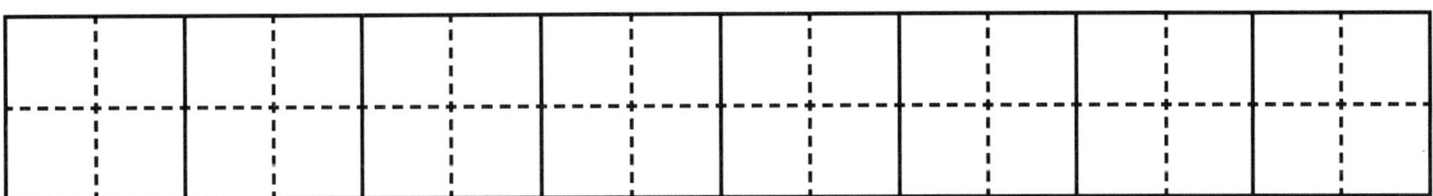

Part 3. Add the radical for each character according to the sample given:

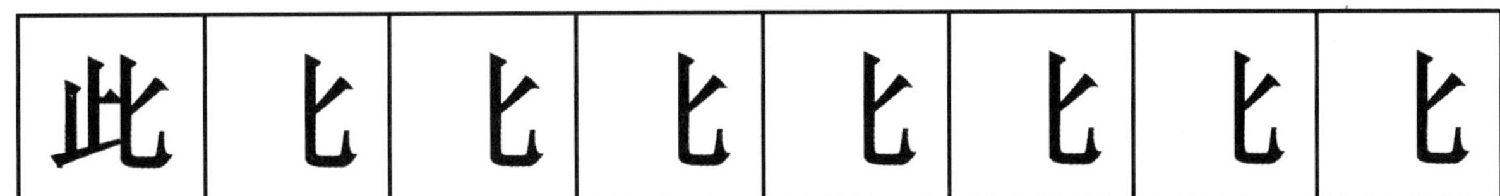

this

Part 4. Find and circle the 止 radical in the characters below:

晾　　些　　步　　武　　负　　走

Part 5. Based on the sound of the 止 radical, please choose the correct *pinyin* for the following characters from the lists below:

1. (　　) 齿　　a. wù　　b. chǐ　　c. fāng
2. (　　) 雌　　a. lǎn　　b. máo　　c. cí
3. (　　) 址　　a. zhǐ　　b. méng　　c. duān

Part 6. Please identify the components you have learned so far for each of the characters below and copy into the brackets:

1. 耻 shame [ ] [ ]
2. 肯 to be willing to [ ] [ ]

Chinese Radical Exercise 95

Part 1. Write out the meaning for the radical below:

Radical	*Pinyin*	Meaning
寸	cùn	

Part 2. Copy the radical 寸：

Part 3. Add the radical for each character according to the sample given:

封	圭	圭	圭	圭	圭	圭	圭

envelop

Part 4. Find and circle the 寸 radical in the characters below:

寿　央　封　财　太　右

Part 5. Please find the component(s) shared by the Chinese characters below and copy into the brackets:

1. 导　时　[　　]
2. 寺　封　[　　][　　]

Part 6. Please identify the components you have learned so far for each of the characters below and copy into the brackets:

1. 对 correct　[　　][　　]
2. 尉 lieutenant　[　　][　　][　　]

Chinese Radical Exercise 96

Part 1. Write out the meaning for the radical below:

Radical	*Pinyin*	Meaning
夂	zhǐ	

Part 2. Copy the radical 夂 :

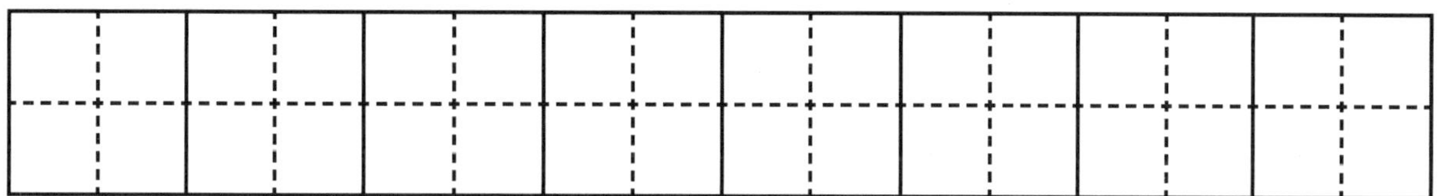

Part 3. Add the radical for each character according to the sample given:

a long narrow strip or piece

Part 4. Find and circle the 夂 radical in the characters below:

冬　政　处　吹　各　夏

Part 5. Based on your understanding of each radical's meaning, please choose an appropriate meaning for the following characters from the three possible choices:

1. (　　) 趾　a. shoulder　b. elbows　c. toes
2. (　　) 备　a. to test　b. to prepare　c. to hurry
3. (　　) 务　a. affair　b. plate　c. fence

Part 6. Please identify the components you have learned so far for each of the characters below and copy into the brackets:

1. 咎 to blame [ ][ ][ ]
2. 惫 tired [ ][ ][ ]

Chinese Radical Exercise 97

Part 1. Write out the meaning for the radical below:

Radical	*Pinyin*	Meaning
矢 (1 2 3 4 5)	shǐ	

Part 2. Copy the radical 矢 :

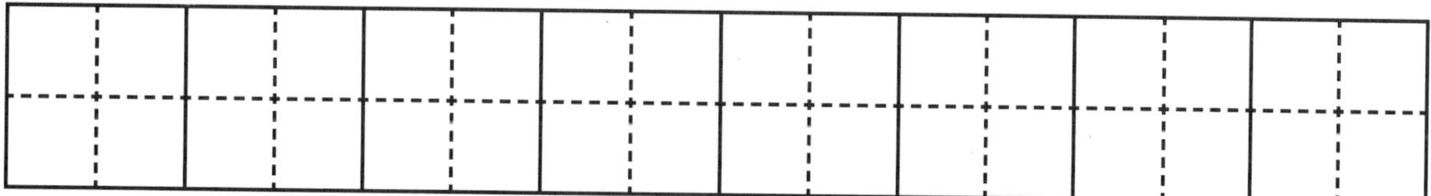

Part 3. Add the radical for each character according to the sample given:

知	日	日	日	日	日	日	日

to know

Part 4. Find and circle the 矢 radical in the characters below:

矫　短　失　鸟　问　矮

Part 5. Please find the components shared by the Chinese characters below and copy into the brackets:

医　矩　　[　　][　　]

Part 6. Please identify the components you have learned so far for each of the characters below and copy into the brackets:

1. 矮 short　　[　　][　　][　　]
2. 雉 pheasant　[　　][　　]

Chinese Radical Exercise 98

Part 1. Write out the meaning for the radical below:

Radical	*Pinyin*	Meaning
斤	jīn	

Part 2. Copy the radical 斤 :

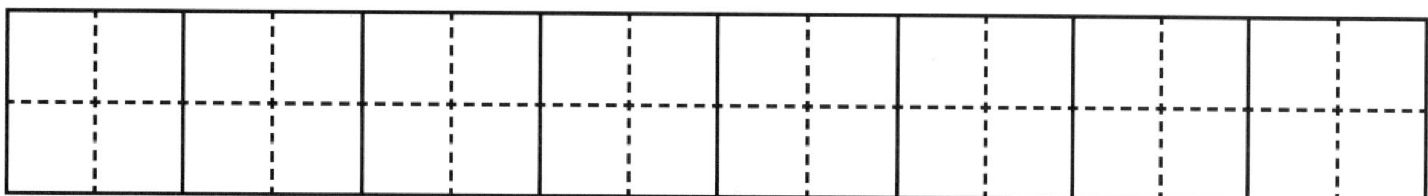

Part 3. Add the radical for each character according to the sample given:

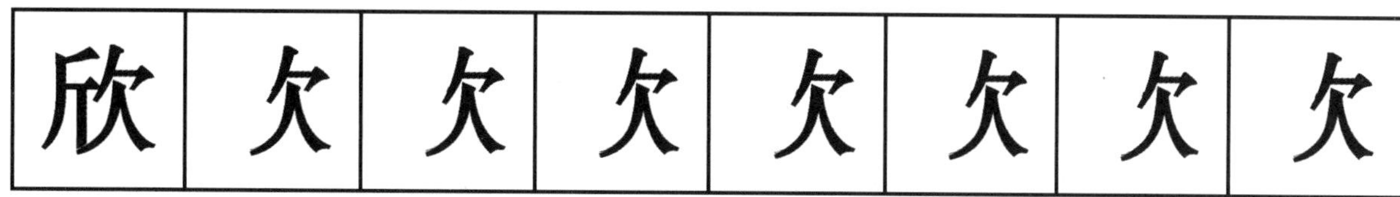

glad

Part 4. Find and circle the 斤 radical in the characters below:

新　订　断　斯　易　望

Part 5. Based on the meaning of the 斤 radical, please choose an appropriate meaning for the following characters from the three possible choices:

1. (　　) 斧　a. griddle　b. axe　c. straw
2. (　　) 断　a. to peek　b. to shed　c. to break
3. (　　) 斥　a. to bask　b. to exclude　c. to admire

Part 6. Please identify the components you have learned so far for each of the characters below and copy into the brackets:

1. 欣 glad [ ][ ]
2. 颀 tall [ ][ ]

Chinese Radical Exercise 99

Part 1. Write out the meaning for the radical below:

Radical	*Pinyin*	Meaning
舌	shé	

Part 2. Copy the radical 舌 :

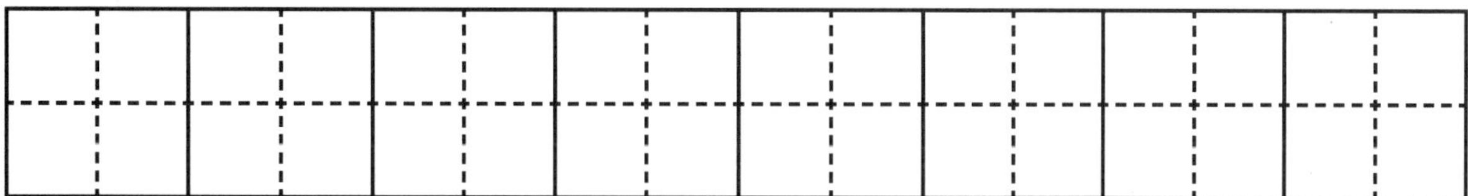

Part 3. Add the radical for each character according to the sample given:

乱	乚	乚	乚	乚	乚	乚	乚

in a mess

Part 4. Find and circle the 舌 radical in the characters below:

乱　码　的　虾　舔　辞

Part 5. Based on the meaning of the 舌 radical, please choose an appropriate meaning for the following characters from the three possible choices:

1. (　　) sweet　a. 甜　b. 斯　c. 短
2. (　　) to lick　a. 各　b. 些　c. 舔

Part 6. Please identify the components you have learned so far for each of the characters below and copy into the brackets:

1. 敌 enemy [ ][ ]
2. 刮 to scrape [ ][ ]

Chinese Radical Exercise 100

Part 1. Write out the meaning for the radical below:

Radical	*Pinyin*	Meaning
身	shēn	

Part 2. Copy the radical 身 :

Part 3. Add the radical for each character according to the sample given:

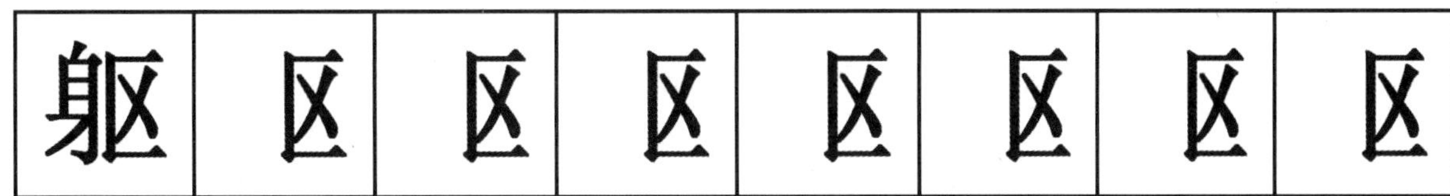

body

Part 4. Find and circle the 身 radical in the characters below:

射　躺　粗　放　解　躲

Part 5. Based on the meaning of the 身 radical, please choose an appropriate meaning for the following characters from the three possible choices:

1. (　　) 躺　a. to browse　b. to lie　c. to sound
2. (　　) 躲　a. to scream　b. to design　c. to hide

Part 6. Please identify the components you have learned so far for each of the characters below and copy into the brackets:

1. 躬 to bow [ ][ ]
2. 射 to shoot [ ][ ]

Comprehensive Radical Lesson Exercises

Lesson 2

水、艸、口、木、手、人、金、心、土、月

Section : ____________________

Chinese name : ____________________

English name : ____________________

Part 1. Based on your understanding of each radical's meaning, please choose the most appropriate meaning for the following characters from the three provided choices:

1. ( ) 地 a. ground b. iron c. plants
2. ( ) 针 a. needle b. glass c. grass
3. ( ) 泪 a. arms b. tears c. hair
4. ( ) 众 a. river b. tongue c. crowd
5. ( ) 茶 a. cup b. tea c. pot
6. ( ) 吃 a. to eat b. to dance c. to worry
7. ( ) 拉 a. to chew b. to pull c. to kick
8. ( ) 森 a. forest b. sea c. mine
9. ( ) 怕 a. to scold b. to run c. to be afraid
10. ( ) 唱 a. to sing b. to push c. to think

Part 2. Based on the sound of each radical we have learned in this lesson, please choose the correct *pinyin* for the following characters from the lists below:

1. ( ) 芯 a. qù b. xīn c. píng
2. ( ) 认 a. sāi b. dù c. rèn
3. ( ) 吐 a. tǔ b. ná c. yuè

Part 3. Based on the meanings of the radicals in this lesson, please choose the appropriate Chinese characters for the following English equivalents:

1. ( ) juice a. 汁 b. 铁 c. 壁
2. ( ) garden a. 急 b. 苑 c. 快
3. ( ) affection a. 情 b. 叫 c. 拿
4. ( ) to wipe a. 抹 b. 草 c. 钥
5. ( ) dust a. 杯 b. 吵 c. 尘
6. ( ) to blow a. 从 b. 吹 c. 城
7. ( ) he a. 他 b. 可 c. 错
8. ( ) copper a. 坐 b. 高 c. 铜
9. ( ) tree a. 去 b. 树 c. 加
10. ( ) to drink a. 喝 b. 服 c. 护

Part 4. Based on the sounds of the radicals in this lesson, please choose the appropriate characters for the following spellings from the choices below:

1. (　　) kòu　a. 脸　b. 扣　c. 杯
2. (　　) yuè　a. 钥　b. 铜　c. 后
3. (　　) mù　a. 喝　b. 念　c. 沐
4. (　　) dù　a. 忙　b. 肚　c. 鑫

Part 5. Please find the component shared by the three Chinese characters in the lists below and copy into the brackets:

1. [　　] 节　药　英
2. [　　] 床　本　李
3. [　　] 报　扫　拍
4. [　　] 老　在　坏
5. [　　] 借　价　假
6. [　　] 胖　服　朋
7. [　　] 有　背　能
8. [　　] 忘　怎　必
9. [　　] 求　录　绿
10. [　　] 吃　员　吗

Part 6. There is a missing component in each of the following characters. Given the provided English meanings, and based on the meanings of radicals as presented in this lesson, please 1) find the appropriate component for each character, and 2) fill in the blanks in order to complete the character. For your reference all the radicals of the lesson are listed below:

氵、艹、口、木、扌、亻、钅、忄、土、月

1. □化　Meaning: flower

2 □丁　Meaning: to hit; to play (ball)

3 □戋　Meaning: money

Comprehensive Radical Lesson Exercises

Lesson 3

糸、虫、言、女、竹、火、王、日、石、鱼

Section : ____________________

Chinese name : ____________________

English name : ____________________

Part 1. Based on your understanding of each radical's meaning, please choose the appropriate meaning for the following characters from the three possible choices:

1. (　　) 渔　a. jogging　b. fishing　c. biking
2. (　　) 纱　a. gauze　b. pin　c. boat
3. (　　) 讲　a. to say　b. to do　c. to take
4. (　　) 暖　a. freezing　b. cool　c. warm
5. (　　) 蚕　a. pine　b. snapper　c. silkworm
6. (　　) 妇　a. children　b. woman　c. man
7. (　　) 烤　a. to bake　b. to sweep　c. to freeze
8. (　　) 笋　a. statue　b. trout　c. bamboo shoot
9. (　　) 绑　a. to tie　b. to find　c. to rock
10. (　　) 热　a. fast　b. hot　c. noisy

Part 2. Based on the sound of each radical we have learned in this lesson, please choose the correct *pinyin* for the following characters from the lists below:

1. (　　) 伙　a. huǒ　b. shǐ　c. qǔ
2. (　　) 枉　a. dōng　b. bǐ　c. wǎng
3. (　　) 渔　a. wù　b. dì　c. yú

Part 3. Based on the meanings of the radicals in this lesson, please choose the appropriate Chinese phrases for the following English equivalents:

1. (　　) Miss　a. 女士　b. 岩石　c. 铅笔
2. (　　) sea bass　a. 树木　b. 花草　c. 鲈鱼
3. (　　) bamboo cage　a. 蚯蚓　b. 竹笼　c. 细丝
4. (　　) language　a. 点灯　b. 妈妈　c. 语言
5. (　　) imperial jade seal　a. 照片　b. 玉玺　c. 蛇蝎

Part 4. Please find the component shared by the three Chinese characters in the lists below and copy into the brackets:

1. [　　] 给　紧　绿
2. [　　] 要　好　姓
3. [　　] 算　篇　第

4. [ ] 点 照 然
5. [ ] 玩 球 理
6. [ ] 间 音 时
7. [ ] 灯 烧 秋
8. [ ] 研 硬 破
9. [ ] 虽 蚁 蛋
10. [ ] 谢 罚 谁

Part 5. Please identify the components you have learned and copy into the brackets:

1. 噬 [ ][ ][ ]
2. 烛 [ ][ ]
3. 始 [ ][ ]
4. 认 [ ][ ]
5. 绍 [ ][ ]

Comprehensive Radical Lesson Exercises

Lesson 4

山、足、鸟、疒、辵、衣、犬、目、刀、邑

Section : ________________

Chinese name : ________________

English name : ________________

Part 1. Based on your understanding of each radical's meaning, please choose the appropriate meaning for the following characters from the three possible choices:

1. (　　) 病 a. curiousness b. excitement c. illness
2. (　　) 猫 a. cat b. gloves c. ankle
3. (　　) 过 a. to pass b. to laugh c. to sit
4. (　　) 眼 a. nose b. eye c. foot
5. (　　) 裙 a. hill b. nest c. skirt
6. (　　) 剑 a. spoon b. sword c. bottle
7. (　　) 拉 a. to chew b. to pull c. to kick
8. (　　) 郡 a. county b. bookstore c. restaurant
9. (　　) 刃 a. eyelashes b. cliff c. blade
10. (　　) 路 a. road b. coat c. toast

Part 2. Based on the sound of each radical we have learned in this lesson, please choose the correct *pinyin* for the following characters from the lists below:

1. (　　) 倒 a. chén b. hù c. dǎo
2. (　　) 袅 a. jùn b. niǎo c. kè
3. (　　) 汕 a. shàn b. fěn c. hé

Part 3. Based on the meanings of the radicals in this lesson, please choose the appropriate Chinese characters for the following English equivalents:

1. (　　) ache a. 疼 b. 衫 c. 出
2. (　　) dove a. 睛 b. 速 c. 鸽
3. (　　) patrol a. 痛 b. 巡 c. 想
4. (　　) hillock a. 岗 b. 色 c. 个
5. (　　) to dispart a. 你 b. 分 c. 妈

Part 4. Based on the sounds of the radicals in this lesson, please choose the appropriate characters for the following spellings from the choices below:

1. (　　) yī a. 依 b. 念 c. 沐
2. (　　) dāo a. 脸 b. 扣 c. 叨
3. (　　) yì a. 苜 b. 挹 c. 后

Part 5. Please find the component shared by the three Chinese characters in the lists below and copy into the brackets:

1. [ ] 都 邮 那
2. [ ] 岁 岸 屹
3. [ ] 刚 别 前
4. [ ] 看 睡 着
5. [ ] 狗 猪 猴
6. [ ] 袖 裤 衬
7. [ ] 适 边 这
8. [ ] 跳 跑 跟
9. [ ] 疼 病 瘦
10. [ ] 鹃 鸿 鸥

Part 6. Please identify the components you have learned and copy into the brackets:

1. 踹 [ ][ ]
2. 猪 [ ][ ][ ]
3. 裂 [ ][ ]
4. 急 [ ][ ]
5. 碳 [ ][ ][ ]
6. 罚 [ ][ ]

Comprehensive Radical Lesson Exercises

Lesson 5

宀、禾、马、贝、车、阜、示、食、酉、八

Section : ________________

Chinese name : ________________

English name : ________________

Part 1. Based on your understanding of each radical's meaning, please choose the appropriate meaning for the following characters from the three possible choices:

1. (　　) 贿　a. to kill　b. to bribe　c. to harvest
2. (　　) 祠　a. ancestral temple　b. studio　c. stall
3. (　　) 餐　a. truck　b. beer　c. meal
4. (　　) 酿　a. to brew　b. to train　c. to drive
5. (　　) 种　a. to climb　b. to sow　c. to buy

Part 2. Based on the sound of each radical we have learned in this lesson, please choose the correct *pinyin* for the following characters from the lists below:

1. (　　) 妈　a. mā　b. zhēn　c. fèi
2. (　　) 扒　a. liàng　b. yǎn　c. bā
3. (　　) 猷　a. dǎ　b. yóu　c. zhuǎn

Part 3. Based on the meanings of the radicals in this lesson, please choose the appropriate Chinese phrases for the following English equivalents:

1. (　　) blessing　a. 鱼饵　b. 车轮　c. 福祉
2. (　　) restaurant　a. 饭馆　b. 驾驶　c. 暖和
3. (　　) car　a. 客官　b. 车辆　c. 心意

Part 4. Based on the sounds of the radicals in this lesson, please choose the appropriate characters for the following spellings from the choices below:

1. (　　) bù　a. 埠　b. 完　c. 和
2. (　　) bei　a. 呗　b. 转　c. 福
3. (　　) ma　a. 酒　b. 吗　c. 秋

Part 5. Please find the component shared by the three Chinese characters in the lists below and copy into the brackets:

1. [　　] 真　弟　关
2. [　　] 饮　饺　饼
3. [　　] 醋　酒　配
4. [　　] 视　祝　社

5. [ ] 除 院 险
6. [ ] 轻 转 载
7. [ ] 贵 货 贴
8. [ ] 吗 妈 蚂
9. [ ] 定 寄 字
10. [ ] 秦 香 和

Part 6. Please identify the components you have learned and copy into the brackets:

1. 密 [ ][ ][ ]
2. 晕 [ ][ ]
3. 馅 [ ][ ]
4. 猷 [ ][ ][ ]
5. 剪 [ ][ ][ ][ ]
6. 总 [ ][ ][ ]

Part 7. Differentiate the radicals that look similar. Please fill in meanings for the radicals below and give one character for each of them (You might want to look for characters in previous lessons):

Number	Radicals	Meanings	A character that contains the radical
1	木		
2	禾		
3	衤		
4	礻		
5	钅		
6	饣		

汉字部首教程

Comprehensive Radical Lesson Exercises

Lesson 6

页、巾、门、广、大、米、田、十、彳、革

Section : ________________

Chinese name : ________________

English name : ________________

Part 1. Based on your understanding of each radical's meaning, please choose the appropriate meaning for the following characters from the three possible choices:

1. (　　) 粒　a. granule　b. trunk　c. belt
2. (　　) 鞋　a. opener　b. banner　c. shoes
3. (　　) 闭　a. to type　b. to shut　c. to think
4. (　　) 带　a. square　b. box　c. strip

Part 2. Based on the sound of each radical we have learned in this lesson, please choose the correct *pinyin* for the following characters from the lists below:

1. (　　) 迷　a. xuē　b. mí　c. lè
2. (　　) 佃　a. hěn　b. zuò　c. tián
3. (　　) 锦　a. nán　b. jǐn　c. wǔ

Part 3. Based on the meanings of the radicals in this lesson, please choose the appropriate Chinese characters for the following English equivalents:

1. (　　) stuffy　a. 闷　b. 衫　c. 出
2. (　　) brown rice　a. 睛　b. 速　c. 糙
3. (　　) wealthy　a. 酒　b. 富　c. 林
4. (　　) extremly　a. 鞋　b. 烦　c. 太

Part 4. Please find the component shared by the three Chinese characters in the lists below and copy into the brackets:

1. [　　] 帅　常　帮
2. [　　] 床　麻　腐
3. [　　] 题　顺　颜
4. [　　] 间　们　问
5. [　　] 华　克　直
6. [　　] 行　往　衍
7. [　　] 靴　鞭　鞋
8. [　　] 美　夸　套
9. [　　] 粗　类　糖
10. [　　] 男　思　略

Part 5. Please identify the components you have learned and copy into the brackets:

1. 糜 [ ][ ][ ]
2. 阁 [ ][ ]
3. 留 [ ][ ]
4. 衔 [ ][ ]
5. 鞋 [ ][ ]
6. 烦 [ ][ ]
7. 纂 [ ][ ][ ][ ]
8. 谜 [ ][ ][ ]
9. 座 [ ][ ][ ]
10. 焖 [ ][ ][ ]

Part 6. Differentiate the radicals that look similar. Please fill in meanings for the radicals below and give one character for each of them (You might want to look for characters in previous lessons):

Number	Radicals	Meanings	A character that contains the radical
1	彳		
2	亻		
3	疒		
4	广		
5	页		
6	贝		

Comprehensive Radical Lesson Exercises

Lesson 7

支、戈、尸、穴、力、舟、口、雨、厂、又

Section : ____________________

Chinese name : ____________________

English name : ____________________

Part 1. Please find the component shared by the three Chinese characters in the lists below and copy into the brackets:

1. [ ] 暖 变 难
2. [ ] 屏 局 剧
3. [ ] 窗 穿 究
4. [ ] 戴 我 或
5. [ ] 船 盘 般
6. [ ] 努 加 劝
7. [ ] 雷 雪 霜
8. [ ] 厕 厚 厨
9. [ ] 四 园 回
10. [ ] 救 教 改

Part 2. Based on your understanding of each radical's meaning, please choose the appropriate meaning for the following characters from the three possible choices:

1. ( ) 划 a. to design b. to bark c. to draw
2. ( ) 空 a. brilliant b. redundant c. empty
3. ( ) 势 a. force b. intelligence c. beauty
4. ( ) 国 a. tripod b. abyss c. country
5. ( ) 男 a. man b. woman c. kid

Part 3. Based on the sound of each radical you have been introduced in this lesson, please choose the correct *pinyin* for the following characters from the lists below:

1. ( ) 历 a. fán b. chū c. lì
2. ( ) 屎 a. shǐ b. fù c. yuàn
3. ( ) 友 a. yǒu b. tīng c. bà

Part 4. Please identify the components you have learned and copy into the brackets:

1. 剧 [ ][ ][ ][ ]
2. 威 [ ][ ]

3. 败 [ ][ ]
4. 做 [ ][ ][ ][ ]
5. 厌 [ ][ ]
6. 紧 [ ][ ]
7. 拐 [ ][ ][ ]
8. 尿 [ ][ ]
9. 裁 [ ][ ][ ]
10. 劝 [ ][ ]

Part 5. Please find the character that contains the targeted radical listed in the table below and fill in the table with the corresponding number of the character:

①空 ②店 ③国 ④吃 ⑤劈 ⑥病 ⑦家 ⑧厅

Number	Radicals	The character that contains the radical
1	厂	
2	广	
3	疒	
4	宀	
5	穴	
6	刀	
7	口	
8	囗	

Comprehensive Radical Lesson Exercises

Lesson 8

牛、皿、夂、羽、羊、弓、歹、小、欠、子

Section : ________________

Chinese name : ________________

English name : ________________

漢字部首教程

Part 1. Please find the component shared by the three Chinese characters in the lists below and copy into the brackets:

1. [ ] 习 次 准
2. [ ] 栩 翻 耀
3. [ ] 差 洋 样
4. [ ] 张 弟 湾
5. [ ] 好 学 存
6. [ ] 盆 盘 益
7. [ ] 当 光 尚
8. [ ] 歌 欢 吹
9. [ ] 残 死 列
10. [ ] 件 牵 牟

Part 2. Based on your understanding of each radical's meaning, please choose the appropriate meaning for the following characters from the three possible choices:

1. ( ) 孩 a. man b. woman c. child
2. ( ) 牲 a. domestic animal b. national flag c. political issue
3. ( ) 群 a. minority b. individual c. flock
4. ( ) 翼 a. wing b. thigh c. breast
5. ( ) 羔 a. bean b. lamb c. beef

Part 3. Based on the sound of each radical you have been introduced in this lesson, please choose the correct *pinyin* for the following characters from the lists below:

1. ( ) 养 a. fán b. zhuàng c. yǎng
2. ( ) 肖 a. zhēn b. lì c. xiào
3. ( ) 冰 a. bīng b. gǒu c. lè
4. ( ) 字 a. shàn b. zì c. qún

Part 4. Based on the meanings of the radicals in this lesson, please choose the appropriate Chinese characters for the following English equivalents:

1. ( ) freeze a. 告 b. 冻 c. 热
2. ( ) pregnant a. 孕 b. 软 c. 死
3. ( ) hover a. 冷 b. 盘 c. 翱

Part 5. Please identify the components you have learned and copy into the brackets:

1. 净 [ ][ ]
2. 羡 [ ][ ][ ]
3. 弱 [ ][ ]
4. 孺 [ ][ ]
5. 盘 [ ][ ]
6. 第 [ ][ ]
7. 璨 [ ][ ][ ][ ]
8. 弘 [ ][ ]
9. 温 [ ][ ][ ]

Part 6. Please circle the words that share the same component and write down the component in the brackets:

1. [ ] 凉 渴 减
2. [ ] 欧 歌 收
3. [ ] 光 前 尊
4. [ ] 汤 凄 泪
5. [ ] 字 孩 打
6. [ ] 欲 放 敬
7. [ ] 常 肖 关
8. [ ] 找 提 孤

Comprehensive Radical Lesson Exercises

Lesson 9

佳、耳、白、骨、立、见、厶、毛、卜、齿

Section : ________________

Chinese name : ________________

English name : ________________

Part 1. Please find the component shared by the three Chinese characters in the lists below and copy into the brackets:

1. [　　] 百　伯　的
2. [　　] 骼　骷　骸
3. [　　] 视　规　觉
4. [　　] 笔　毫　毯
5. [　　] 售　雕　难
6. [　　] 闻　聋　联
7. [　　] 意　童　端
8. [　　] 台　去　县
9. [　　] 上　占　贞
10. [　　] 龄　龈　龉

Part 2. Based on your understanding of each radical's meaning, please choose the appropriate meaning for the following characters from the three possible choices:

1. (　　) 视　a. to watch　b. to create　c. to compose
2. (　　) 私　a. worldwide　b. national　c. personal
3. (　　) 髓　a. marrow　b. juice　c. egg white
4. (　　) 聊　a. to chat　b. to dance　c. to sleep
5. (　　) 啮　a. to leap　b. to gnaw　c. to ride

Part 3. Based on the sound of each radical you have been introduced in this lesson, please choose the correct *pinyin* for the following characters from the lists below:

1. (　　) 锥　a. zhuī　b. chāo　c. jiān
2. (　　) 柏　a. jú　b. hù　c. bǎi
3. (　　) 饵　a. ěr　b. kōng　c. xiē
4. (　　) 牦　a. zǒu　b. máo　c. chà

Part 4. Based on the meanings of the radicals in this lesson, please choose the appropriate Chinese characters for the following English equivalents:

1. (   ) the female of bird   a. 雌   b. 站   c. 觉
2. (   ) acute hearing   a. 聪   b. 雀   c. 观
3. (   ) bright   a. 桌   b. 能   c. 皓

Part 5. Please identify the components you have learned and copy into the brackets:

1. 毡 [   ][   ][   ]
2. 准 [   ][   ]
3. 贞 [   ][   ]
4. 尾 [   ][   ]
5. 帛 [   ][   ]
6. 雄 [   ][   ]
7. 部 [   ][   ][   ]
8. 酥 [   ][   ]

Part 6. Based on the sounds and meanings of the radicals that you have been introduced, please match the characters on the left to their sounds and meanings on the right:

1. 补 ●   ● jiàn (naval vessel)
2. 怕 ●   ● ěr (bait)
3. 笠 ●   ● bǔ (to patch)
4. 舰 ●   ● lì (a large bamboo hat)
5. 饵 ●   ● pà (to fear)

Part 7. Please circle the words that share the same component and write down the component in the brackets:

1. [   ] 怕 的 时
2. [   ] 惯 视 赔
3. [   ] 笔 拿 掌
4. [   ] 照 春 百
5. [   ] 厕 现 觉

6. [　　] 笔　尾　拳
7. [　　] 补　处　直
8. [　　] 颜　觅　烦

Comprehensive Radical Lesson Exercises

Lesson 10

方、黑、殳、儿、彡、气、勹、爪、瓦、走

Section : ____________________

Chinese name : ____________________

English name : ____________________

Part 1. Please find the component shared by the three Chinese characters in the lists below and copy into the brackets:

1. [ ] 泡 狗 够
2. [ ] 房 族 旁
3. [ ] 先 允 兄
4. [ ] 默 黛 黝
5. [ ] 段 股 毅
6. [ ] 形 参 须
7. [ ] 汽 氨 氧
8. [ ] 采 妥 爱
9. [ ] 起 趁 越
10. [ ] 瓶 瓷 瓮

Part 2. Based on your understanding of each radical's meaning, please choose the appropriate meaning for the following characters from the three possible choices:

1. ( ) 受 a. to ask b. to breath c. to receive
2. ( ) 瓶 a. bottle b. park c. cookie
3. ( ) 役 a. light b. war c. van
4. ( ) 包 a. street b. swan c. package
5. ( ) 旗 a. round table b. gloves c. flag

Part 3. Based on the sound of each radical you have learned in this lesson, please choose the correct *pinyin* for the following characters from the lists below:

1. ( ) 旁 a. qǐ b. páng c. hū
2. ( ) 衫 a. shān b. yě c. jiàng
3. ( ) 饱 a. qù b. dé c. bǎo
4. ( ) 汽 a. qì b. rú c. fù
5. ( ) 防 a. guī b. mò c. fáng

Part 4. Based on the meanings of the radicals in this lesson, please choose the appropriate Chinese characters for the following English equivalents:

1. (　　) to look for　　a. 颜　　b. 克　　c. 觅
2. (　　) fluorine　　a. 氟　　b. 影　　c. 元
3. (　　) to catch up with　　a. 放　　b. 句　　c. 赶
4. (　　) ink　　a. 墨　　b. 段　　c. 氮
5. (　　) beard　　a. 投　　b. 须　　c. 旅

Part 5. Please identify the components you have learned and copy into the brackets:

1. 衫 [　　][　　]
2. 说 [　　][　　][　　][　　]
3. 竞 [　　][　　][　　]
4. 殉 [　　][　　][　　]
5. 搬 [　　][　　][　　]

Part 6. The following words share the same phonetic component 勹. Based on the meanings of the radicals that you have learned, please match the characters on the left to their meanings on the right:

1. 跑 pǎo ●	● full
2. 抱 bào ●	● bud
3. 炮 pào ●	● robe
4. 鲍 bào ●	● to hug
5. 饱 bǎo ●	● to run
6. 苞 bāo ●	● firecrackers
7. 咆 páo ●	● to shout
8. 泡 pào ●	● blister
9. 袍 páo ●	● bubble
10. 疱 pào ●	● ormer; abalone

汉字部首教程

Part 7. Please write down the meaning for each of the radicals and circle the word which contains the radical:

Number	Radicals	Meanings	Circle the character
1	亻		他　往　彰
2	彳		彬　什　行
3	彡		很　须　狗
4	犭		澎　街　猫
5	丷		当　关　妥
6	⺍		肖　美　乳
7	⺥		总　尝　采

Comprehensive Radical Lesson Exercises

Lesson 11

匚、户、工、止、寸、夊、矢、斤、舌、身

Section : ____________________

Chinese name : ____________________

English name : ____________________

Part 1. Please find the component shared by the three Chinese characters in the lists below and copy into the brackets:

1. [ ] 巫 式 项
2. [ ] 巨 医 区
3. [ ] 时 封 导
4. [ ] 肩 房 扇
5. [ ] 嘴 武 些
6. [ ] 谢 躺 躲
7. [ ] 适 乱 辞
8. [ ] 所 断 折
9. [ ] 短 矮 疑
10. [ ] 备 条 复

Part 2. Based on your understanding of each radical's meaning, please choose the appropriate meaning for the following characters from the three possible choices:

1. ( ) 差 a. taste b. frost c. errand
2. ( ) 甜 a. sad b. sweet c. broken
3. ( ) 房 a. room b. waist c. ring
4. ( ) 斩 a. to drift b. to chop c. to return
5. ( ) 匠 a. carpenter b. lawyer c. cosmetics

Part 3. Based on the sound of each radical you have been introduced in this lesson, please choose the correct *pinyin* for the following characters from the lists below:

1. ( ) 沪 a. hù b. luàn c. xiàng
2. ( ) 红 a. nán b. chóu c. hóng
3. ( ) 攻 a. gōng b. fàn c. lǐ
4. ( ) 新 a. huà b. bǎn c. xīn
5. ( ) 址 a. chōng b. zhǐ c. láo

Part 4. Please identify the components you have learned and copy into the brackets:

1. 谢 [ ][ ][ ]
2. 疼 [ ][ ]

3. 对 [ ][ ]
4. 砸 [ ][ ][ ]
5. 话 [ ][ ]
6. 欣 [ ][ ]
7. 知 [ ][ ]
8. 处 [ ][ ]
9. 房 [ ][ ]
10. 趾 [ ][ ]

Part 5. Based on the sounds and meanings of the radicals that you have learned introduced, please match the characters on the left to their sounds and meanings on the right:

1. 趾 ●	● gōng (to bow)
2. 护 ●	● cūn (village)
3. 躬 ●	● zhǐ (toes)
4. 村 ●	● gōng (work)
5. 功 ●	● hù (to protect)

Part 6. Please write down *pinyin* and meanings for each of the radicals in the following table. Additionally, find the word that contains the targeted radical and fill its corresponding number in the list below:

① 放 ② 局 ③ 此 ④ 功 ⑤ 启 ⑥ 地 ⑦ 备

Number	Radicals	*Pinyin*	Meanings	The character that contains the radical
1	尸			
2	户			
3	工			
4	土			
5	止			
6	夂			
7	攵			

Answer Key for Individual Radical Exercises

Chinese Radical Exercise 1 水（氵氺）

Part 5	1. b	2. a	3. c	4. a
Part 6	1. 氵	2. 水		

Chinese Radical Exercise 2 艸（艹）

Part 5	1. a	2. c	3. a
Part 6	艹 氵		

Chinese Radical Exercise 3 口

Part 5	1.c	2. b
Part 6	1. 艹 口	2. 氵 口

Chinese Radical Exercise 4 木（朩）

Part 5	1. b	2. b	3. a
Part 6	1. 木 氵	2. 木 口	

Chinese Radical Exercise 5 手（龵扌）

Part 5	1. a	2. c	3. b
Part 6	1. 扌	2. 手	3. 龵 手

Chinese Radical Exercise 6 人（亻）

Part 5	1. c	2. a	3. b
Part 6	1. 亻 口 木	2. 亻 木	3. 亻 口

Chinese Radical Exercise 7 金（钅）

Part 5	1.a	2. a	3. c

Part 6 **钴** 吵 **铝** **镍** **银** 伯 **铁** 波 **铜**

Chinese Radical Exercise 8 心（忄⺗）

Part 5　1. 忄　2. 心　3. ⺗

Part 6　1. 口 心　2. 忄 艹

Chinese Radical Exercise 9 土

Part 5　1. c　2. b　3. c

Part 6　1. 艹 土　2. 人 土

Chinese Radical Exercise 10 月（⺝）

Part 5　1. 月　2. ⺝　3. 月

Part 6　1. 月土　2. 月口

Chinese Radical Exercise 11 糸（糹纟）

Part 5　1. b　2. a　3. a

Part 6　1. 纟人　2. 纟 口

Chinese Radical Exercise 12 虫

Part 5　1. c　2. b　3. c

Part 6　1. 虫 糸　2. 口 虫

Chinese Radical Exercise 13 言（讠）

Part 5　1. b　2. c　3. a

Part 6　1. 亻 言　2. 讠 人

Chinese Radical Exercise 14 女

Part 5　1. a　2. b　3. b

Part 6　1. 氵 女　2. 女 木

Chinese Radical Exercise 15 竹（⺮）

Part 5　1. a　2. a　3. c

Part 6　1. ⺮ 木　2. ⺮ 土　3. ⺮ 人 口

Chinese Radical Exercise 16 火（灬）

Part 5　1. b　2. b　3. a

Part 6　1. 讠 火　2. 火 灬　3. 亻 口 木 火

Chinese Radical Exercise 17 王（玉）

Part 5　(琳) (琅) (玛) 竽 (瑙) 社 (琥) (珀) 纽 (珠) (珥)

Part 6　1. 王 口　2. 钅 玉　3. 月 王

Chinese Radical Exercise 18 日（⺜）

Part 5　1. a　2. b

Part 6　1. 艹 曰　2. 日 口 灬　3. 日 月

Chinese Radical Exercise 19 石

Part 5　1. c　2. b　3. b

Part 6　1. 石 月　2. 石 水

Chinese Radical Exercise 20 鱼（魚）

Part 5　1. a　2. a　3. b

Part 6　1. 鱼 日　2. 鱼 土　3. 鱼 月

Chinese Radical Exercise 21 山

Part 5　1. a　2. c　3. a

Part 6　1. 山 石　2. 山 火　3. 山 土

Chinese Radical Exercise 22 足（⻊）

Part 5　1. b　2. c　3. b

Part 6　1. ⻊ 石　2. ⻊ 水 曰　3. ⻊ 山 月

Chinese Radical Exercise 23 鸟（鳥）

Part 5　1. a　2. b　3. c

Part 6　1. 口 鸟　2. 月 鸟　3. ⻊ 口 鸟

Chinese Radical Exercise 24 疒

Part 5　1. a　2. b　3. a

Part 6　1. 疒口山　2. 疒火

Chinese Radical Exercise 25 辵（辶）

Part 5　1. c　2. b　3. a

Part 6　辶王

Chinese Radical Exercise 26 衣（衤）

Part 5　1. b　2. a　3. b

Part 6　1. 衤亻口木　2. 衣口

Chinese Radical Exercise 27 犬（犭）

Part 5　1. 犭　2. 犬

Part 6　(猫)　杀　(狗)　(狮)　遛　(狐)　(猴)　吼　(猿)

Chinese Radical Exercise 28 目

Part 5　1. a　2. a　3. c

Part 6　1. 木目心

Chinese Radical Exercise 29 刀（刂 ⺈）

Part 5　1. 刀　2. 刂　2. ⺈

Part 6　1. c　2. b

Chinese Radical Exercise 30 邑（阝）

Part 5　1. c　2. a　3. c

Part 6　1. 刀口阝　2. 土日阝

Chinese Radical Exercise 31 宀

Part 5　1. b　2. b　3. a

Part 6　1. 宀火　2. 宀玉　3. 宀女

Chinese Radical Exercise 32 禾

Part 5	1. c	2. b	3. a
Part 6	1. 禾 刂	2. 禾 日	3. 禾 火

Chinese Radical Exercise 33 马（馬）

Part 5	1. a	2. c	3. c
Part 6	1. 女 马	2. 口 马	3. 马 糸

Chinese Radical Exercise 34 贝（貝）

Part 5	1. b	2. a
Part 6	1. 宀 贝	2. 口 月 贝

Chinese Radical Exercise 35 车（車 车）

Part 5	1. c	2. b	3. b
Part 6	1. 纟 车 口	2. 车 口	

Chinese Radical Exercise 36 阜（阝）

Part 5	1. a	2. c	
Part 6	1. 阝 车	2. 阝 人	3. 阝 日

Chinese Radical Exercise 37 示（礻）

Part 5	1. 示	2. 礻	3. 礻
Part 6	1. 阝（left）示	2. 木 示	3. 礻 阝（right）

Chinese Radical Exercise 38 食（飠 饣）

Part 5	1. b	2. a	3. b
Part 6	1. 饣 虫	2. 饣 宀	3. 饣 𠂉

Chinese Radical Exercise 39 西

Part 5	1. b	2. c	3. a
Part 6	1. 西 禾	2. 西 日	

Chinese Radical Exercise 40 八（丷）

Part 5　1. 丷　2. 八
Part 6　1. 八刀贝　2. 丷酉　3. 丷日

Chinese Radical Exercise 41 页（頁）

Part 5　1. b　2. c
Part 6　1. 火页　2. 石页

Chinese Radical Exercise 42 巾

Part 5　1. b　2. c　3. c
Part 6　1. 阝（right）巾　2. 卄曰巾

Chinese Radical Exercise 43 门（門）

Part 5　1. c　2. b
Part 6　1. 门马　2. 门木

Chinese Radical Exercise 44 广

Part 5　1. a　2. c　3. b
Part 6　1. 广巾　2. 广木

Chinese Radical Exercise 45 大

Part 5　1. a　2. a　3. b
Part 6　1. 大示　2. 丷酉大

Chinese Radical Exercise 46 米

Part 5　1. c　2. b　3. b
Part 6　1. 米宀示　2. 米大

Chinese Radical Exercise 47 田

Part 5　1. a　2. c
Part 6　1. 田糸　2. 田月

Chinese Radical Exercise 48 十

Part 5　1. 日 十　2. 十 口

Part 6　1. 十 大　2. 人 十

Chinese Radical Exercise 49 彳

Part 5　1. a　2. c

Part 6　1. 彳 十 心　2. 彳 曰

Chinese Radical Exercise 50 革

Part 5　1. c　2. a

Part 6　1. 革 宀 安　2. 革 亻

Chinese Radical Exercise 51 攴（攵）

Part 5　1. a　2. c

Part 6　1. 十 口 攵　2. 贝 攵　3. 米 女 攵

Chinese Radical Exercise 52 戈

Part 5　1. a　2. b　3. c

Part 6　田 戈

Chinese Radical Exercise 53 尸

Part 5　1. c　2. a

Part 6　1. 尸 米　2. 尸 十 口

Chinese Radical Exercise 54 穴

Part 5　1. b　2. c

Part 6　1. 穴 犬　2. 穴 巾

Chinese Radical Exercise 55 力

Part 5　1. a　2. a　3. c

Part 6　1. 田 力　2. 力 口 木

Chinese Radical Exercise 56 舟

Part 5　1. b　2. c　3. a

Part 6　1. 舟人　2. 舟口　3. 舟宀

Chinese Radical Exercise 57 囗

Part 5　1. a　2. c　3. a

Part 6　1. 囗口　2. 囗玉　3. 囗大

Chinese Radical Exercise 58 雨（⻗）

Part 5　1. a　2. b

Part 6　1. 雨革月　2. 雨田

Chinese Radical Exercise 59 厂

Part 5　1. b　2. b　3. a

Part 6　1. 厂贝刂　2. 厂力

Chinese Radical Exercise 60 又

Part 5　1. a　2. b　3. b

Part 6　1. 又戈　2. 忄日又

Chinese Radical Exercise 61 牛（牜）

Part 5　1. b　2. a　3. a

Part 6　1. 禾刂牛　2. 牜攵

Chinese Radical Exercise 62 皿

Part 5　1. c　2. b　3. c

Part 6　1. 戈皿　2. 日月皿

Chinese Radical Exercise 63 仌（冫）

Part 5　1. b　2. c

Part 6　1. 冫马　2. 冫囗口示

Chinese Radical Exercise 64 羽

Part 5   1. a   2. c   3. b

Part 6   1. 羽田八   2. 大十羽

Chinese Radical Exercise 65 羊（⺶⺷）

Part 5   1. b   2. c   3. a

Part 6   1. ⺶ 目   2. ⺷ 大

Chinese Radical Exercise 66 弓

Part 5   1. a   2. b   3. a

Part 6   1. 弓土田   2.弓米   3.女又弓

Chinese Radical Exercise 67 歹（歺）

Part 5   1. c   2. b

Part 6   1. 歺 又 食   2. 歹 刂

Chinese Radical Exercise 68 小（⺌）

Part 5   1. c   2. c

Part 6   1. 小 大   2. ⺌ 口衣

Chinese Radical Exercise 69 欠

Part 5   1. a   2. a   3. b

Part 6   1.车欠   2. 又欠

Chinese Radical Exercise 70 子

Part 5   1. c   2. a

Part 6   1. 木子   2. 子 皿

Chinese Radical Exercise 71隹

Part 5   1. b   2. c   3. a

Part 6   1. 隹口   2. ⺌ 羽 隹

Chinese Radical Exercise 72 耳

Part 5　1. c　2. b　3. b

Part 6　1. 耳又　2. 耳火

Chinese Radical Exercise 73 白

Part 5　1. a　2. a　3. c

Part 6　1. 白王　2. 白水

Chinese Radical Exercise 74 骨

Part 5　1. b　2. a　3. b

Part 6　1. 骨米女　2. 骨又

Chinese Radical Exercise 75 立

Part 5　1. c　2. b　3. c

Part 6　1. 立曰十　2. 立曰心

Chinese Radical Exercise 76 见（見）

Part 5　1. a　2.a　3. b

Part 6　1.礻见　2. 王见

Chinese Radical Exercise 77 厶

Part 5　1. 月（⺼）厶　2. 忄厶

Part 6　1. ⺮目大厶　2. 厶牛

Chinese Radical Exercise 78 毛

Part 5　1. c　2. b

Part 6　1. ⺮毛　2. 尸毛

Chinese Radical Exercise 79 卜（⺊）

Part 5　1. b　2. c　3. a

Part 6　1.土卜　2.⺊曰木

Chinese Radical Exercise 80 齿（齒）

Part 5　1. a　2. b　3. c

Part 6　齿足

Chinese Radical Exercise 81 方

Part 5　1. a　2. c　3. c

Part 6　1. 方攵　2. 方毛

Chinese Radical Exercise 82 黑

Part 5　1. b　2. b　3. a

Part 6　1. 黑 立 日　2. 口 黑

Chinese Radical Exercise 83 殳

Part 5　1. c　2. a　3. b

Part 6　1. 月殳　2. 扌殳

Chinese Radical Exercise 84 儿

Part 5　1. 口儿　2. 立儿

Part 6　1. 厶儿　2. 口儿

Chinese Radical Exercise 85 彡

Part 5　1. b　2. a　3. c

Part 6　1. 木彡　2. 彡页

Chinese Radical Exercise 86 气

Part 5　1. a　2. b　3. b

Part 6　1. 氵气　2. 气 宀 女

Chinese Radical Exercise 87 勹

Part 5　1. c　2. c　3. b

Part 6　1. 勹 冫　2. 钅勹厶　3. 勹日

Chinese Radical Exercise 88 爪（爫）

Part 5	1. c	2. a	3. b
Part 6	1. 爫木彡	2. 爫女	

Chinese Radical Exercise 89 瓦

Part 5	1. c	2. b
Part 6	1. 八厶瓦	2. 冫欠瓦

Chinese Radical Exercise 90 走

Part 5	1. a	2. c	3. b
Part 6	1. 走耳又	2. 走卜	

Chinese Radical Exercise 91 匚

Part 5	1. b	2. c
Part 6	1. 石匚巾	2.⺮匚王

Chinese Radical Exercise 92 户

Part 5	1. a	2. b
Part 6	1. 户羽	2.户隹

Chinese Radical Exercise 93 工

Part 5	1. c	2. a	3. c
Part 6	1. 工攵	2. 工页	

Chinese Radical Exercise 94 止

Part 5	1. b	2. c	3. a
Part 6	1. 耳止	2. 止月	

Chinese Radical Exercise 95 寸

Part 5	1. 寸	2. 土寸
Part 6	1. 又寸	2. 尸示寸

Chinese Radical Exercise 96 夂

Part 5	1. c	2. b	3. a
Part 6	1. 夂卜口	2. 夂 田 心	

Chinese Radical Exercise 97 矢

Part 5	匚矢	
Part 6	1. 矢禾女	2. 矢隹

Chinese Radical Exercise 98 斤

Part 5	1. b	2. c	3. b
Part 6	1. 斤欠	2. 斤 页	

Chinese Radical Exercise 99 舌

Part 5	1. a	2. c
Part 6	1. 舌攵	2. 舌刂

Chinese Radical Exercise 100 身

Part 5	1. b	2. c
Part 6	1. 身弓	2. 身寸

Answer Key for Comprehensive Radical Lesson Exercises

Lesson 2

Part 1 1. a 2. a 3. b 4. c 5. b 6. a 7. b 8. a 9. c 10. a

Part 2 1. b 2. c 3. a

Part 3 1. a 2. b 3. a 4. a 5. c 6. b 7. a 8. c 9. b 10. a

Part 4 1. b 2. a 3. c 4. b

Part 5 1. 艹 2. 木 3. 扌 4. 土 5. 亻 6. 月 7. ⺼ 8. 心 9. 氺 10. 口

Part 6 1. 花 2. 打 3. 钱

Lesson 3

Part 1 1. b 2. a 3. a 4. c 5. c 6. b 7. a 8. c 9. a 10. b

Part 2 1. a 2. c 3. c

Part 3 1. a 2. c 3. b 4. c 5. b

Part 4 1. 糸（纟） 2. 女 3. ⺮ 4. 灬 5. 王 6. 日 7. 火
8. 石 9. 虫 10. 讠

Part 5 1. 口⺮人 2. 火虫 3. 女口 4. 讠人 5. 纟口

Lesson 4

Part 1 1. c 2. a 3. a 4. b 5. c 6. b 7. b 8. a 9. c 10. a

Part 2 1. c 2. b 3. a

Part 3 1. a 2. c 3. b 4. a 5. b

Part 4 1. a 2. c 3. b

Part 5 1. 阝 2. 山 3. 刂 4. 目 5. 犭 6. 衤 7. 辶 8. ⻊ 9. 疒 10. 鸟

Part 6 1. ⻊山 2. 犭土日 3. 刂衣 4. ⺈心 5. 石山火 6. 讠刂

Lesson 5

Part 1 1. b 2. a 3. c 4. a 5. b

Part 2 1. a 2. c 3. b

Part 3 1. c 2. a 3. b

Part 4 1. c 2. a 3. b

Part 5 1. 八（丷） 2. 饣 3. 酉 4. 衤 5. 阝 6. 车 7. 贝 8. 马
9. 宀 10. 禾

Part 6 1. 宀心山 2. 曰 车 3. 饣⺈ 4. 丷酉犬 5. 丷月刂刀 6. 丷口心

Part 7

Number	Radicals	Meanings	A character that contains the radical
1	木	tree	李
2	禾	grain	秋
3	衤	clothes; clothing	衫
4	礻	to show	福
5	钅	gold; metal	钱
6	饣	food	饭

Lesson 6

Part 1 1. a 2. c 3. b 4. c

Part 2 1. b 2. c 3. b

Part 3 1. a 2. c 3. b 4. c

Part 4 1. 巾 2. 广 3. 页 4. 门 5. 十 6. 彳 7. 革 8. 大 9. 米 10. 田

Part 5 1. 广木米 2. 门⺈ 3. 刀田 4. 彳钅 5. 革 土 6. 火页
7. ⺮目大糸 8. 讠辶米 9. 广人土 10. 火门心

Part 6

Number	Radicals	Meanings	A character that contains the radical
1	彳	small steps	行
2	亻	person	你
3	疒	sickness	病
4	广	big house	床
5	页	head	额
6	贝	seashell	贵

Lesson 7

Part 1　1. 又　2. 尸　3. 穴　4. 戈　5. 舟　6. 力　7. ⻗　8. 厂　9. 囗　10. 攵

Part 2　1. c　2. c　3. a　4. c　5. a

Part 3　1. c　2. a　3. a

Part 4　1. 尸十口刂　2. 女戈　3. 贝攵　4. 亻十口攵　5. 厂犬　6. 又糸
7. 扌口力　8. 尸水　9. 十戈衣　10. 又力

Part 5　1. ⑧　2. ②　3. ⑥　4. ⑦　5. ①　6. ⑤　7. ④　8. ③

Lesson 8

Part 1　1. 冫　2. 羽　3. 羊　4. 弓　5. 子　6. 皿　7. ⺍　8. 欠　9. 歹　10. 牛

Part 2　1. c　2. a　3. c　4. a　5. b

Part 3　1. c　2. c　3. a　4. b

Part 4　1. b　2. a　3. c

Part 5　1. 冫⺈　2. 羊冫欠　3. 弓冫　4. 子⻗　5. 舟皿　6. ⺮弓
7. 王歺又米　8. 弓厶　9. 氵曰皿

Part 6
1. [冫]　(凉)　渴　(减)
2. [欠]　(欧)　(歌)　收
3. [丷]　光　(前)　(尊)
4. [氵]　(汤)　凄　(泪)
5. [子]　(字)　(孩)　打
6. [攵]　欲　(放)　(敬)
7. [⺍]　(常)　(肖)　关
8. [扌]　(找)　(提)　孤

Lesson 9

Part 1　1. 白　2. 骨　3. 见　4. 毛　5. 隹　6. 耳　7. 立　8. 厶　9. 卜　10. 齿

Part 2　1. a　2. c　3. a　4. a　5. b

Part 3　1. a　2. c　3. a　4. b

Part 4　1. a　2. a　3. c

Part 5　1. 毛卜口　2. 冫隹　3. 卜贝　4. 尸毛　5. 白巾
6. 厶隹　7. 立口阝　8. 西禾

Part 6　1. 补　bǔ　to patch
2. 怕　pà　to fear

3. 笠 lì a large bamboo hat
4. 舰 jiàn naval vessel
5. 饵 ěr bait

Part 7
1. [白] **怕** **的** 时
2. [贝] **惯** 视 **赔**
3. [手] 笔 **拿** **掌**
4. [日] **照** **春** 百
5. [见] 厕 **现** **觉**
6. [毛] **笔** **尾** 拳
7. [卜] **补** **处** 直
8. [页] **颜** 觅 **烦**

Lesson 10

Part 1 1. 勹 2. 方 3. 儿 4. 黑 5. 殳 6. 彡 7. 气 8. 罒 9. 走 10. 瓦

Part 2 1. c 2. a 3. b 4. c 5. c

Part 3 1. b 2. a 3. c 4. a 5. c

Part 4 1. c 2. a 3. c 4. a 5. b

Part 5 1. 衤彡 2. 讠丷口儿 3. 立口儿 4. 歹勹日 5. 扌舟殳

Part 6
1. 跑 to run
2. 抱 to hug
3. 炮 firecrackers
4. 鲍 ormer; abalone
5. 饱 full
6. 苞 bud
7. 咆 to shout
8. 泡 bubble
9. 袍 robe
10. 疱 blister

Part 7

Number	Radicals	Meanings	Circle the character
1	亻	person	(他) 往 彰
2	彳	small steps	彬 什 (行)
3	彡	to embellish	很 (须) 狗
4	犭	dog; animal	澎 街 (猫)
5	丷	to divide; to separate	当 (关) 妥
6	⺌	small	(肖) 美 乳
7	爫	claw	总 尝 (采)

Lesson 11

Part 1 1. 工 2. 匚 3. 寸 4. 户 5. 止 6. 身 7. 舌 8. 斤 9. 矢 10. 夂

Part 2 1. c 2. b 3. a 4. b 5. a

Part 3 1. a 2. c 3. a 4. c 5. b

Part 4 1. 讠身寸 2. 疒夂 3. 又寸 4. 石匚巾 5. 讠舌 6. 斤欠 7. 矢口 8. 夂卜 9. 户方 10. 耳止

Part 5
1. 趾 zhǐ toes
2. 护 hù to protect
3. 躬 gōng to bow
4. 村 cūn village
5. 功 gōng work

Part 6

Number	Radicals	*Pinyin*	Meanings	The character that contains the radical
1	尸	shī	house; corpse	②
2	户	hù	single leaf door	⑤
3	工	gōng	ruler	④
4	土	tǔ	soil; earth	⑥
5	止	zhǐ	foot	③
6	夂	zhǐ	arriving	⑦
7	攵	pū	action by using hands	①

Pinyin:

Meaning:

Shape:

Pinyin:

Meaning:

Shape:

Pinyin:

Meaning:

Shape:

Pinyin:

Meaning:

Shape:

Pinyin:

Meaning:

Shape:

Pinyin:

Meaning:

Shape:

Pinyin:

Meaning:

Shape:

Pinyin:

Meaning:

Shape:

Pinyin:

Meaning:

Shape:

Pinyin:

Meaning:

Shape:

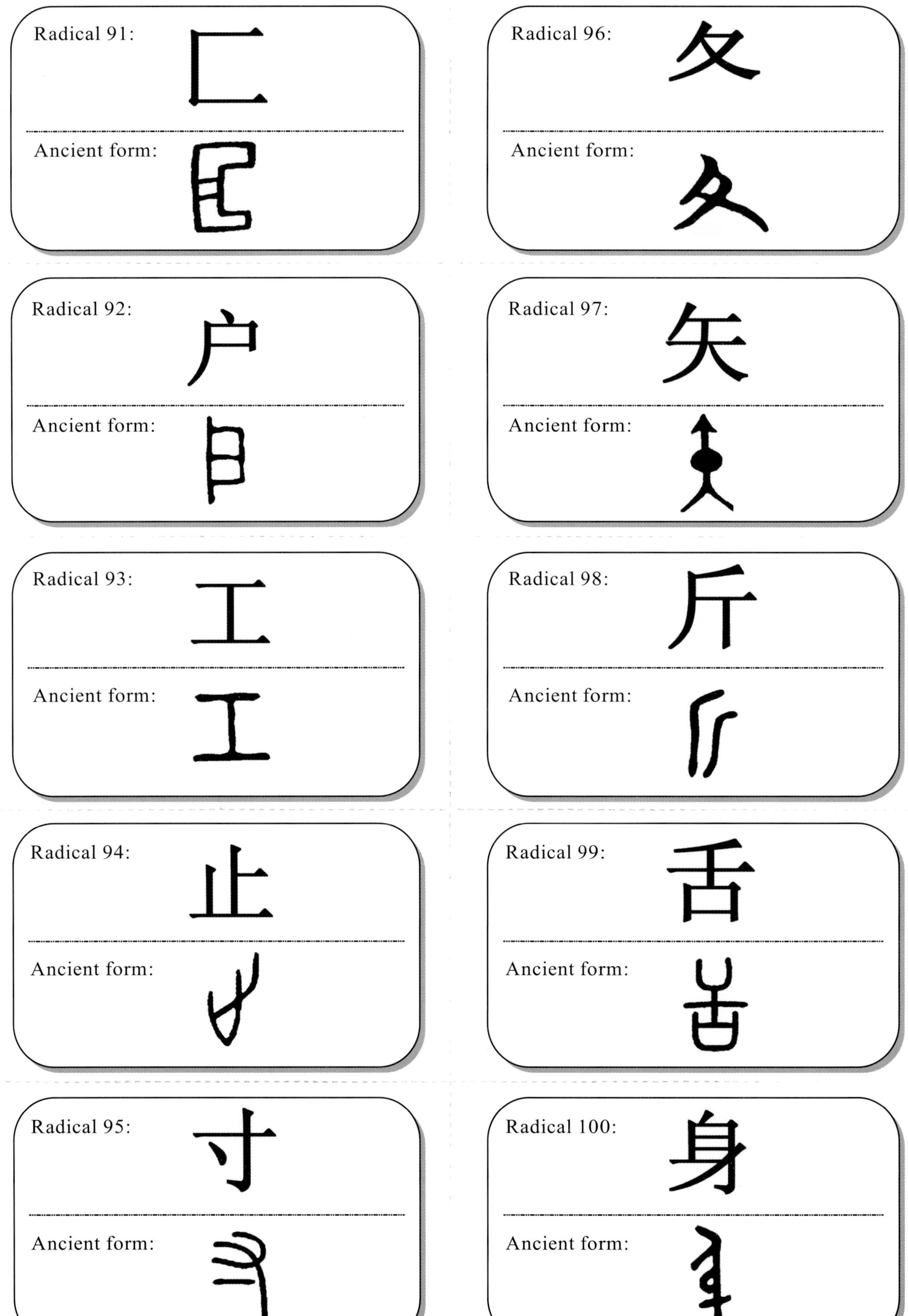

Radical 91:
匚
Ancient form:
Radical 96:
夂
Ancient form:
Radical 92:
户
Ancient form:
Radical 97:
矢
Ancient form:
Radical 93:
工
Ancient form:
Radical 98:
斤
Ancient form:
Radical 94:
止
Ancient form:
Radical 99:
舌
Ancient form:
Radical 95:
寸
Ancient form:
Radical 100:
身
Ancient form:

Pinyin:

Meaning:

Shape:

Pinyin:

Meaning:

Shape:

Pinyin:

Meaning:

Shape:

Pinyin:

Meaning:

Shape:

Pinyin:

Meaning:

Shape:

Pinyin:

Meaning:

Shape:

Pinyin:

Meaning:

Shape:

Pinyin:

Meaning:

Shape:

Pinyin:

Meaning:

Shape:

Pinyin:

Meaning:

Shape:

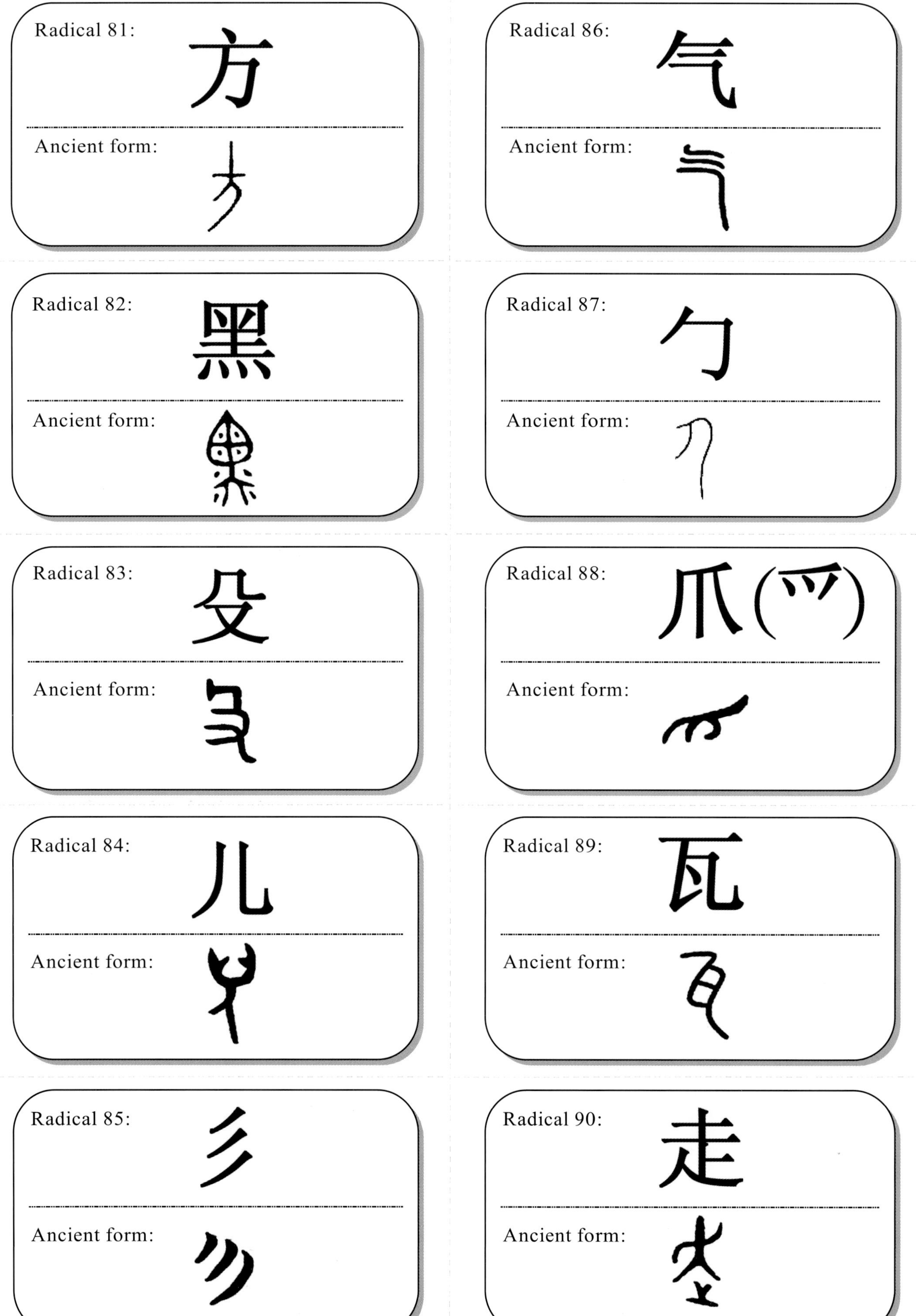
Radical 81:
方
Ancient form:
Radical 82:
黑
Ancient form:
Radical 83:
殳
Ancient form:
Radical 84:
儿
Ancient form:
Radical 85:
彡
Ancient form:
Radical 86:
气
Ancient form:
Radical 87:
勺
Ancient form:
Radical 88:
爪(爫)
Ancient form:
Radical 89:
瓦
Ancient form:
Radical 90:
走
Ancient form:

Pinyin:

Meaning:

Shape:

Pinyin:

Meaning:

Shape:

Pinyin:

Meaning:

Shape:

Pinyin:

Meaning:

Shape:

Pinyin:

Meaning:

Shape:

Pinyin:

Meaning:

Shape:

Pinyin:

Meaning:

Shape:

Pinyin:

Meaning:

Shape:

Pinyin:

Meaning:

Shape:

Pinyin:

Meaning:

Shape:

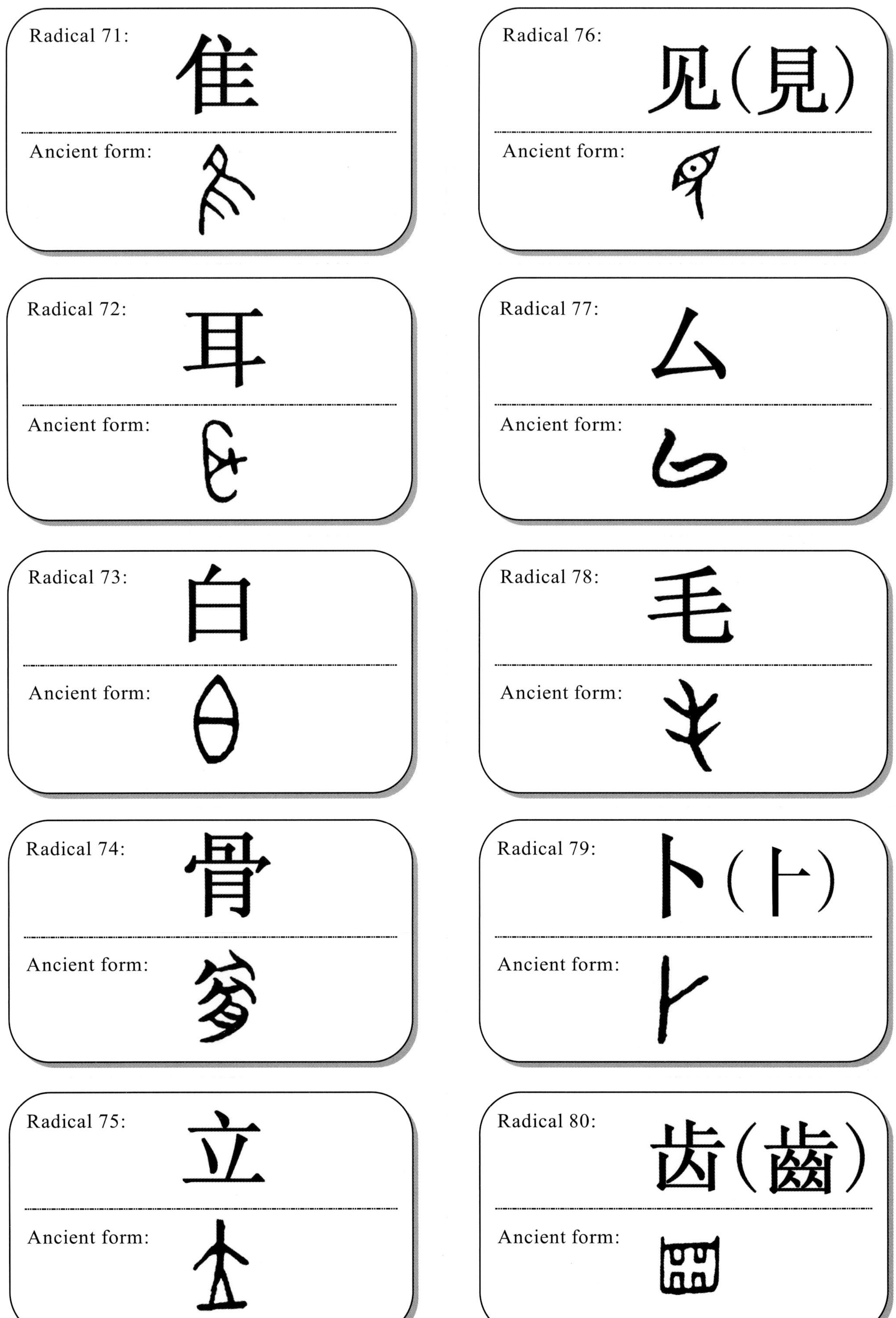
Radical 71:
隹
Ancient form:
Radical 72:
耳
Ancient form:
Radical 73:
白
Ancient form:
Radical 74:
骨
Ancient form:
Radical 75:
立
Ancient form:
Radical 76:
见(見)
Ancient form:
Radical 77:
厶
Ancient form:
Radical 78:
毛
Ancient form:
Radical 79:
卜(⺊)
Ancient form:
Radical 80:
齿(齒)
Ancient form:

Pinyin:

Meaning:

Shape:

Pinyin:

Meaning:

Shape:

Pinyin:

Meaning:

Shape:

Pinyin:

Meaning:

Shape:

Pinyin:

Meaning:

Shape:

Pinyin:

Meaning:

Shape:

Pinyin:

Meaning:

Shape:

Pinyin:

Meaning:

Shape:

Pinyin:

Meaning:

Shape:

Pinyin:

Meaning:

Shape:

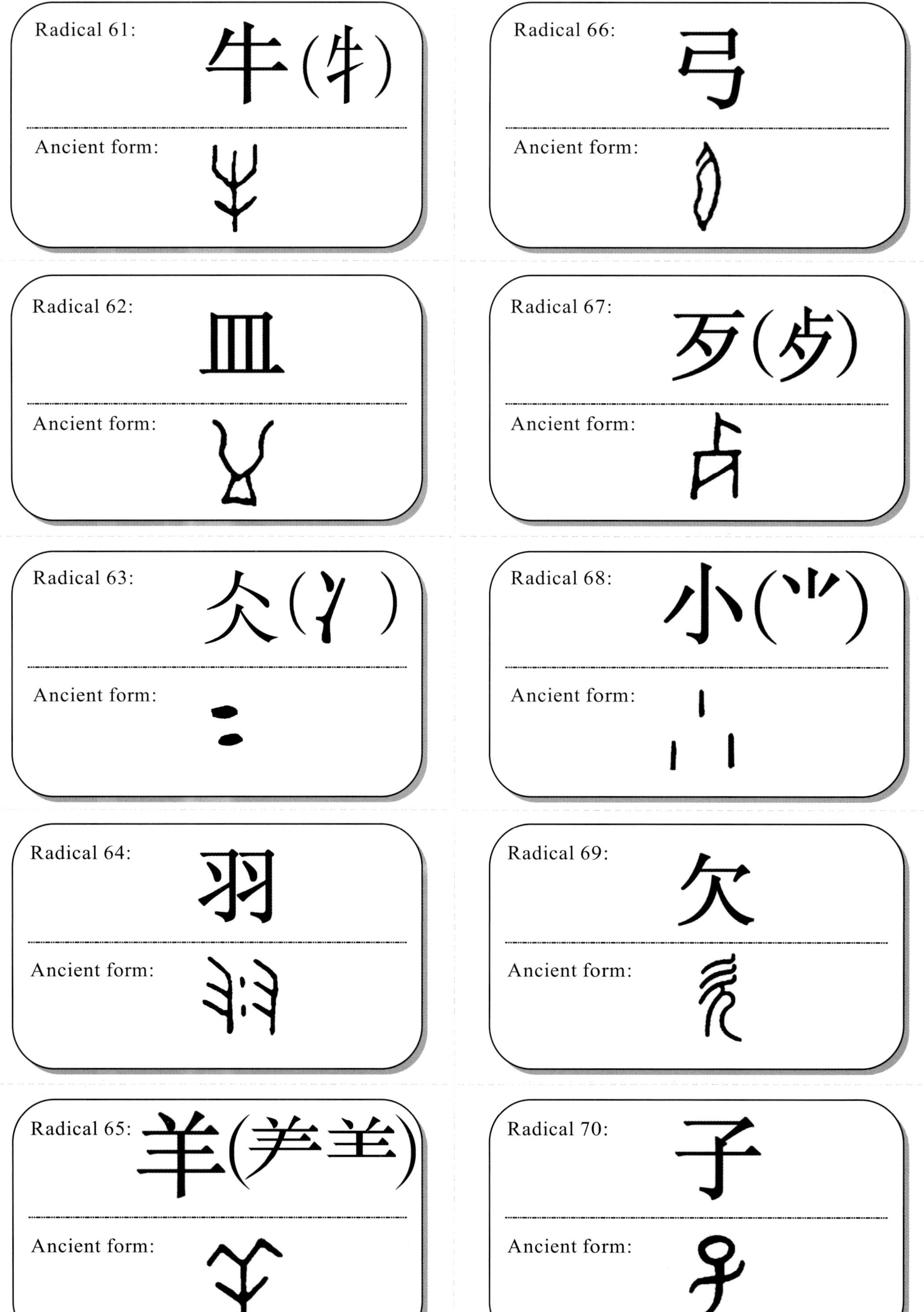
Radical 61: 牛(牜)
Ancient form:
Radical 62: 皿
Ancient form:
Radical 63: 仌(冫)
Ancient form:
Radical 64: 羽
Ancient form:
Radical 65: 羊(⺶⺷)
Ancient form:
Radical 66: 弓
Ancient form:
Radical 67: 歹(歺)
Ancient form:
Radical 68: 小(⺌)
Ancient form:
Radical 69: 欠
Ancient form:
Radical 70: 子
Ancient form:

Pinyin:

Meaning:

Shape:

Pinyin:

Meaning:

Shape:

Pinyin:

Meaning:

Shape:

Pinyin:

Meaning:

Shape:

Pinyin:

Meaning:

Shape:

Pinyin:

Meaning:

Shape:

Pinyin:

Meaning:

Shape:

Pinyin:

Meaning:

Shape:

Pinyin:

Meaning:

Shape:

Pinyin:

Meaning:

Shape:

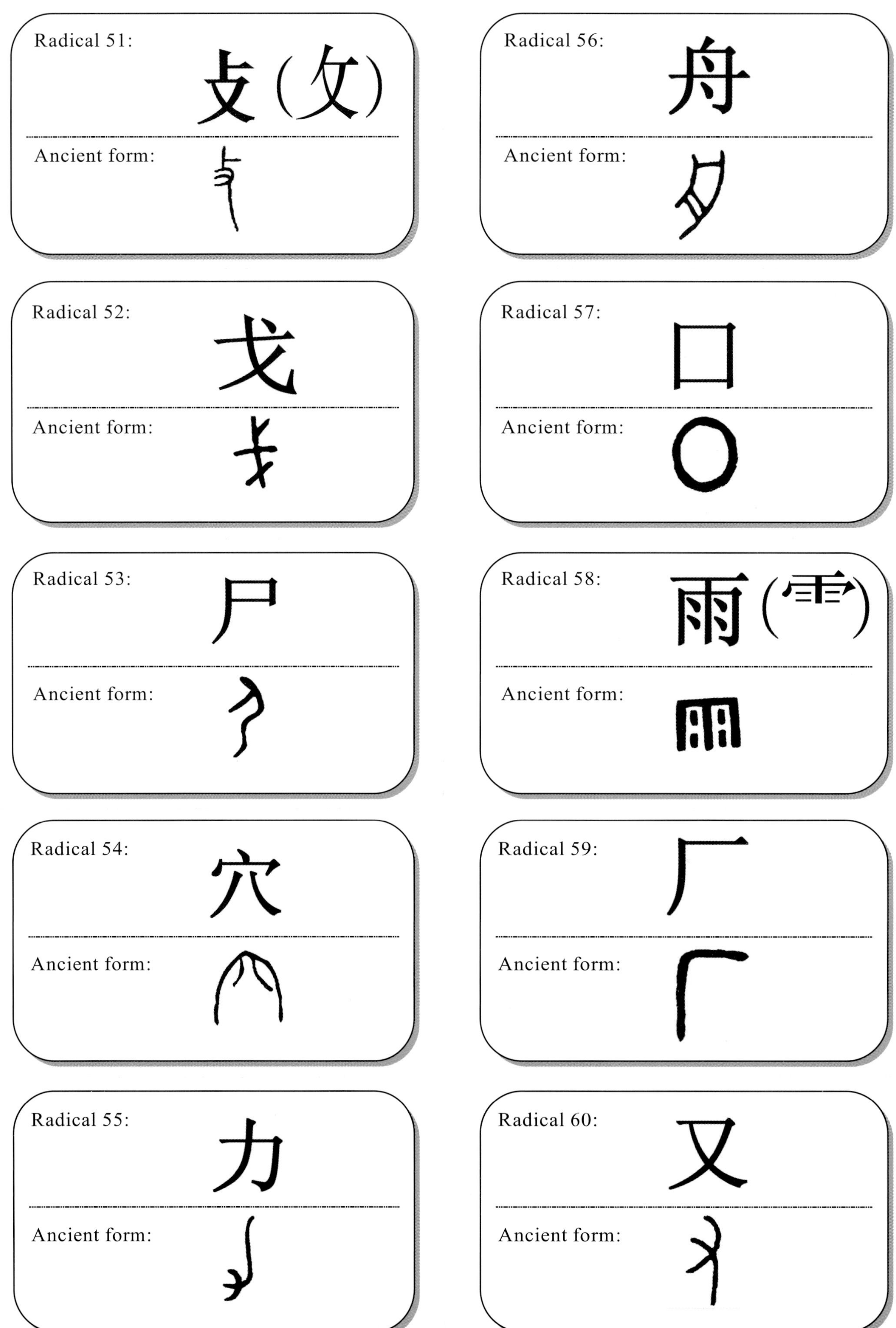
Radical 51:
攴(攵)
Ancient form:
Radical 52:
戈
Ancient form:
Radical 53:
尸
Ancient form:
Radical 54:
穴
Ancient form:
Radical 55:
力
Ancient form:
Radical 56:
舟
Ancient form:
Radical 57:
口
Ancient form:
Radical 58:
雨(⻗)
Ancient form:
Radical 59:
厂
Ancient form:
Radical 60:
又
Ancient form:

Pinyin:

Meaning:

Shape:

Pinyin:

Meaning:

Shape:

Pinyin:

Meaning:

Shape:

Pinyin:

Meaning:

Shape:

Pinyin:

Meaning:

Shape:

Pinyin:

Meaning:

Shape:

Pinyin:

Meaning:

Shape:

Pinyin:

Meaning:

Shape:

Pinyin:

Meaning:

Shape:

Pinyin:

Meaning:

Shape:

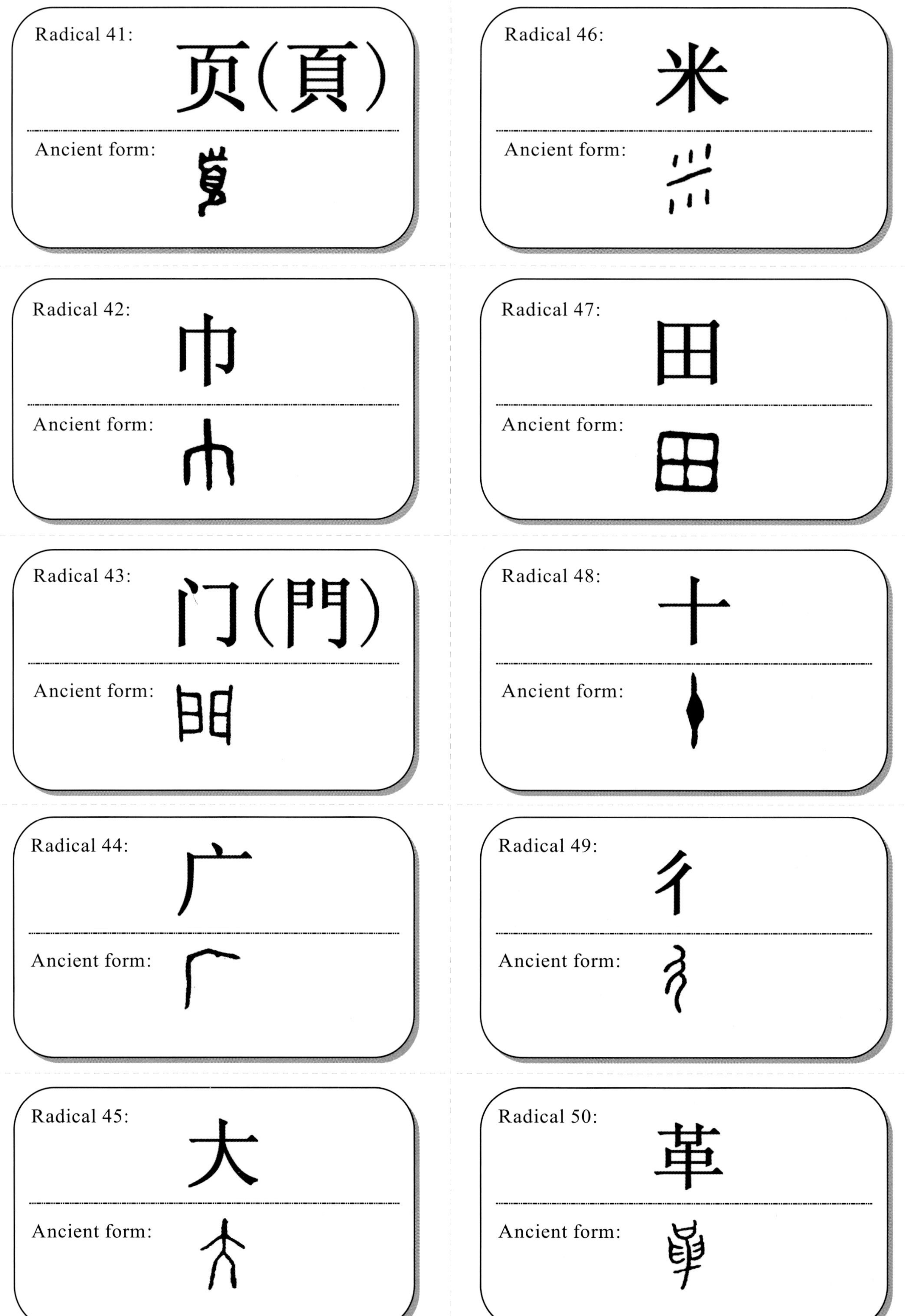
Radical 41:
页(頁)
Ancient form:
Radical 42:
巾
Ancient form:
Radical 43:
门(門)
Ancient form:
Radical 44:
广
Ancient form:
Radical 45:
大
Ancient form:
Radical 46:
米
Ancient form:
Radical 47:
田
Ancient form:
Radical 48:
十
Ancient form:
Radical 49:
彳
Ancient form:
Radical 50:
革
Ancient form:

Pinyin:

Meaning:

Shape:

Pinyin:

Meaning:

Shape:

Pinyin:

Meaning:

Shape:

Pinyin:

Meaning:

Shape:

Pinyin:

Meaning:

Shape:

Pinyin:

Meaning:

Shape:

Pinyin:

Meaning:

Shape:

Pinyin:

Meaning:

Shape:

Pinyin:

Meaning:

Shape:

Pinyin:

Meaning:

Shape:

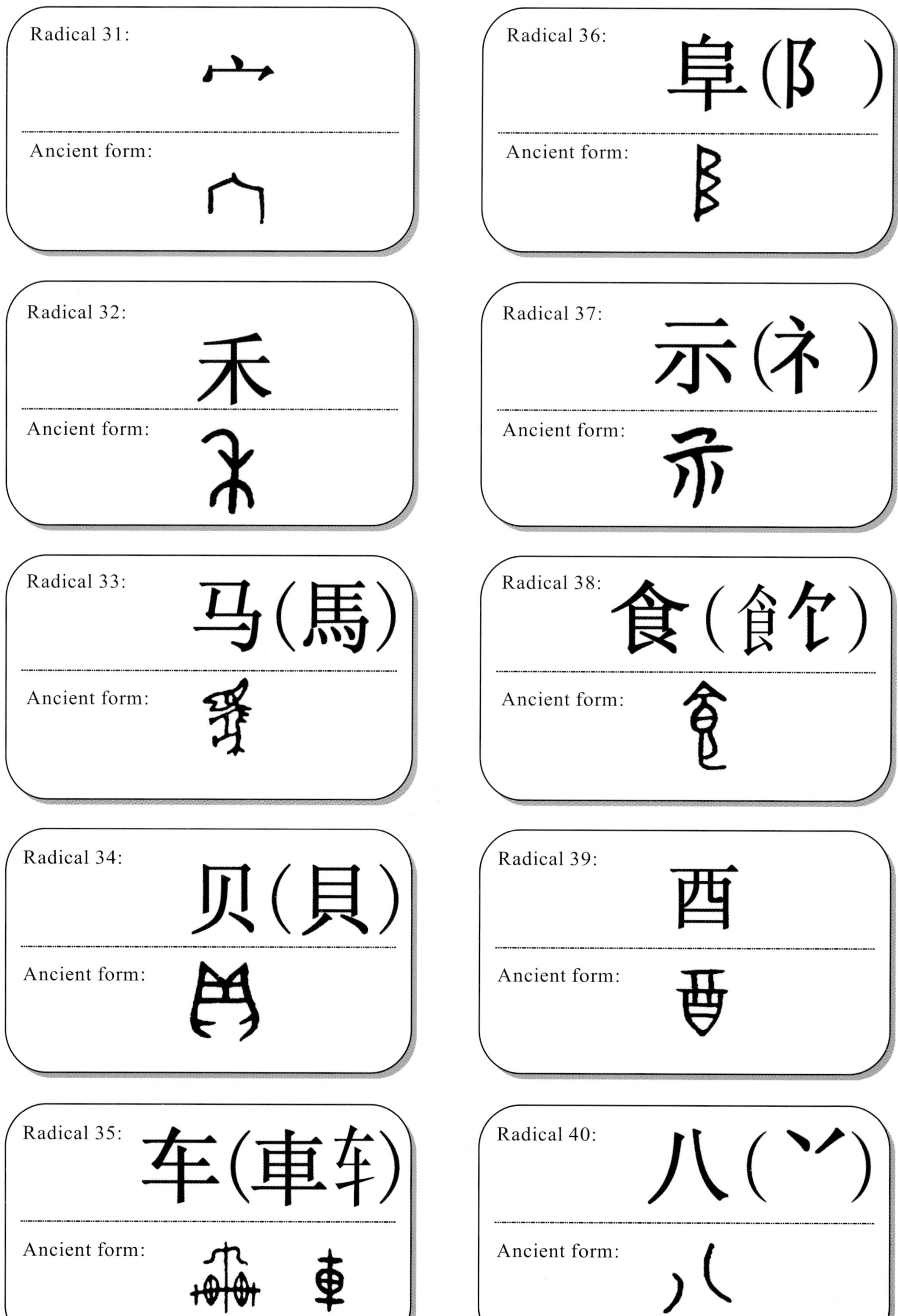
Radical 31:
宀
Ancient form:
Radical 32:
禾
Ancient form:
Radical 33:
马(馬)
Ancient form:
Radical 34:
贝(貝)
Ancient form:
Radical 35:
车(車 车)
Ancient form:
Radical 36:
阜(阝)
Ancient form:
Radical 37:
示(礻)
Ancient form:
Radical 38:
食(飠饣)
Ancient form:
Radical 39:
酉
Ancient form:
Radical 40:
八(丷)
Ancient form:

Pinyin:

Meaning:

Shape:

Pinyin:

Meaning:

Shape:

Pinyin:

Meaning:

Shape:

Pinyin:

Meaning:

Shape:

Pinyin:

Meaning:

Shape:

Pinyin:

Meaning:

Shape:

Pinyin:

Meaning:

Shape:

Pinyin:

Meaning:

Shape:

Pinyin:

Meaning:

Shape:

Pinyin:

Meaning:

Shape:

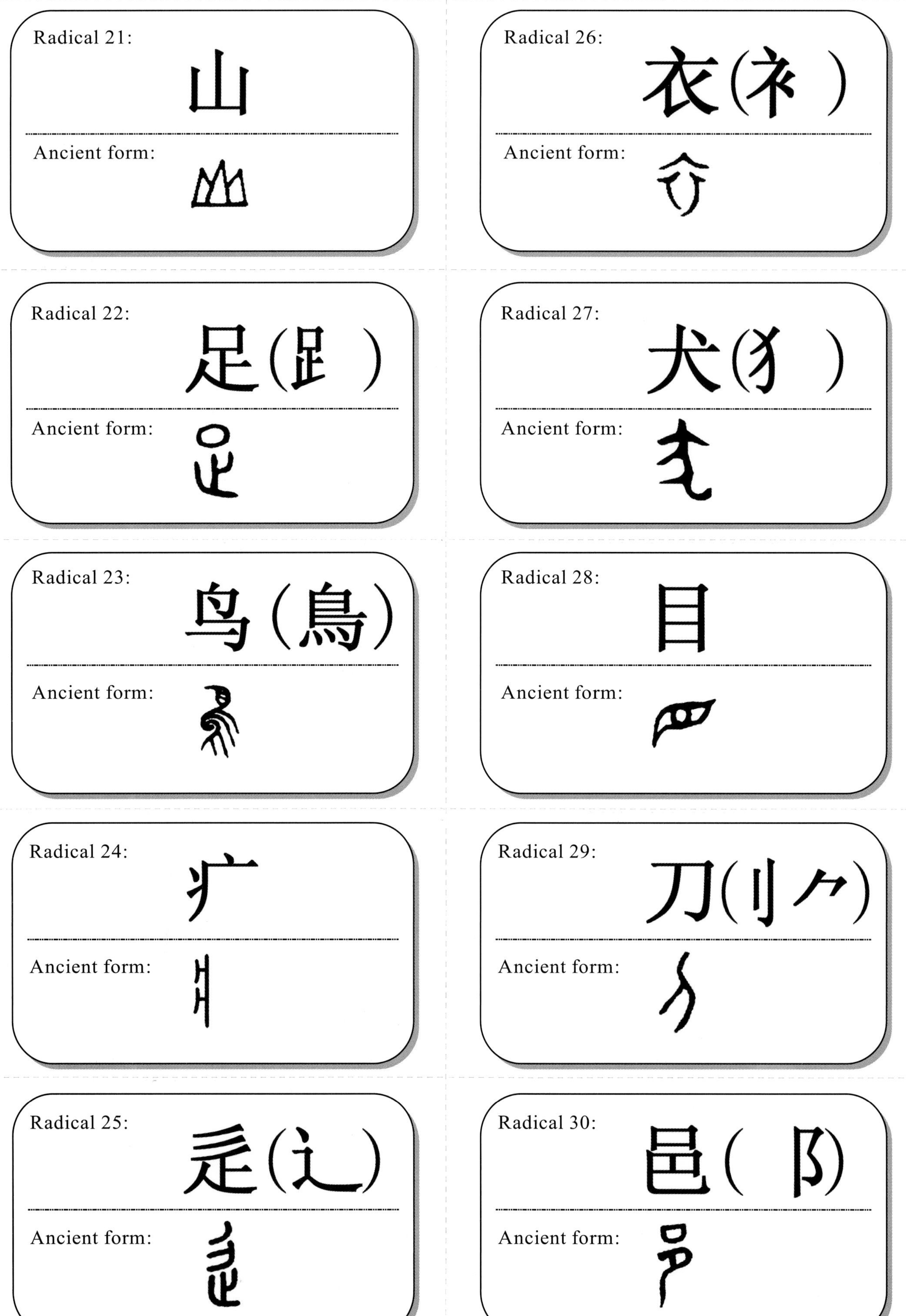
Radical 21:
山
Ancient form:
Radical 22:
足(⻊)
Ancient form:
Radical 23:
鸟(鳥)
Ancient form:
Radical 24:
疒
Ancient form:
Radical 25:
辵(辶)
Ancient form:
Radical 26:
衣(衤)
Ancient form:
Radical 27:
犬(犭)
Ancient form:
Radical 28:
目
Ancient form:
Radical 29:
刀(刂⺈)
Ancient form:
Radical 30:
邑(阝)
Ancient form:

Pinyin:

Meaning:

Shape:

Pinyin:

Meaning:

Shape:

Pinyin:

Meaning:

Shape:

Pinyin:

Meaning:

Shape:

Pinyin:

Meaning:

Shape:

Pinyin:

Meaning:

Shape:

Pinyin:

Meaning:

Shape:

Pinyin:

Meaning:

Shape:

Pinyin:

Meaning:

Shape:

Pinyin:

Meaning:

Shape:

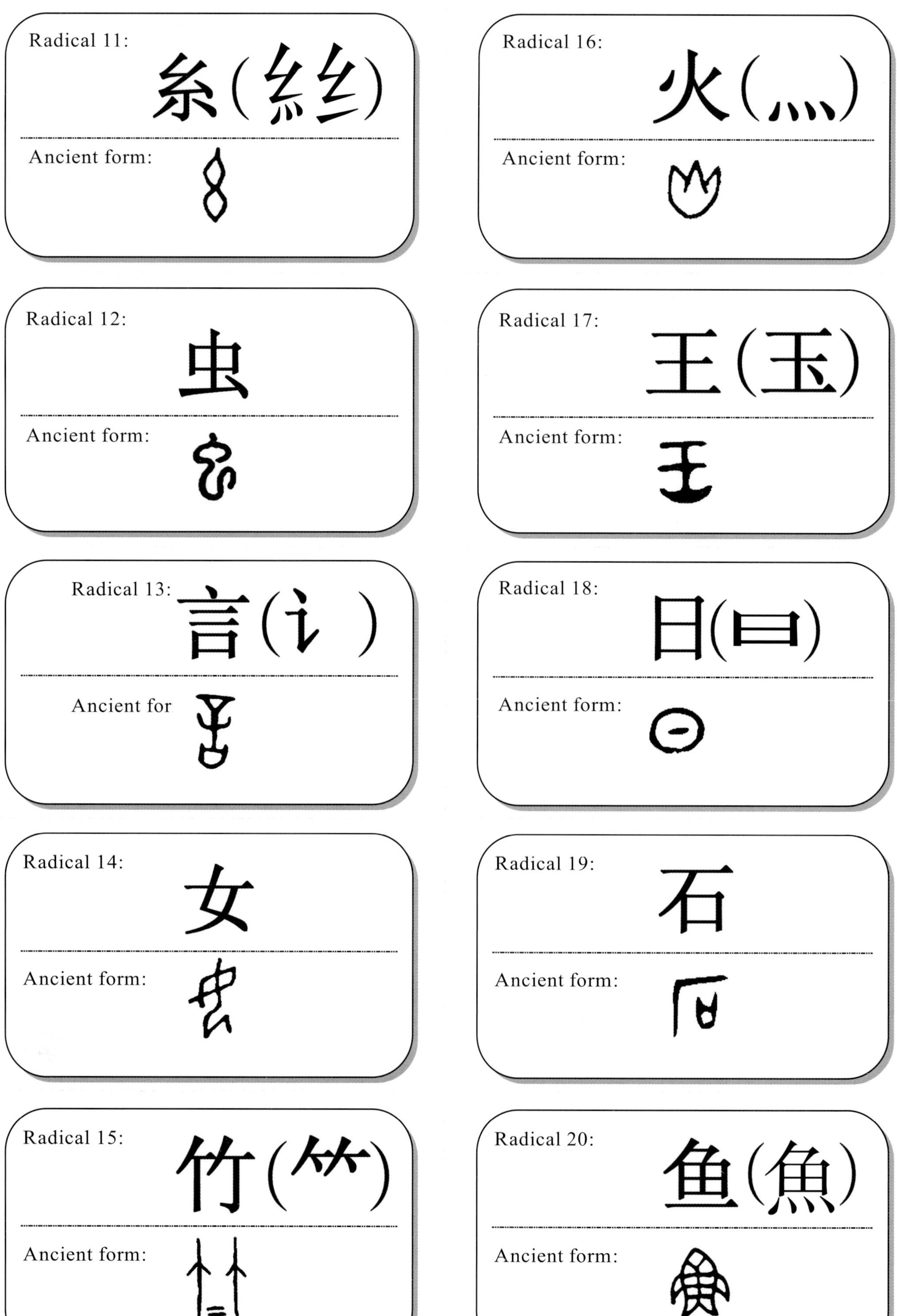

Radical 11:
糸(纟纟)
Ancient form:
Radical 12:
虫
Ancient form:
Radical 13:
言(讠)
Ancient for
Radical 14:
女
Ancient form:
Radical 15:
竹(⺮)
Ancient form:
Radical 16:
火(灬)
Ancient form:
Radical 17:
王(玉)
Ancient form:
Radical 18:
日(⺜)
Ancient form:
Radical 19:
石
Ancient form:
Radical 20:
鱼(魚)
Ancient form:

Pinyin:

Meaning:

Shape:

Pinyin:

Meaning:

Shape:

Pinyin:

Meaning:

Shape:

Pinyin:

Meaning:

Shape:

Pinyin:

Meaning:

Shape:

Pinyin:

Meaning:

Shape:

Pinyin:

Meaning:

Shape:

Pinyin:

Meaning:

Shape:

Pinyin:

Meaning:

Shape:

Pinyin:

Meaning:

Shape:

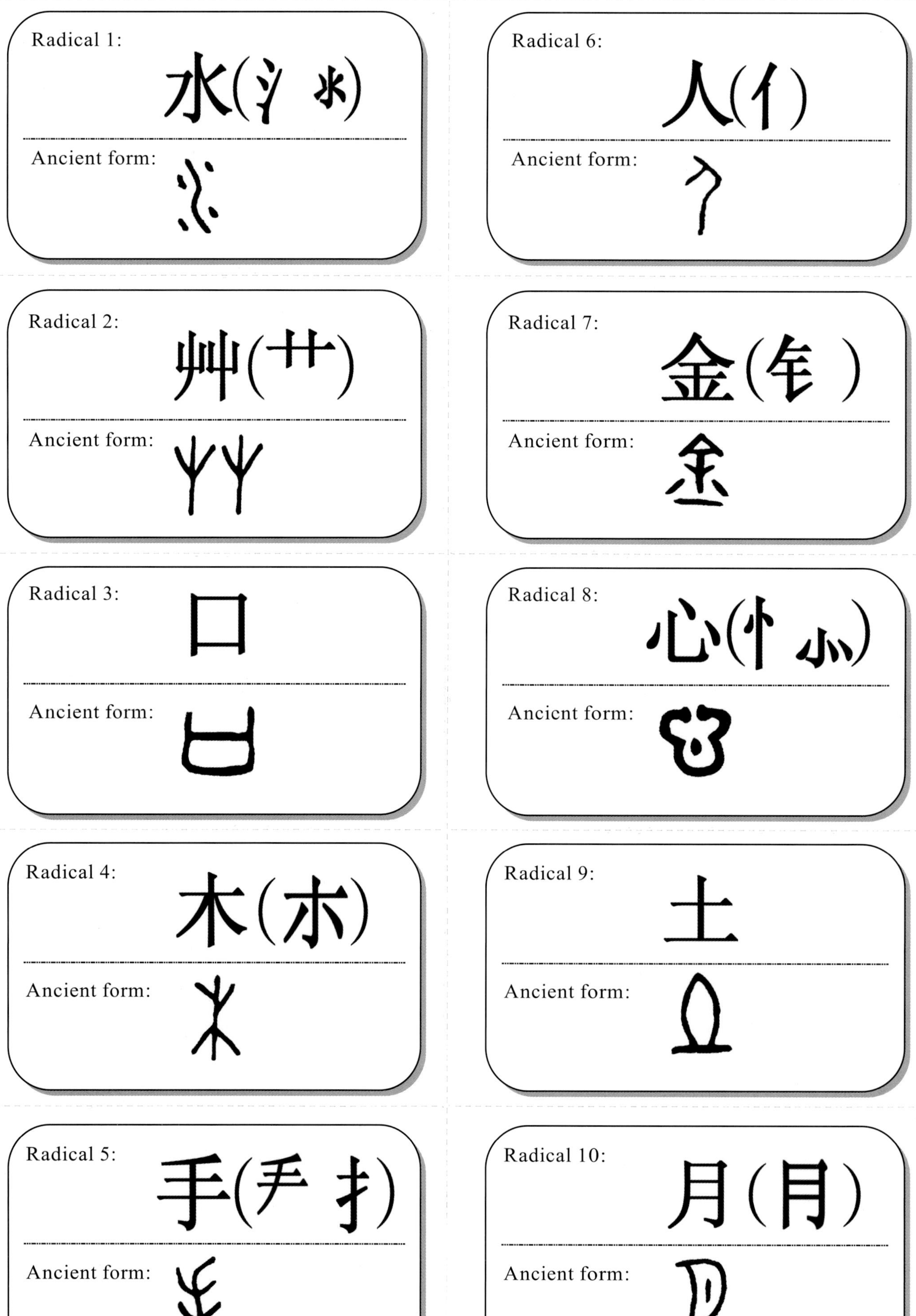

Radical 1:
水(氵 氺)
Ancient form:
Radical 2:
艸(艹)
Ancient form:
Radical 3:
口
Ancient form:
Radical 4:
木(朩)
Ancient form:
Radical 5:
手(龵 扌)
Ancient form:
Radical 6:
人(亻)
Ancient form:
Radical 7:
金(钅)
Ancient form:
Radical 8:
心(忄 ⺗)
Ancient form:
Radical 9:
土
Ancient form:
Radical 10:
月(⺼)
Ancient form: